Solving Problem Solving

Solving Problem Solving

A Potent Force for Effective Management

ROBERT LOUIS FLOOD

JOHN WILEY & SONS

Chichester · New York · Brisbane · Toronto · Singapore

Other Wiley Editorial Offices

John Wiley & Sons, Inc., 605 Third Avenue,
New York, NY 10158-0012, USA

Jacaranda Wiley Ltd, 33 Park Road, Milton,
Queensland 4064, Australia

John Wiley & Sons (Canada) Ltd, 22 Worcester Road,
Rexdale, Ontario M9W 1L1, Canada

John Wiley & Sons (SEA) Pte Ltd, 37 Jalan Pemimpin #05-04,
Block B, Union Industrial Building, Singapore 2057

Library of Congress Cataloging-in-Publication Data
Flood, Robert L.
  Solving problem solving : a potent force for effective management / Robert
Louis Flood.
      p.   cm.
  Includes bibliographical references and index.
  ISBN 0-471-95590-6
  1. Problem solving.   2. Management science.   I. Title.
  HD30.29.F58   1995   95–2364
  658.4′03—dc20   CIP

British Library Cataloguing in Publication Data

A catalogue record for this book is available from the British Library

ISBN 0-471-95590-6

Typeset in 11/13 pt Palatino from author's disks by Photo·graphics, Honiton, Devon
Printed and bound in Great Britain by Biddles Ltd, Guildford

To my admirable son
Ross Louis
*who I have taught for 14 years – only to discover that I did
most of the learning*

Contents

Preface   xi

Acknowledgements   xiv

PART 1. GETTING STARTED WITH TSI

1. **Critical Success Factors for a New Problem
    Solving System**   3

2. **Overview of the Problem Solving System: TSI**   9

PART 2. EXPLAINING TSI

3. **Understanding Organisation for Problem
    Solving – 'The Philosophy'**   19

4. **Key Principles for Problem Solving – 'The
    Principles'**   26

5. **How to Problem Solve – 'The Process'**   29
    5.1 Critical Review Mode   31
    5.2 Problem Solving Mode   32
         5.2.1 Creativity   34
         5.2.2 Choice   36
         5.2.3 Implementation   41
    5.3 Critical Reflection Mode   41

PART 3. DO'S AND DON'TS OF PROBLEM SOLVING WITH TSI

6. **What is Happening When You Problem Solve?** 47
   6.1 Design – 'How?' 48
   6.2 Debate – 'What?' 50
   6.3 Disimprison – 'Why and for Whom?' 52

7. **Pitfalls in Problem Solving and How to Avoid Them** 57
   7.1 The Systemic Principle 57
   7.2 Motivation Style 58
   7.3 Leadership Style 59
   7.4 Facilitation Style 61
   7.5 Personal Style 64
   7.6 Problem Solving Style 64
   7.7 Time Constraints 66
   7.8 Aesthetics 66
   7.9 Measurement 67
   7.10 Training and Competence 68
   7.11 What is Meant By 'Organisation' 69
   7.12 What is Meant By 'Problem' 71
   7.13 Choosing and Using Consultants 74

8. **Choosing and Using Consultants** 75

PART 4. TSI IN ACTION

9. **How to Problem Solve – 'The Methods'** 83
   9.1 Critical Review Mode 84
   9.2 Problem Solving Mode 86
      9.2.1 Creativity 88
         9.2.1.1 Idea generation and evaluation – The 'For what reason?' method 92
         9.2.1.2 Idea generation and evaluation – Brainstorming 94
         9.2.1.3 Idea generation and evaluation – Nominal Group Technique 97

9.2.1.4 Image generation and
evaluation – Metaphors   100
9.2.2 Choice   107
9.2.3 Implementation   114
9.2.3.1 Process design – Continuous
improvement: Quality
Management   115
9.2.3.2 Process design – Radical
Change: Business Process
Reengineering   131
9.2.3.3 Organisational design –
Diagnosis for Effective
Organisation   139
9.2.3.4 Implementing Designs and
Decisions   171
9.2.3.5 Debating – Exploring and
Choosing Designs   177
9.2.3.6 Debating – Exploring and
Making Decisions   185
9.2.3.7 Debating – Testing Polarised
Viewpoints   197
9.2.3.8 Disimprisoning – Critically
Evaluating Designs and
Decisions   211
9.3 Critical Reflection Mode   227
9.4 Other Problem Solving Methods   229
9.5 Endnote   232

10. Nine Cases Employing TSI, Written by
Managers and Consultants – 'An International
Perspective'   233
Case 10.1   Normet Pty Ltd (Australia and Asia):
Phil Hearse, Managing Director. Focus: Strategic
Management – planning the future.   235
Case 10.2   Sintech Construction Pty Ltd and
Nakamaya Corporation (Singapore and Japan):
Chow Kok Fong, Director of Projects. Focus:
Human dimension of establishing an international
joint venture.   268
Case 10.3   Helderberg Boeing 747 Disaster

(**South Africa and International**): Johan
Strumpfer, Principal Researcher. Focus: Problem
solving in deep ocean search planning.   268
**Case 10.4   North Yorkshire Police (United
Kingdom)**: Steve Green, Commander of York
Division. Focus: Managing and developing a
police division in a large bureaucracy.   279
**Case 10.5   Southern Life Association (South
Africa)**: Warren Topp, Senior Project Manager.
Focus: Critical evaluation within Business Process
Reengineering (BPR).   294
**Case 10.6   The Halesworth Partnership Pty Ltd
(Australia)**: Tony Tregurtha and Annmaree
Desmond, Directors. Focus: Consulting in the
Australian financial sector.   320
**Case 10.7   ABC and Co. (Hong Kong and
Taiwan)**: Peter C.Y. Wong, Managing Director.
Focus: Implementing Quality Management (QM)
principles in an ageing family-owned company.   349
Case 10.8   Utopia-Aire Pty Ltd (Singapore):
Jeremy Chia, Managing Director. Focus:
Entrepreneurship, creativity and change –
building innovativeness into organisational
processes.   360
**Case 10.9   Trent Health Authority (United
Kingdom)**: Wendy Gregory, Norma Romm and
Michael Walsh, Research Consultants. Focus: User
participation in defining quality standards within
the National Health Service.   367
Overview   390

11.   **Concluding Comments**   393

Further Reading   399

Preface

This book explains organisation and problem solving, identifies types of action to take when problem solving, establishes a problem solving system to do this, explains what is happening when using this system, marks pitfalls to avoid when using the system, provides guidelines for choosing and using consultants to problem solve for/with you and illustrates with an international outlook the problem solving system through its many applications, written by managers and consultants.

Case studies in this book report on problem solving in Australia, Hong Kong, Japan, Singapore, South Africa, Taiwan, the United Kingdom, the United States of America and a country in the Middle East. The case studies cover problem solving in air transportation, bunker transfer, car sales, community projects, computer site preparation, the construction industry, consumer products, custody of offenders, entertainments, financial services, health care, hospital administration, management consultancy, mining, policing, search and recovery and tourism.

The problem solving system is called Total Systems Intervention (TSI). It is explained and brought to life in this book in four parts. Part 1 comprises Chapters 1 and 2. Chapter 1 sets out Critical Success Factors for TSI. Chapter 2 brings forward an abridged version of TSI with the aim of getting managers thinking with and using it whilst time is invested reading the rest of the book. Part 2 comprises Chapters 3 to 5, which explain TSI as a problem solving system. The chapters construct a clear understanding of TSI in terms of its philosophy, principles and process – the three Ps of TSI. The remainder of the book adds detail to TSI in two parts. Part 3 comprises Chapters 6 to 8. These chapters run through the do's and don'ts of problem solving with TSI. And Part 4 comprises Chapters 9 and 10, which provide methods and their principles that operationalise TSI and case studies that illustrate TSI in action. Chapter 11 concludes and Further Reading rounds off the book. Abstracts of the chapters are given below.

Part 1. Getting Started with TSI

1. Critical Success Factors for a New Problem Solving System

Chapter 1 states what must be achieved in terms of Critical Success Factors to ensure that managers are adequately supported in efforts made to improve their problem solving skills.

2. Overview of the Problem Solving System: TSI

Chapter 2 gives an up-front overview of the problem solving system TSI, aimed at getting managers started, getting them thinking and using TSI.

Part 2. Explaining TSI

3. Understanding Organisation for Problem Solving – 'The Philosophy'

Chapter 3 is the first in a series of three chapters that explain TSI as a problem solving system. Chapter 3 introduces the *philosophy*, or main ideas, about organisation and problem solving that TSI assumes and explains TSI's understanding of organisation for problem solving.

4. Key Principles for Problem Solving – 'The Principles'

Chapter 4 continues the explanation of TSI with an account of its key *principles* for problem solving and explains the kinds of action to take if TSI's philosophy is adopted.

5. *How to Problem Solve – 'The Process'*

Chapter 5 extends the explanation of TSI with a description of the *process* of the problem solving system. It explains how to implement TSI's principles using three modes by which TSI is operated: the Critical Review Mode which incorporates methods into TSI's system of methods, the Problem Solving Mode which employs the system of methods in problem solving and the Critical Reflection Mode which assesses the adequacy of the results of the Problem Solving Mode.

Part 3. Do's and Don'ts of Problem Solving with TSI

6. *What is Happening When You Problem Solve?*

Chapter 6 and remaining chapters add detail to TSI. Chapter 6 begins the treatment with an explanation of what is happening when you problem solve using TSI. It states what you should do – the do's.

7. *Pitfalls in Problem Solving and How to Avoid Them*

Chapter 7 reviews the main pitfalls in problem solving with TSI and how to avoid them. It states what you should not do – the don'ts.

8. *Choosing and Using Consultants*

Chapter 8 runs through the pros and cons of different categories of consultant that may be used in the TSI process and supplies guidance on choosing them. It states the do's and don'ts of using consultants.

Part 4. TSI in Action

9. *How to Problem Solve – 'The Methods'*

Chapter 9 provides a user's guide to some key methods and their principles for each of the three modes of TSI and supplies case studies to illustrate their use.

10. Nine Cases Employing TSI, Written by Managers and Consultants – 'An International Perspective'

Chapter 10 presents an international selection of nine case studies that discuss applications of TSI, written by managers and consultants. Each case study appraises a different type of organisational problem solving using TSI. The chapter concludes with an overview of the lessons learnt from the case studies.

11. Concluding Comments

Solving Problem Solving finishes with a summary of the scheme of the book, its findings and some ideas for further development.

Over time, as you explore and put into practice the ideas and methods presented in this book, a fuller, deeper and richer understanding of problem solving will be accomplished. This is not a book to be read once and shelved, however. It is a reference book to be consulted again and again. The spine should get crumpled, the cover bashed-up, pages dog-eared and annotated – then, and only then, will this book have served its purpose.

ACKNOWLEDGEMENTS

I asked two people to be readers of the manuscript of this book as it progressed from early drafts to the final thing. Phil Hearse read from a practitioner's point of view. Norma Romm read from an academic and scholarly point of view. In fact, both contributed in both respects and because of that *Solving Problem Solving* is a much improved system of thought.

I am indebted to the following people who have sacrificed time from already tight working schedules to produce material for the case studies in *Solving Problem Solving*: John Beckford, Jeremy Chia, Loo Wing Chuen, Claire Cohen, Robert Cross, Annmaree Desmond, Chow Kok Fong, Steve Green, Wendy Gregory, Phil Hearse, INTERACT Consortium, Gerald Midgley, Norma Romm, Mark Rowan, Johan Strumpfer, Warren Topp, Tony Tregurtha, Lew Yue Wah, Mike Walsh, Peter Wong and Sharon Wong. All of the above-named people hold at least a masters degree; most masters degrees are held with distinction and seven are PhDs. I am appreciative of the honesty they have shown, giving me a real insight into the ups and downs of their working lives. Recording their names above is barely recognition of the contribution that each one has made to this book. Ultimately, I must take responsibility for the final interpretation of their work.

For inspiring me, for teaching me, but most of all for being a friend to me, I, like many others, have to thank Russell Ackoff.

Robert L. Flood,
January 1995,
Hull, UK.

Part 1
GETTING STARTED WITH TSI

1
Critical Success Factors for a New Problem Solving System

Well-developed problem solving skills are vital possessions that all successful managers must hold. This is because managers essentially are problem solvers. Complementing, expanding and improving problem solving skills as recommended in this book will help managers to cope even more effectively with organisational problems that they face and will broaden their perspective on how to face them (what is meant by 'organis-ation' and 'problem' is detailed in Chapter 3).

Making improvements to problem solving skills is important. Unfortunately several obstacles get in the way. There are per-haps three main obstacles.

- Time available for managers to make improvements is lim-ited.
- Help given to managers seeking to make improvements is not good enough.
- Making improvements means change which may seem threat-ening to managers and not in their interests.

So, what can be done?

It is simple to reason out what can be done and where to begin. Time available for managers can only be increased if they are able to do their work more efficiently and effectively. To do work efficiently means to work without any unnecessary waste in time or resources. To do work effectively means to achieve chosen tasks. Being more efficient and effective is only possible if managers' skills are improved. Improving the skills is only possible if the help given is good enough. The help given is not good enough. We need to begin, then, by substantially improving help given to managers and to convince them that it is in their interests, and in the interests of those they work with, to make improvements.

I have come up with nine Critical Success Factors (CSFs) that indicate where help given to managers can be improved. These CSFs state what must be achieved so that managers are adequately supported in their efforts to improve their problem solving skills. The nine CSFs are catalogued below.

- There exists in the literature an enormous and diverse range of problem solving methods. Faced with this enormity and diversity, managers are not surprisingly left stunned. It is impossible for them to know where to begin. The barrier has been allowed to rise because no one has stood back and addressed the broad question 'Which method should be used, when and why?'
  CSF1 *A problem solving system is needed which guides managers through the process of choosing methods relevant to the main problems that they face.*
- Systematic investigation of problem solving methods poses huge difficulties for managers. To become familiar with a diversity of methods means coming to terms with their great number of concepts; concepts that differ from method to method. Some of the concepts are obscure and this accentuates the challenge. It is a challenge made unnecessarily difficult. Again and again, I come across managers each doing their best to learn about and understand new methods, but finally having to admit defeat. They are defeated by the volume and obscurity of the concepts.
  CSF2 *A problem solving system is needed which cuts back on the number of concepts used to explain methods and translates those that are kept into everyday language and then integrates them into one coherent whole system.*
- Managing organisational-enterprises and other forms of organisation is becoming ever more challenging. This state-

ment may sound hackneyed but it is true. Today, managers have to cope with rapidly developing technology for the workplace, escalating amounts of management information moving around at great speed, rising consumer awareness, growing expectations of employees, as well as having to handle corporate culture, office politics and the interests of suppliers, pressure groups and a concerned public. Organisations have become very messy and fuzzy things with problems that are hard to understand. Organisations can no longer be understood as static and easily separable units constrained by the environment in which they operate. Nowadays organisational analysis must focus on cultural and symbolic processes, macro-power processes and other complex issues. Methods that are able to stimulate and provoke creative and perceptive thought about these matters are needed. Methods for creative thinking do exist but are rarely used alongside problem solving methods.

CSF3 *A problem solving system is needed which incorporates powerful tools to stimulate and provoke creative and perceptive thought about organisation and organisational problems.*

- Methods are frequently presented like recipes. They describe what to do without explaining how the method works in terms of principles and purposes. It is essential, however, that an explanation is given and explored so that managers are able to understand the kind of changes that are supposed to occur. This knowledge will improve the likelihood of achieving the desired impact for all concerned.

CSF4 *A problem solving system must be supported by an explanation of what is happening when people use the system properly, according to the principles of the system.*

- There are many pitfalls to avoid when problem solving. They rarely are avoided because managers are not worried about their existence or their intricacies. The pitfalls therefore must be catalogued and organised into a knowledge base. Managers equipped with this knowledge of things to avoid are more likely to achieve the desired impact with the methods they choose.

CSF5 *A problem solving system must be used in the light of knowledge about potential pitfalls to avoid.*

- Shallow and gimmicky books written about problem solving

are extremely common. They lead their readers inevitably to failure because the ideas in the books are without foundation. This can cause uncountable damage by disappointing and putting off managers keen to acquire genuine and worthy problem solving skills.

CSF6 *A problem solving system must not be shallow or gimmicky.*

• Many books on problem solving provide case examples centred on one geographic region, such as the USA, the UK or the Far East. This centricism fails to explore problem solving at an international level. It also means that cases are of limited use to the bulk of managers across the globe. An international perspective on problem solving adds value.

CSF7 *A problem solving system has added value if it is demonstrated to be applicable at an international level.*

• Problem solving is often made to seem gruelling and frustrating. It is true, problem solving can be hard work, but it can often be fun, even funny – especially when a coherent, whole problem solving system is used.

CSF8 *Problem solving should be fun.*

• Problem solving entails being critical. Being critical is usually interpreted as being negative. A cartoon in the *Times Higher Education Supplement* said it all – a note was pinned on the door of a Professor of Critical Theory that read 'Enter, then start knocking'. Two points given below argue that being critical does not mean being negative.

  – Being critical is the most effective way of learning about, understanding and hence making improvements where organisational problems are encountered. As I see it, any organisational improvement is a positive thing.

  – This book is critical of many current problem solving practices. Criticism is based on experiences of hundreds of managers who are well seasoned when it comes to intervention using problem solving methods. They have evaluated methods and their outcomes, learnt from this, achieved better understanding, and with this knowledge helped me to improve the effectiveness of the problem solving system TSI. As I understand it, improving problem solving effectiveness is also a positive thing.

  CSF9 *A problem solving system must include procedures that are critical of outcomes it generates and must include procedures which ensure that the system remains critical of itself.*

This book squares up to the nine CSFs highlighted above. In doing this, it helps managers to make good use of time available to make improvements to their problem solving skills. It also shapes the problem solving system presented in this book so that it is respectful of managers and the management *modus operandi*, in the sense that it takes into account that organisational life requires the work of management and that management skills must be drawn on while extending the experience of managers. The problem solving system reported in this book meets all nine CSFs in the following way.

- It cuts back on the number of concepts used within problem solving, translates the remaining concepts into everyday language and integrates them into one whole system.
- It incorporates powerful tools to stimulate and provoke creative and perceptive thought and in this way helps to develop an informed understanding of problems faced.
- It steers the problem solver through the process of choosing methods relevant to problems faced.
- It comes with an explanation of what is happening when people use the system according to its principles.
- It comes with the knowledge of potential pitfalls in problem solving that need to be avoided.
- It is not shallow or gimmicky.
- It has added value because it is demonstrated to be applicable at an international level.
- It is critical of outcomes it generates and is critical of itself.
- It encourages fun.
- It is called Total Systems Intervention (TSI).
  Total: It draws together and integrates methods for
  - *creativity* (to think creatively and perceptively about problems faced)
  - *choice* (to choose (a) method(s) relevant to those problems)
  - *implementation* (to apply chosen methods to tackle those problems).
  Systems: It guides managers toward a whole or systems view. It takes into account all relevant aspects of a problem solving situation. It deals with whole systems. It is a total problem solving system.
  Intervention: It is an activity that brings about progressive

improvement where problems are found through intervention – Total Systems Intervention.

That is the background. I will return to the CSFs in the concluding chapter when reflecting upon the ways in which each one
is met in the chapters that follow. But now, let's get going. Let's
start right away thinking about and using the problem solving
system TSI.

2
Overview of the Problem Solving System: TSI

This chapter provides managers with an up-front overview of the problem solving system TSI, which is explained in detail as the book progresses. It is an abridged version of TSI aimed at getting managers started, getting you thinking and using TSI. As stated in the first chapter, every manager problem solves in their job every day. This chapter will help you to reflect on your job today, tomorrow and over the next few weeks or so, whilst the rest of the book is read for the first time. It will help you to reflect on how you problem solve, how your skills can be complemented, expanded and improved through TSI.

The crucial idea that makes TSI stand out is its discovery that managers operate three main types of activity when problem solving – Creativity, Choice and Implementation (these are known as the three phases of TSI). Think about it. Surely this is what you do to some extent?

- *You think creatively* about the problems that you face, listening to and incorporating other people's views.
- *You choose a method*, sometimes simple, sometimes sophisticated, that you judge is most likely to tackle those problems effectively.
- *You then implement changes*, using the method to develop proposals that actually tackle those problems.

I agree that it is not normal to think about problem solving in this way, but that is the whole point of TSI, to help to clarify, understand and formalise what we do. Only then will it be possible to complement, expand and improve on the skills that we have. This learning begins by digging deeper into the process, Creativity, Choice and Implementation.

In TSI these three activities are brought together to form the problem solving cycle shown in Figure 2.1. The cycle investigates organisational 'messes', surfaces problems and demonstrates the interacting nature of them and chooses the right method(s) to tackle the problems in the circumstances. The TSI cycle recognises that problem solving is a continuous process. It is not a simple matter of solving a problem and then it is all over and done with. There is no end point. Problem solving is a core component of the continuous process of management. There will always be new problems tomorrow no matter what we do today. The required skill is to be confident when managing those problems, to realise effective organisation and to achieve successfully things that we set out to do. A part of that skill is to be creative in the way that we choose things to do, be it improving procedures, developing strategy and policy,

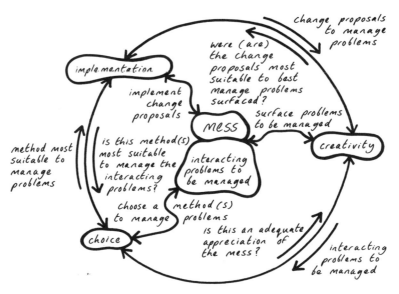

Figure 2.1   *The problem solving cycle of TSI*

influencing the corporate culture, or whatever. Another part of that skill is being able to choose relevant methods that help you do those things well. This is a continuous process – a process of creative thinking, choice of method(s) and implementation of innovative change proposals worked out with the chosen method(s).

We can also observe from Figure 2.1 that the cycle operates in both clockwise and anti-clockwise directions. There is no given start, or finish point. Activities do not actually happen in any preset order. The existence of this fluid approach to problem solving can be demonstrated by further examining what happens in the three phases of TSI.

- *Creativity.* When thinking creatively about interacting problems faced, you will also project your thinking forward. You will ask which method(s) is/are most suitable, what change proposals it/they will generate and what consequences there will be for all involved if those proposals are implemented? You will also reflect on how well previous implementations have gone taking into account other people's viewpoints.
- *Choice.* When choosing a method you will always reflect on creative thinking, reassessing if a good enough understanding of the problems faced has been worked out. You also will make projections about the impact of implementing change proposals that methods will generate if they are chosen.
- *Implementation.* When implementing change proposals arising from the chosen method(s) you will reflect on the suitability of the method and on the adequacy of creative thinking about the problems faced that gave rise to the choice of method(s).

Problem solving is, then, a mixture of creative thinking, choice of method(s) and implementation of change proposals worked out by operating the chosen method(s). Only one of these activities is in focus at any one time. The other two always remain in the picture; but as problem solving continues the focus will change.

Now pause briefly and ask yourself the following questions.

- How do you normally problem solve?
- Can you understand the way that you problem solve in terms

of the three phases, Creativity, Choice, and Implementation, and the problem solving cycle shown in Figure 2.1?

- Does the cycle improve your own understanding about how you problem solve?
- Does the cycle complement the problem solving skills that you already have, perhaps by organising your thoughts more clearly about the problem solving process?
- Is the cycle a more realistic way of thinking about problem solving compared to the traditional finite linear process
  - identify the problem
  - solve it
  - get back to normal organisational life?
- Does the cycle provide a good basis on which to expand and improve further your problem solving skills?

Each one of the phases, Creativity, Choice and Implementation, will now be analysed in a little more detail. TSI identifies the task, the methods that we can use and the expected outcome for each phase. Starting with the Creativity phase, the process of TSI works as follows.

The *task* of the Creativity phase is to gain an appreciation of problems to be dealt with taking into account other people's views, to demonstrate the interacting nature of the problems and to highlight core problems that must be dealt with. No problem exists in isolation. Tackling one problem will also impact on or create other problems. A range of *methods* which promote creative thinking may be employed here (set out in Chapter 9). The *outcome* in the form of a set of core and inter-acting problems to be dealt with is passed on to the Choice phase.

Now take another short break and address the following questions.

- Do you spend enough time thinking creatively and seriously confronting other people's views of problems faced?
- Do you employ tools to aid creative thinking or do you rely on intuition?
- If you do use tools for creative thinking, how effective are they? Are they sufficient to penetrate the complexities of mod-ern-day management?

- Have you explored the possibility of using additional creativity-enhancing methods by reviewing what is available?

The *task* of the Choice phase is to choose (a) method(s) that will help you most effectively to manage the interacting and core problems surfaced during the Creativity phase. The need is to tackle the most pressing problems whilst managing as broad a spread of problems as possible. The key is to remember that the problems are interacting and that each method, which has an immediate and given purpose, will generate change proposals that cut across them in a different way, dealing with many of the problems but managing them differently by concentrating on highlighted problems only. The *method* designed for the Choice phase relates types of method to the problems they are critically assessed as best suited to (explained in detail in Chapter 9). The expected *outcome* is choice of (a) method(s) that will most effectively tackle problems faced. The outcome is passed on to the Implementation phase.

Again, pause and address the following questions.

- Do you use a spread of methods so that choice of method is an issue?
- Do you think that using a spread of methods is more appropriate for problem solving than sticking to just one or two, since the problems that modern-day managers face are so diverse that employing a few methods only will be inadequate?
- Do you choose methods according to experience in a trial-and-error fashion? Is such a pragmatic approach likely to work effectively or is it high-risk roulette, a kind of hit-or-miss?
- Do you ever choose methods that fail to achieve expected results? If so, why do they fail? If they do not fail, then why do they succeed?
- Do you employ an approach that encourages reasoning about which method to use based on critical analysis of what they are and are not good at doing?

The *task* of the Implementation phase is to employ the chosen method(s) from the Choice phase to deal with problems surfaced by creative thinking. The chosen *method(s)* is/are used to develop and implement specific change proposals to tackle the core problems surfaced (a system of methods is described in Chapter 9). The *outcome* in the form of innovative change proposals is implemented and also is passed on to the Creativity phase. The task of the Creativity phase, following changes made, is to continue to surface problems to be dealt with, to demonstrate the interacting nature of these problems and to highlight the core ones. The process continues from hereon in the same manner described above.

Now pause once more and address the following questions.

- What are the main methods that you employ, be they simple or sophisticated?
- What purpose do those methods serve? (To design efficient organisational processes or effective organisational design? To debate and make decisions about what should be done? To evaluate critically whose interests are being served by the designs or the decisions?)
- Can the methods that you employ tackle all of the diverse and complex organisational problems mentioned in the previous bullet point?
- What problems do you face that the methods you employ cannot properly tackle or deal with?

The points made so far can be summarised as follows. The problem solving system called TSI comprises three phases – Creativity, Choice and Implementation. The phases are organised on a cycle and the cycle shows problem solving to be a continuous process. Each phase has its task, methods and outcome. A system of methods usefully employed in TSI is detailed in Chapter 9.

For now, this introduction to TSI will help you to get started, to organise your thoughts about how you problem solve and to question whether or not your problem solving skills can be expanded upon and improved. It raises questions for you to answer such as the following three main ones.

- Are you creative enough in thinking about the diverse problems that you face?
- Are the methods that you employ capable of tackling the diverse problems that you face?

- Do you use methods in a trial-and-error, hit-or-miss manner, or do you reason which method should be used, when and why, to tackle the diverse problems that you face?

These questions direct attention to the strengths and weaknesses of your problem solving skills. They ask you whether you take into account the views and interests of other people. They ask you honestly to assess whether your skills can be complemented, expanded and improved through TSI. They prepare you for the rest of the book.

The aim of the book over the next three chapters is to construct an in-depth explanation of the problem solving system TSI. TSI can usefully be studied through its philosophy, principles and process – the three Ps. Chapter 3 introduces the *philosophy* which explains TSI's understanding of organisation for problem solving. The aim is to develop a foundational understanding of organisation and problem solving. Chapter 4 then sets out the *principles* which propose kinds of action that we should take if TSI's philosophy is adopted. The aim of this chapter is to identify key principles for problem solving. Chapter 5 builds up a comprehensive account of the *process* which implements the principles. The aim here is to explain how to problem solve using the process of TSI. Let us now turn to Chapter 3 and begin the process of learning about the details of TSI.

Part 2
EXPLAINING TSI

3
Understanding Organisation[1] for Problem Solving – 'The Philosophy'

Chapter 3 provides the philosophy of TSI which explains TSI's understanding of organisation for problem solving. The aim is to develop a foundational understanding of organisation and problem solving. This presentation is not a deep philosophy but is representative of one that can be referred to (see Further Reading at the end of the book).

The main idea of TSI's philosophy is that we think about places in which we work as whole human organisations. It is only when a good understanding of organisation as a whole is grasped, by taking into account the viewpoints of all concerned, that effective management can be achieved. If we fail to develop a whole understanding then unnecessary things will happen that foil otherwise well-thought-out plans. When applied to the

---

[1] Attention must be paid to my intended meaning of the term '(an) organisation(s)' in this text. TSI understands '(an) organisation(s)' in terms of relationships between people that transcend the traditional appreciation set by a boundary being drawn between the internal organisation and its external clients. It is more realistic to appreciate '(an) organisation(s)' in terms of various forms of human relationships rather than separate organic social entities. Wherever and however employed in this text, the term '(an) organisation(s)' must be interpreted in the preferred way as just stated. See also section 7.11 What is Meant By 'Organisation'.

many forms of organisation, then, TSI insists that we assume an adaptable and negotiable stance so that we are able to develop and work with a whole view of them.

With TSI, organisation is conceived of as a whole system that comprises parts which are continually interacting. Parts form a system (the horizontal dimension) that is a subsystem of a larger system and has subsystems itself (the vertical dimension). Organisation is therefore thought of as if it were a vertically and horizontally integrated series of systems.

The question remains 'How we can enrich our understanding of the whole organisation in these systemic terms?' The following four key dimensions of organisation guide our thinking. We need to have a thorough understanding of *organisational processes*, the flows and controls from suppliers right through to consumers, including parties such as stakeholders with an interest in events. We need to understand *organisational design* within which the processes happen. This means identifying the possible functions of organisation and how these functions (rather than lines of authority) are controlled and co-ordinated.

We must also appreciate *individual and cultural differences and similarities* that exist between people. People are different. People need different things, respond to things in different ways and understand things differently. In this sense, there is no single organisation. There are as many forms of organisation as there are people thinking about the forms.

Despite this differentiation, cohesion can be attained. This is partly because of the possibility of corporate culture. A strong corporate culture with good cohesion comprises people who share a common history, hold a common understanding and have a common sense of belonging. Corporate culture is where people who feel they belong to a corporation share many ideas, such as social rules and practices, although there will rarely be a total overlap. However, in a dynamic corporation differences of opinion or interest inevitably arise. A number of these will be expressed through organisational politics.

Having an appreciation of *political dynamics* helps to round things off, to complete the whole picture. It is important to know who holds power and how this power is used to serve certain interests. It leads us to explore who is in a position to bring resources or biases to bear to get their own way. The question is, 'Who in the scheme of things may be regarded as influential in determining strategy, policy and what people do?' It also allows us to examine how power may be spread in ways which indeed subvert official positions of power.

It is therefore the argument of TSI that we can only get to know about forms of whole organisation if we develop understanding in terms of 'control' in the following four key dimensions.

- *Organisational processes* – flows, and controls over flows.
- *Organisational design* – functions, their organisation, co-ordination and control.
- *Organisational culture* – mediation of behaviour in terms of people's relationship to social rules and practices.
- *Organisational politics* – power and potency to influence the flow of events.

Unless all four key dimensions of organisation are taken into account, i.e., a whole system view is developed, then problem solving is bound to be ineffective. It will be ineffective because crucial influential factors will have been neglected. Leaving influential things hidden gives rise to a predominance of unexpected and usually unwanted changes. Allowing organisational activities to be run in this way leads to ineffective management.

The problem solving system TSI must therefore operate a system of methods that is able to deal with problems arising from each of the four key dimensions. There are methods available to do this. Methods can be grouped according to which key dimension they are best suited to, i.e., what types of problem they are judged by their users to be best at tackling. Each of the key dimensions of organisation is the source of a type of problem, which accordingly means that there must be four main types of problem solving method.

In a nutshell, there are four key dimensions to organisation and four main types of problem solving method that tackle problems which arise respectively in each key dimension. Every problem solving method with its own immediate and given purpose can be categorised in this way.

The image of organisation pieced together above builds a

framework on which an ideal whole system view can be constructed. The ideal can be captured as a model of organisational dynamics which helps to achieve effective management. The model is an ideal because it represents the ideal dynamic of organisation from a TSI perspective. It is an ideal picture of organisational dynamics that we would like to achieve by employing TSI. Of course, ideals can never be achieved. The point is that we should try to approximate the ideal as best as possible. The ideal whole system view has six stages of construction as set out below.

- *Organisational forms comprise technical and human activities.* Organisational activities are represented by an interactive mixture of technical (organisational processes and organisational design) and human (organisational culture and organisational politics) activities. The whole system framework is, then, a horizontally and vertically integrated set of technical and human activities.
- *Organisational activities must be efficiently and effectively controlled (i.e., co-ordinated and mediated) whilst maintaining viability in line with TSI's principles (see next chapter).* Activities are co-ordinated and mediated by technical procedures and socio-cultural and socio-political rules and practices. Procedures, rules and practices must attune, so that viability is achieved.
- *Organisational activities must be directed to achieve some purpose.* Human organisations normally have an officially declared mission to which activities are directed. Ideally this purpose will allow for interpretation and feedback between the declaration and implementation of purpose.
- *People appreciate organisational events in different ways.* Individuals and groups naturally make their own interpretations of events, the way they are controlled, as well as organisational purpose. They hold a view of their own role and purpose in organisational activities. It is this divergence that generates vital organisational dynamism. However, it can cause fruitless discord, a lack of cohesion, inefficiency, ineffectiveness and, ultimately, non-viability. It can lead to polarisation with people rigidly adhering to their own position. Even shades of difference can lead to non-negotiable conflict in the long run. People's views therefore must be taken into account as a mat-

ter of course and conflict must be resolved or measures taken to accommodate differences fairly.

- *The previous two stages must be harmonised through organisational design and management style.* An organisational design and management style must be chosen that balance people's needs with organisational needs, remembering that organisational needs will also reflect the business or organisational context.
- *Managers and problem solvers must accept responsibility for the impact of their decisions and policies on the physical, biological and social environment (e.g., see Case 10.3 in Chapter 10).*

A summary of the chapter so far sees TSI holding an ideal picture of organisational dynamics that managers should strive to achieve. It is the view of TSI that unless managers do strive toward the ideal they will be dogged constantly by inefficiency, ineffectiveness, fruitless conflict and strife. The ideal can be achieved, firstly, by constructing a whole system view of organisational dynamics according to four key dimensions – organisational processes, organisational design, organisational culture and organisational politics. (You may also share with me the need to strive for the ideal on moral, as well as practical, grounds.)

Clearly TSI must provide principles, processes and methods for problem solving that help us to intervene in those dimensions of organisation that do not match up to the ideal. Only then will it be possible to approximate the ideal. Happily, I can say that these components of an ideal problem solving system are provided in *Solving Problem Solving*. TSI helps managers to approximate the ideal.

When applied to organisational problem solving, TSI extends this systemic understanding of organisation. Of great importance here is TSI's awareness of the process of problem solving. For TSI, problem solving actually means getting to know about and then managing interacting issues as opposed to solving identifiable problems.[2] Problems arise from the interaction of

---

[2] Despite adoption of the term 'problem' in this text – for readability – TSI's actual position is that there is no such thing as a problem, only interacting issues to be managed. 'Problem' must be read in this text to mean 'interacting issues'. See also section 7.12 What is Meant By 'Problem'.

technical and human activities, how they are co-ordinated and mediated, interaction of organisational activities with other factors, organisational mission, organisational design and management style, people's interpretations of these and how people choose to exert the power that they hold. Problem solving is a particular type of human activity that by definition is also a part of organisational activities. Organisation, then, can be understood as a complex of interacting activities and problem solving as a continuous process of managing them. Problem solving is a part of the problem to be dealt with.

Intervention, accordingly, will go something like this. Problems are surfaced through creative thinking. By undertaking careful and communicative reasoning, an approach most suitable to tackle the problems surfaced is chosen. Change proposals to deal with the problems are worked out using the chosen approach. Implementation of change proposals takes place. Some problems are dealt with purposefully and directly, some purposefully but indirectly (an oblique use of methods which is discussed in subsequent chapters), whilst others are surprisingly impacted on as a result of our never having an absolute understanding of the whole organisation. These surprises are counter-intuitive, i.e., things that occur counter to our intuitive understanding where formal analysis has not penetrated. New problems arise as a further consequence of implementation. Organisational dynamics, described in the form of problems, changes and reformulated implementation directed at new problems takes place. TSI therefore is a continuous process of dealing with problems throughout whole organisations.

In this chapter an understanding of organisation has been developed from a TSI perspective. TSI paints a picture of organisational forms as if they were whole systems that have an ideal dynamic. To help to achieve that ideal dynamic organisational events must first be understood in terms of four key dimensions – organisational processes, organisational design, organisational culture and organisational politics. Methods relevant to each key dimension are therefore needed to manage organisational dynamics and move them toward the ideal dynamic. Organisational problems are understood as interacting problems. Problem solving, however, must be understood as part of the overall organisational activities and therefore as part of the continuous process of dealing with interacting problems. This is the philosophy of TSI. Let us now move on to the next chapter and to the principles of TSI.

4

Key Principles for Problem Solving – 'The Principles'

Chapter 3 explains the philosophy of TSI. Chapter 4 now sets out the principles which propose kinds of action that we should take if the philosophy about organisation for problem solving constructed in the last chapter is adopted. The aim is to identify key principles for problem solving from the philosophy. In other words, the principles must be drawn out of the philosophy.

Principles are extremely important. They provide a mechanism to evaluate intervention. A TSI intervention must be evaluated against its own principles. If and only if intervention operates according to the principles established in this chapter can the intervention be said to be a valid use of TSI. As a minimum, this means in practice endeavouring to achieve the principles.

There are four main principles to be extracted from the philosophy – being systemic, achieving meaningful participation, being reflective and the goal of enhancing human freedom.

The foundational principle tells us to study organisational forms as if they were *systemic*. This means 'take into account the whole'. It also means that there is a form of hierarchy. 'The system' under study is a part of a greater whole. It also comprises interacting parts. For TSI the hierarchy comprises technical (organisational processes and organisational design) and human (organisational culture and organisational politics) activities at three hierarchical levels – 'the system', 'the subsystems' and 'the suprasystem'. 'The system' is always the hierarchical level that becomes the focus of attention, although the level focused on may change during analysis. All interactions between all parts, of technical and human sorts, at the three levels must be taken into account during the process of continuous management of problems. This principle helps to prevent undesirable counter-intuitive consequences from occurring. It therefore leads to more effective management.

The principle of *meaningful participation* follows the systemic principle. If we are to develop an adequate appreciation of all interactions between all parts, of technical and human sorts, at three levels at any one time, then the perceptions of all people involved and affected must be drawn into the picture. To a large extent organisational events are what people think they are. It is important therefore that we know what people think. If participation is not achieved then only a limited understanding of organisation can be developed. This is not a whole system perspective, meaning the systemic principle is violated. This will lead to less than effective management.

The principle of *reflection* follows the previous two principles. There are two reflective needs with TSI.

- To reflect upon the relationship between different organisational interests – demonstrating that people may be dominated who, as a result, cannot meaningfully participate.
- To reflect upon the dominance of favoured approaches to intervention – demonstrating where the use of one (or a few) method(s) prevails, restricting the capability of managers to tackle effectively the full range of technical and human issues that they face.

The first reflective need is to pinpoint where power is exerted and domination over people exists, throughout the organisation. Often a dominant view holds sway. Domination prevents meaningful participation of involved and affected people and the inclusion of their viewpoints in decision making. This in turn means that less than a whole system understanding is achieved during analysis and that fair practice in generating change proposals is hence compromised.

The second reflective need is to overcome a common mistake

made by problem solvers. Normally they use a small number of methods with restricted problem solving capability. They do not know about the limitations in the methods they are using. Each method is limited, however, in the kinds of problem that it is best employed to tackle. A full range of approaches is required, sufficient to tackle all sorts of technical and human problems in the four key dimensions of organisation. This can be achieved through critical reflection on the strengths and weaknesses of each method, thus bringing these matters to the fore and so linking methods to the sort of problem they are best directed at. Alternatively, if methods are being used to deal with problems they were not originally designed to address, the consultant or manager should be made aware of this through critical reflection.

The reflective principle can be summarised neatly as follows. The first reflective need is to ensure that a whole system understanding is achieved – surfacing all problems to be dealt with. The second reflective need is to ensure that all problems are dealt with – employing methods as and when relevant. Achieving both needs promotes fair and effective management.

The fourth principle introduces TSI's ideology and indeed its moral justification. TSI argues that an explicit ideology of human freedom must enter management practice. This ideology is a personal commitment for some people, but I am also introducing it in TSI as part of a coherent theory about effective management. It logically follows the preceding three principles. Freedom is enhanced through the process of reflection. Reflection helps to achieve meaningful participation, which in turn promotes being systemic and taking into account the whole. Taking into account the whole is an important step toward better informed management, effective problem solving and minimising counter-intuitive consequences.

In this chapter the four main principles of TSI have been set out. They are the four cornerstones of TSI. The principles are interrelated and support each other. The principles must be adhered to if we are to claim a valid use of TSI. The principles reflect the philosophy reported in Chapter 3 and shape the process of TSI explained in the next chapter, to which we now turn our attention.

5
How to Problem Solve – 'The Process'

In Chapter 3 the philosophy of TSI is presented. It explains TSI's understanding of organisation for problem solving. In Chapter 4 the principles of TSI are set out. These propose kinds of action that we should take if the philosophy constructed in Chapter 3 is adopted. The task for this chapter is to explain how to implement the principles through the process of TSI.

The process of TSI has three modes of operation.

- Critical Review Mode.
- Problem Solving Mode.
- Critical Reflection Mode.

The Critical Review Mode reviews critically methods bidding to be incorporated in the Problem Solving Mode of TSI. It does this by assessing the ways in which the method under review can be incorporated within and operated by the process of TSI. There are three stages to this process.

- Test problem solving methods using the three phases of TSI (introduced in Chapter 2), Creativity, Choice and Implementation, to judge which of these the method under review may contribute to.
- Further review problem solving methods by assessing which

of the four key dimensions of organisation (described in Chapter 3) the method is capable of engaging.
- Ultimately, ask whether TSI can learn anything from methods reviewed in terms of its own philosophy, principles, process and its own methods such as the method to operationalise the Critical Review Mode.

The Problem Solving Mode of TSI employs a system of methods for problem solving brought together through the Critical Review Mode. It operates through the three phases of TSI as follows.

- Think creatively about problems faced and identify the core ones.
- Choose the most suitable method(s) in the circumstances to deal with the core problems.
- Use the chosen method(s) to develop and implement innovative change proposals that tackle the core problems.

The term 'circumstances' is used above in a systemic sense to mean the whole situation. The whole situation means everyone and everything. The notion of suitability therefore is subject to those circumstances. It is not the case that there is literally a right method independent of the problem solvers. If circumstances change such that there is a different mix of people, the decision on suitability may change too. It all depends on circumstances and the involved people are part of those circumstances. The Critical Reflection Mode helps to judge suitability in the circumstances – a point that must be remembered throughout this book and whenever problem solving.

The Critical Reflection Mode uses the three phases of TSI to help problem solvers to reflect upon the adequacy of the output of the Problem Solving Mode. It asks the following questions about each phase. In the circumstances

- Is/are the method(s) in use the most suitable one(s)?
- Is/are the output of the method(s) appropriate?

The three modes are discussed below. (Procedures that operationalise the three modes are detailed in Chapter 9.)

5.1 CRITICAL REVIEW MODE

The process of TSI guides the problem solving process by employing methods for creative thinking, choice of method(s) for implementation and the use of those method(s) to develop and implement innovative change proposals. To do this TSI must incorporate problem solving methods in its schema. It does this by critically reviewing methods bidding to be incorporated in the system of methods operated through the Problem Solving Mode, using to structure the critique the three phases of TSI and the four key dimensions of organisation. The critical review has two starting assumptions which are tested out. The two starting assumptions enrich the process of TSI by encouraging variety in the methods employed in each of the three phases.

The first starting assumption is that each method undergoing review advocates forms of creativity, choice and implementation. Procedures are given that help problem solvers to learn about each method in terms of the three phases. Assessing a range of methods in this way provides a wide knowledge about what can be done within each phase of TSI. Procedures are given that then help problem solvers to choose the most suitable way of carrying out each phase taking into account the circumstances.

The second starting assumption is that each method asks four questions which reflect the four key dimensions of organisation: 'How can we efficiently design processes?', 'How can we realise effective organisational design?', 'What options should we debate and decide upon?' and 'Why should we accept a design or a decision, who is likely to benefit and has fair practice operated in generating these change proposals?' The questions help us to highlight which of the key dimensions each method addresses. Procedures are given that help problem solvers to understand exactly in what way the methods address the four questions. On the basis of this, problem solvers, when using TSI in the Problem Solving Mode, will be able to choose the most suitable method(s) for implementation in the circumstances.

The Critical Review Mode is needed so that a system of methods is prepared, capable of tackling the complex and diverse problems that we face today. It is not possible to problem solve in a satisfactory way with TSI unless an adequate base of methods has been reviewed and incorporated in the system of methods. But remember, the critical review process is never complete in the sense that there will always be more methods to review! (Chapter 9 provides a suggested base system of methods for the Problem Solving Mode following my own use of the Critical Review Mode.)

5.2 PROBLEM SOLVING MODE

The process of TSI has three phases in the Problem Solving Mode: Creativity, Choice and Implementation. You will be very familiar with these by now. The activities are brought together in Chapter 2 to form a problem solving cycle that is repeated in Figure 5.1. The cycle is a continuous process with no predetermined start or finish point. It is a continuous process that promotes creative thinking about the organisational 'mess', surfaces and demonstrates the interacting nature of problems and helps problem solvers to deal with them. (Remember, TSI actually assumes that managers manage issues rather than solve problems.) The problems are an appreciation of organisational

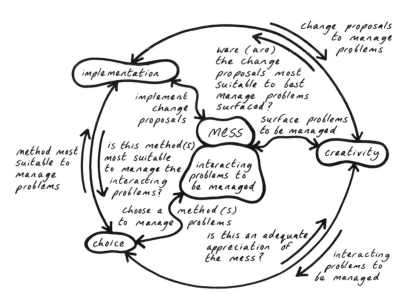

Figure 5.1   *The problem solving cycle of TSI (repeat of Figure 2.1)*

complexity arising from technical and human activities (discussed in Chapter 3). The circular process operates in both clockwise and anti-clockwise directions. The clockwise direction is the Problem Solving Mode dealt with in this section. The anti-clockwise direction is the Critical Reflection Mode that is picked up in the next section.

The process (Creativity, Choice and Implementation) in the Problem Solving Mode operates in the following way. Each phase has a task, methods and expected outcome. The outcome is passed on to the next phase. That next phase uses the outcome from the previous phase to help achieve its given task drawing upon methods relevant to its task. The resulting outcome is passed on to the next phase, and so the process continues.

Starting with the Creativity phase, the process works as follows. The task of creative thinking is to surface problems to be dealt with, to demonstrate the interacting nature of the problems and to identify the core ones. It does this by using methods for creative thinking that break out of current assumptions and get to grips with core problems to be dealt with. A range of methods that promote creative analysis is employed here (discussed in Chapter 9). The outcome is a set of interacting problems with the core ones highlighted. This appreciation is passed on to the Choice phase.

The task of the Choice phase is to choose (a) method(s) which has/have an immediate and given purpose for implementation that will deal with the problems surfaced by creative thinking, concentrating on the core problems that have been located. The need is to tackle the most pressing problems, the core ones, whilst managing as broad a spread of the interacting problems as possible. The trick is to remember that the problems are interacting and that each method will generate change proposals that cut across them in a different way, affecting many problems but dealing with them differently by concentrating on the most pressing ones to start with. The task then becomes a matter of choosing the most suitable method(s) in the circumstances. The outcome, which is a choice of method(s) that will be used to come up with innovative change proposals, is passed on to the Implementation phase.

The task of the Implementation phase is to employ the chosen method(s) from the Choice phase to deal with the problems surfaced by creative thinking. The chosen method(s) is/are used to develop and implement innovative change proposals that tackle the given problems. The outcome in the form of innovative change proposals is implemented and is also passed on to the Creativity phase.

The task of the Creativity phase is to continue to surface problems to be dealt with, to demonstrate the interacting nature of these problems and to highlight the core ones. By this time problems will have changed because proposals will already have been implemented. The process continues from hereon in the manner described above, taking into account changes occurring as a consequence of implementation of proposals.

The process of TSI in the Problem Solving Mode is best thought of as a singularity, that is, it is one integrated whole. The purpose of separating out three activities, Creativity, Choice and Implementation, is to explain the singularity and the process. Each one distinguishes and focuses on a type of activity that is carried out in the process of TSI; however, as stressed in Chapter 2, no phase exists independently as might be mistakenly assumed from the above presentation. At any one time each phase comes into play, although one of the phases may be in sharper focus than the other two. A description of the process of each of the three phases in the Problem Solving Mode will now be given.

5.2.1 Creativity

Each of the three phases of TSI can be found actually within each of the three phases. That is, the three phases coexist in a recursive structure. Figure 5.2 illustrates this point. Creativity, the first phase to be covered, is best understood therefore as the subactivities, creativity, choice and implementation. However, each subactivity takes on its own meaning within the Creativity phase as seen later.

The aim of the Creativity phase is to surface problems to be dealt with using creative thinking. This involves both divergent and convergent thinking. These two forms of thinking are briefly discussed below.

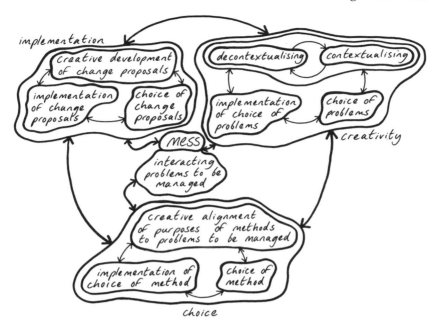

Figure 5.2 *Subactivities of the three phases of TSI*

Divergent thinking helps people to get unstuck by appreciating the situation from many different angles and considering the viewpoints that others may have on the situation. Appreciating things in this way surfaces problems to be dealt with that are otherwise hidden or not previously thought of. Divergent thinking is therefore creative.

Convergent thinking works in co-operation with divergent thinking, converging on problems to be dealt with. Convergent thinking makes sense of the diversity of possible problems generated. It converges on core problems that must be dealt with.

So, in terms of the recursive structure, divergent thinking provides the *creative* input necessary to surface a wide range of problems to be dealt with. It does this by looking at organisational complexity from many angles taking into account other people's viewpoints. Convergent thinking then *chooses* the core problems that must be dealt with. *Implementation* of the choice of core problems follows by passing them on to the Choice phase.

5.2.2 Choice

The aim of the Choice phase is to choose (a) method(s) which has/have an immediate and given purpose for implementation that will best deal with the problems surfaced by creative thinking, concentrating on the core problems that have been located. The process of Choice has choice of method as the main concern, although aspects of creativity and implementation are also found.

The process of choice of method for implementation is built upon the philosophy of TSI and its systemic view of organisation. In Chapter 3, on the philosophy of TSI, it was stated that organisation, to be understood as a whole, must be analysed in terms of control in the following four key dimensions.

- *Organisational processes* – flows and controls over flows.
- *Organisational design* – functions, their organisation, co-ordination and control.
- *Organisational culture* – mediation of behaviour in terms of people's relationship to social rules and practices.
- *Organisational politics* – power and potency to influence the flow of events.

Problem solving must take into account all four key dimensions to be effective. The problem solving system must therefore incorporate the following four types of problem solving method that each tackles problems found in one of the four key dimensions of organisation.

- Methods that address the question 'How can we design the most efficient organisational processes and arrange their implementation?'
- Methods that address the question 'How can we achieve effective organisation?'
- Methods that ask 'What options should we decide upon that debate technical and human issues that arise in organisational dynamics and lead to decisions on what to do about them?'
- Methods that ask 'Why a design or a decision should be adopted that merely serve the interests of dominant groups, rather than balancing individual and organisational needs,

taking into account physical, biological and social environments?'

Table 5.1 summarises how the ideas mentioned above fit together. The essence of the table's contents is that technical issues are dealt with through design whilst human issues are dealt with through debate; but the two are not separate as pointed out below. Also, the table makes it clear that the four key dimensions of organisation can only be managed if problem solving methods are used in a complementary way. Methods are employed when they are most suitable in the circumstances to address core problems identified, but will be replaced by another method(s) when core problems change. Core problems change because all forms of organisation are dynamic and part of that dynamic is intervention using problem solving methods.

The process of choice of method for implementation is in line with the principles of TSI. The arrangement of ideas shown in Table 5.1 accords with the principle of human freedom which in turn provides support to the three other principles, reflection, participation and being systemic (discussed in the previous chapter). The four main types of problem solving method necessary to deal with problems arising in the four key dimensions of organisation address the need to guarantee as far as possible human freedom. This guarantee can be shown to exist for each one as summarised below.

Technical activities centre on the desire for some level of prediction and control. This is catered for by methods that *design freedom into organisational activities in the form of efficient organisational processes and effective organisational design*. For human

Table 5.1 *Summary of the main ideas of the Choice phase from the Problem Solving Mode of TSI*

Technical		Human	
Design of organisational processes	Effective organisational design	Debating what to do	Debating why something should be done
Asking the question 'How?'	Asking the question 'How?'	Asking the question 'What?'	Asking the question 'Why?'

activities methods have been established that encourage *freedom through open and meaningful debate.* Also focusing on human activities are methods that generate debate about individual and group *freedom, freeing people from dominating designs and decisions.* TSI's principle of human freedom is therefore supported by each of the four main types of problem solving method used in TSI's process, but, interestingly, support comes in four different although mutually reinforcing ways.

Each type of method is reciprocal. We need to have efficient designs for processes and effective organisation that meaningfully involve people at all levels and across all functions so that activities operate well. The amount of efficiency and effectiveness realised from the designs depends upon there being an adequate understanding about how to operate the designs, roles to be played by people according to the designs (and their interpretation of the designs), how each role contributes and fits into the whole design, appreciation of the benefits and meaningfulness of the whole, etc. This means that people must learn about and understand these things, which requires open and free debate. Now, when designs or outcome of debate are subject to dominating forces a means of overcoming the forces is essential so that meaningful participation is achieved. Explicit questions about why designs or decisions should be adopted helps to achieve more genuine debate, enhancing learning and understanding, making fairer decisions, leading to more meaningful work and maximum effectiveness and efficiency from designs. This allows argument into the dynamics of organisation. Designs and decisions are therefore operated through the principle of human freedom – which all adds up to maximum freedom.

This leads on to the process of choosing (a) most suitable method(s) to tackle the interacting and core problems brought forward from the Creativity phase. This is relatively straightforward. There are two steps.

- *Choose type of method* by linking problems to be managed to one of the four key dimensions of organisation.
- *Choose actual method(s)* from the set of methods grouped according to the key dimension that it/they serve(s), by

assessing which one most clearly tackles the problem(s) in detail according to its immediate and given purpose.

These two steps are operationalised in Chapter 9. Also, guidelines are given that suggest what to do if none of the methods incorporated in the problem solving system can tackle the problems surfaced by the Creativity phase. This in itself is a *creative* process. *Choice* of method is then *implemented*. The method(s) chosen is/are taken forward to the Implementation phase.

There is an extremely important point that must be recorded here which adds an extra dimension to problem solving with TSI. With careful handling, methods can be used obliquely to achieve purposes that are not their immediate or given purpose. An example is the use of effective organisational design to address coercion. What is happening when you problem solve in such a case is more complex than so far explained. The method used has an immediate and given purpose to find a solution to effective organisational design. The oblique purpose which is really the whole point of the exercise is to ensure that people are not coerced. So, the way the method is used is with an oblique purpose in mind. This can be true of any method

In choosing methods, then, problem solvers are faced with options such as which one(s) to use. But they also have options about how to use them. This is best explained through an enhanced understanding of the process of Choice.

The enhanced process of Choice in TSI can be put across quite easily. Figure 5.3 shows the relationship between the four main

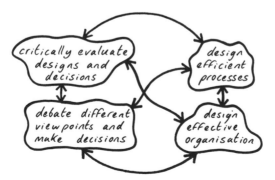

Figure 5.3 *Relationship between the four main types of problem solving method employed in TSI*

types of problem solving method. The figure shows how a manager may move from one type of problem solving method to another in any direction at any time, depending on circumstances. It shows types of method being used according to their immediate and given purpose.

Figure 5.4 expresses an alternative way of relating the four main types of problem solving method using six straight lines that represent the oblique use of methods. The lines are directed with arrowheads. Each line has two arrowheads at either end, meaning that it is possible to move in both directions of the line. There are 12 possible oblique uses of types of method shown in Figure 5.4. An oblique use occurs when a method of a given type is drawn along any one of the arrows, piercing a method of another given type that it is directed at and dominating it as depicted at the tip of the arrowhead.

A hypothetical illustration will help. Take it that problem solvers have moved around the circular part of the diagram by employing the process of TSI and have chosen 'Why?' type methods as most relevant to the issues faced. In other words, the problem solvers judge the problem context to be coercive. Another feature of the problem context may be, however, that

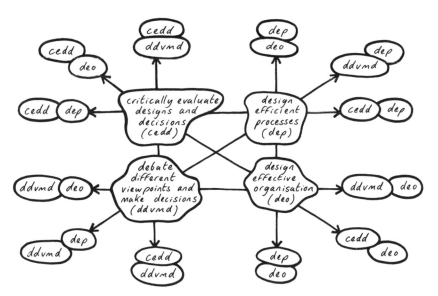

Figure 5.4 *Oblique use of the four main types of problem solving method employed in TSI*

management feel edgy about the explicit use of a method that directly questions the appropriateness of their previous actions and indeed their integrity as managers (an excuse often used to justify disregarding politically sensitive problems). Yet they understand the need to accommodate the free will of those affected, if for no other reason than maintaining organisational viability. Then a good choice of method might be to pull in a method of a different type but to operate it with principles of human freedom drawn from a 'why?' ethic. The operation must of course adhere to these principles to be a valid oblique use of the method. In this way it may be possible for managers to permit sensitive practice 'through the back door' (i.e., through another argument). A further illustration of this can be found in Chapter 9.

5.2.3 Implementation

The aim of Implementation is to employ the method(s) chosen for implementation to deal with the problems surfaced by creative thinking. The chosen method(s) is/are used *creatively* to develop, *choose* and *implement* innovative change proposals that address the given problems. The process of Implementation employs the method(s) for implementation as its main concern, although, as just intimated, aspects of creativity and choice are also found (see Figure 5.2). The process of implementation is carried out in line with the immediate and given purpose, and guidelines of the chosen method(s), or some other method if an oblique use is the intention.

Output of all three phases of TSI in the Problem Solving Mode is subject to further analysis through TSI's Critical Reflection Mode.

5.3 CRITICAL REFLECTION MODE

The process Creativity, Choice and Implementation, in the Critical Reflection Mode, works as follows (refer also to Figure 5.1). The Critical Reflection Mode operates in the anti-clockwise direction, raising questions about the outcome of the three phases. It does this by asking in the circumstances the following questions about the output of the phases.

- Is/are the method(s) used the most suitable one(s)?
- Is/are the output(s) of the method(s) appropriate?

This form of analysis is explained below for each of TSI's three phases.

- The Implementation phase receives (a) method(s) reasoned to be most suitable for managing the problems surfaced by the Creativity phase. It also generates innovative change proposals using the(se) method(s). Implementation's critically reflective position asks 'Is/are this/these method(s) and the innovative change proposals it/they generate(s) most suitable given the circumstances?'.
- The Choice phase receives details of problems to be managed and on the basis of this chooses a method for implementation. Choice's critically reflective position asks 'Is this an adequate appreciation of organisational events and is the method for choice capable of leading to the most suitable choice of method for implementation in the circumstances?'
- The Creativity phase receives details of change proposals judged to be most adequate to manage problems surfaced by creative thinking. Creativity employs methods to continue the process of creative thinking. Creativity's critically reflective position asks 'Were/are the change proposals most suitable to best deal with problems surfaced, and was/were/is/are the method(s) used for creative thinking the most suitable one(s) to surface core problems to be dealt with?' It questions whether current practice needs to be altered.

Each phase, then, passes its outcome to the next phase in the clockwise Problem Solving Mode, but receives critical reflections on that outcome from the next phase in the anti-clockwise Critical Reflection Mode.

The process of TSI has now been put in place and its three modes explained. Chapter 9 sets out the methods and procedures employed through the process of TSI that operationalises the three modes. Before revealing the operationalisation of TSI there is an important job to be done, and that is to understand properly the process by drawing attention to the do's and don'ts of problem solving with TSI.

Part 3

DO'S AND DON'TS OF
PROBLEM SOLVING WITH TSI

6
What is Happening When You Problem Solve?

So far in this book we have reviewed the philosophy, principles and process – the three Ps of TSI. This explains TSI's understanding of organisation for problem solving, sets out the kind of action that we should take if that view is adopted and explains how the principles can be implemented in practice. It is essential now to explain in broad terms the sort of changes that should occur in practice when different types of method are used. This will improve the understanding of what is happening when you problem solve and will improve the likelihood of achieving any desired impact.

As we have already seen, there are four main types of problem solving method, each tackling problems arising from one of the four key dimensions of organisation. The four types of method and the general question that they address are repeated below.

- Methods that address the question 'How can we design the most efficient organisational processes and arrange their implementation?'
- Methods that address the question 'How can we achieve effective organisation?'
- Methods that ask 'What options should we decide upon that debate technical and human issues that characterise organis-

ational activities and lead to decisions on what to do about them?'

- Methods that ask 'Why a design or a decision should be adopted that merely serve the interests of dominant groups, rather than balancing individual and organisational needs, taking into account the physical, biological and social environments?'

Each type of method and the question it addresses can be studied to determine the sort of changes that are supposed to occur when they are put into action, if a valid use is to be claimed. Each one is explored below under the categories 'Design – How?', 'Debate – What?', and 'Disimprisoning – Why and for Whom?'.

6.1 DESIGN – 'HOW?'

When the consultant and/or the manager has decided what needs to be done, why and whose interests are likely to be served, then it remains to determine 'How best to do it?' How to do it is essentially about design, that is, design of organisational processes or organisational design. The aim is to employ the first principle of TSI, being systemic, in the sense of design. This is achieved through efficient and/or effective designs. Process design aims to achieve efficient organisational processes. Organisational design aims to realise an effective form of organisation.

When answering 'How?' questions, we operate methods that are means-end approaches. Ends are set, such as specifications or standards that have to be achieved. The means to achieve them are then identified, such as methods, materials, manpower or machinery. It is then a matter of utilising the means to achieve the ends. This is essentially a linear process that is explored further below.

In general, problem solving accomplishes two things.

- Those that emerge from the process.
- The output of the process.

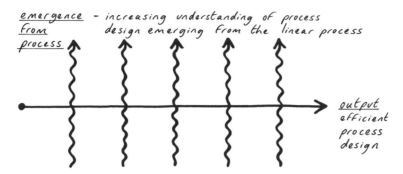

Figure 6.1   *What is happening during the linear process – process design*

Understanding these two things helps to explain what is happening when we problem solve. Figure 6.1 illustrates the point for the linear process – process design.

In Figure 6.1 the output of the problem solving process is shown as a solution which is the most efficient process design. The solution is the main point of the exercise. It is what the process is all about. Emerging out of the problem solving process, however, is increasing understanding of organisational processes. This understanding supports the solution.

Figure 6.2 shows the linear process for organisational design. Achieving the most effective organisational design is the whole point of the exercise. Emerging out of the process, however, is increasing understanding of organisational design as such. This understanding provides support knowledge and also allows people using the design to reinterpret its relevance.

There is a potentially wider benefit from this type of process.

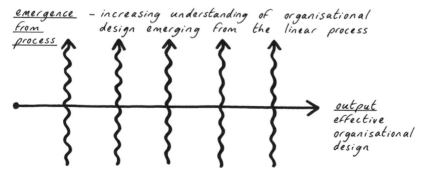

Figure 6.2   *What is happening during the linear process – organisational design*

In both cases the designs, as argued in Chapter 5, can lead to greater human freedom, the fourth main principle of TSI. Human freedom in one respect can be achieved through efficient organisational processes and effective organisational design. This prevents human organisation from being dragged down by its own inefficiency and ineffectiveness. Being inefficient and ineffective traps people in the muddle which ensues. Then people are not free, save for those who benefit from and possibly cause the muddle (a part of the complexity a consultant or manager must be aware of).

In summary, the changes that occur when using methods that answer the question 'How?' achieve the following.

- A solution – efficient organisational processes or effective organisational design – the main point of the exercise.
- Support knowledge – increasing understanding of organisational processes or organisational design emerging from the linear process.
- Wider benefit – human freedom through efficient organisational processes or effective organisational design; especially if the discussion of the design is an ongoing process.

6.2 DEBATE – 'WHAT?'

When it is not clear what needs to be done, or there is disagreement about this, or it is necessary to reassess what is being done, then the main problem to tackle is 'What should we do?' A satisfactory answer to the question 'What?' demands open and meaningful debate between people involved in the decision-making process as well as those who will be affected by it. The aim is to support the first principle of TSI, being systemic, by upholding the second principle of participation. Debate is usually in the form of strategic options analysis aiming to come up with a favoured option, accepted for the time being as having taken into account all factors and the viewpoints of all interested parties.

When answering 'What?' questions, we are operating methods that are cyclical and are employing a process that is theoretically never-ending. Debate is a never-ending process of learning and understanding, although in practice there are limits dictated by time and resource constraints (but even these are debatable). The ideal debate would include representatives of all viewpoints contributing equally. Debate would be open, meaningful and free from power distortions. Debate would ideally conclude in working agreements about options to take forward. These working agreements contain divergence in interpretation and these ongoing differences must be accounted for as part of organisational structure. Figure 6.3 illustrates the cyclical process of debate.

Figure 6.3 shows that the main benefit of the exercise evidently is learning and understanding generated through debate about people's possible roles, people's beliefs, how they fit together, why differences in opinion exist, whether they are negotiable, the generation of new ideas, people's cherished ideas being challenged, and so on. These components of the process are most vital and importantly lead to people shifting their attitudes and beliefs. This amounts to changes in corporate or organisational culture (unless the culture itself incorporates flexibility of attitude or mindset as part of its principles). A

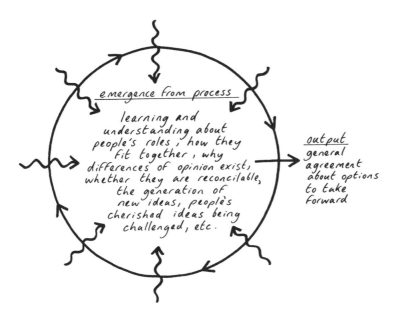

Figure 6.3 *What is happening during the cyclical process of debate*

consequence of the learning and understanding may be negotiated working agreements about options to take forward.

A wider benefit of such a process is that meaningful debate can lead to another sort of human freedom, i.e., freedom of the mind. This means that people are able to escape from mind-traps such as preconceptions, biases and an inability to appreciate things due to a lack of relevant understanding of alternative viewpoints. Participation in debate enables people to see more clearly the horizons of those they work with. Ideally, these horizons are drawn together in a negotiated map that offers new possibilities for all. This might involve, for example, in a commercial company, working out the value of new technology, why sales and distribution sections are at loggerheads or the pros and cons of a Total Quality Management programme for the organisational-enterprise.

In summary, the changes that occur when using methods that answer the question 'What?' achieve the following.

- Learning and understanding, and in most cases a change in people's beliefs and attitudes, and consequently a change in corporate or organisational culture – the main point of the exercise.
- Ideally, negotiated working agreements about options to take forward – although if not achieved this does not negate the value of learning and understanding.
- Wider benefit – freedom of the mind.

6.3 DISIMPRISON – 'WHY AND FOR WHOM?'

When coercive forces are suspected, it is necessary to investigate whose interests are being served. The aim is to ensure that the fourth principle of TSI, achieving human freedom, is upheld by employing the third principle, the reflective principle. This means reflection through debate on whose interests are being served in the current situation. There must also be reflection on the outputs of 'How?' and 'What?' approaches, to consider whether the outputs support a primarily dominant person or group and, if so, why this should be so.

When operating 'Why?' questions, we are operating methods

that are cyclical and, as said before, theoretically never-ending, although the same practical limits apply. Disimprisoning is a process of learning, understanding and challenging the rationale behind designs and decisions. Since the situation is not thought to be free from power distortions, it is legitimate for the process to be strategic and tactical so that designs and decisions can be effectively challenged. All people involved and affected by the designs or decisions must be involved in the process. If this is not feasible because there are too many people, then a fair means of representation must be worked out. The process ideally would conclude, where coercive forces exist, with a demonstration of the need to rethink how things are currently done, or the need to carry out redesign, or the need to rework decisions made through debate, or the need to reconsider the process of apparent pseudo-debate. Figure 6.4 illustrates this cyclical process.

Figure 6.4 illustrates two main benefits that arise when asking the question 'Why and for whom?' The first one is learning and understanding about designs and decisions, in particular in the light of whose interests are being served and an orientation to re-examine the legitimacy of designs and decisions. This may

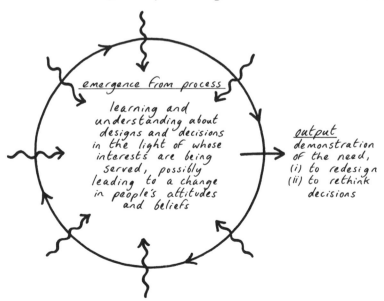

Figure 6.4   *What is happening during the cyclical process of disimprisoning*

also lead to a change in people's attitudes and beliefs. Secondly, as a separate issue, there may be a clear demonstration of the need to redesign or to rethink decisions. These benefits arise from research into whose interests are being served, linking organisational power structures to biases in society (e.g., sex, race or class), or by identifying experts and their position in the power structure, or identifying other forms of the operation of power through, for example, pseudo-debate, or one-sided interpretation of relevant information to support decisions. Reflection of these sorts all adds up to disimprisoning because they help to prevent designs and decisions from becoming prisons for people.

In summary, the changes that occur when using methods that answer the question 'Why and for whom?' achieve the following.

- Learning and understanding about designs and decisions in the light of whose interests are being served, possibly leading to a change in people's attitudes and beliefs.
- Ideally, in coercive contexts, a demonstration of the need
  - to redesign, and/or
  - to rethink decisions.
- Preventing designs and decisions from becoming prisons for people – disimprisoning, which is the main point of the exercise. This disimprisoning process implies the development of a propensity to relinquish the belief that one's concerns must relate to fulfilment of predefined interests. This relinquishment in turn may make possible negotiated options that go beyond initial standpoints and look towards novel change proposals that transcend the initial definition of interests.

There is one final point to make. In the previous chapter it was explained that methods can be used obliquely to achieve purposes that are not their immediate or given purpose. The example given in Chapter 5 cites the use of effective organisational design in an effort to tackle coercion. So, what is happening when you problem solve can be more complex than explained above. Any method used has an immediate and given purpose but the whole point of the exercise may be found in an oblique

Table 6.1 *Summary of what is happening when you problem solve*

	Designing	Debating	Disimprisoning
Type of process	Linear	Cyclical	Cyclical
Main point of the exercise	To find a solution to either efficient processes or effective organisational design	To change people's beliefs and attitudes, and organisational culture	To prevent designs and decisions from becoming prisons
How is the main point achieved?	As the output of the process	Emerges from the process	A combination of the output of *and* what emerges from the process
Supporting changes	Knowledge emerging from the process about organisational processes or organisational design	–	Knowledge emerging from the process about designs and decisions in the light of whose interests are being served; possible changes to people's attitudes and beliefs; leading to the output of the process which is demonstration of the need (i) to redesign or (ii) to rethink decisions
Other benefits	–	Possible decisions made about options to be taken forward	–
Wider benefits	Freedom through design	Freedom of the mind	–

purpose. The method is therefore used with an oblique purpose in mind.

The information in this chapter explains in broad terms what is happening when we problem solve. The main points are recorded in Table 6.1. This enables us to compare and contrast what is happening when we problem solve with each of the four main types of method, either through direct use of immediate and given purpose or through an oblique use. This consolidation reminds us of the main point of employing each of the four types of methods and will, therefore, improve the likelihood of achieving what we set out to do when we choose a method (even if choice is made with an oblique purpose in mind). These are the do's of problem solving with TSI.

There are other details that must be taken into account if we are set on achieving successful and fair problem solving. These details are usefully thought of as potential pitfalls in problem solving. Pitfalls are don'ts in problem solving. The next chapter identifies some of the more important don'ts and discusses how to avoid them.

7
Pitfalls in Problem Solving and How to Avoid Them

The previous chapter focuses on what is happening when you problem solve. The chapter works with TSI's four main purposes for problem solving and explains what should be done to achieve those purposes. It spells out some of the do's in problem solving. Abiding by these do's, however, is not enough. On their own they do not guarantee success because beyond the do's are don'ts that trip up problem solvers and snag the problem solving process. These are the pitfalls. This chapter aims to identify some of the common pitfalls and suggests how they can be overcome. There are 13 don'ts discussed below starting with the systemic principle.

7.1 THE SYSTEMIC PRINCIPLE

A good place to start is with the principles of TSI. The potential pitfall when it comes to being systemic is that, whilst principles can be read and understood, in practice they are easily forgotten. It is difficult to remember to keep the problem solving activities in line with established principles as time progresses.

For TSI, successful problem solving begins with the systemic principle. The systemic principle is the grounding principle of TSI. This principle, if you remember, wants problem solvers to think about and manage the whole. Only when a whole understanding is gained can change proposals be implemented with any sense of justification or confidence. The trouble with systemic thinking is that our education programmes train us from a very early age to reason in a reductionist and not a systemic way. Reductionism means breaking things down into parts, literally reducing them down and then dealing separately with the parts. Consequently, instead of building whole pictures of problems, it feels natural for people to think about and deal with problems in a fragmented way. Problem solving ends up tackling pieces of the problem without considering the consequences of change proposals on the whole problem and whole organisation.

The difficulty is deep rooted. Reductionist thinking is institutionalised in schools, colleges and universities in most countries, although there are pockets of people trying to teach systemic skills. The conventional influence, however, is so strong that most people are unaware that their thought processes are shaped by reductionist thought. Evidently reductionist thinking presents a serious potential pitfall for our problem solving system.

> *Pitfall 1*. Reductionism is institutionalised in a great majority of educational establishments. Consequently, reductionism dominates management thinking and organisational problem solving. A reductionist approach leads to ineffective problem solving.

> *Suggestion*. Continually assess whether the problem solving process is adhering to the systemic principle. Extend this by checking against the other three principles since the systemic principle is supported by them.

7.2 MOTIVATION STYLE

Not all problem solving needs or ought to involve senior management. This is implicit in the four principles of TSI. For example, in a company that practices quality management according to genuine quality principles (or indeed TSI according to its principles), *all people are considered to be managers* because they take responsibility for managing their own work. Everyone is a problem solver. When an innovative idea is thought out by one or a group of people they are allowed to implement it. If the idea requires resources beyond the set allocation, or impinges some way on established strategy, then a proposal must be submitted or placed on an agenda of a meeting for discussion. It is vital that these proposals are taken seriously by senior management who co-ordinate and control the resources asked for, by entering into discussion with those who initiated the proposals and those who would be affected by them. Even if the proposal has to be turned down, the initiators must feel that it was given a good and fair hearing and that the reasons for rejection are understandable (this is best achieved through negotiation and discussion). If they do not, then the would-be problem solvers are bound to be demotivated. They will be much less likely to contribute to organisational problem solving in the future.

Pitfall 2. Senior management demoralise people who are keen and willing to participate in organisational problem solving if they pay only lip service to innovations brought forward.

Suggestion. Make it policy that innovative ideas are implemented by their originators, as long as they do not impinge on strategy, budgeting, etc. If they do impinge on these things, then the people concerned should submit a proposal for improvement which must be given a fair and proper hearing, ideally through negotiation and discussion, ensuring that the innovators get complete feedback on the outcome. This naturally implies the need for good leadership, the subject of the next pitfall.

7.3 LEADERSHIP STYLE

Leadership style influences the way a problem solving system such as TSI operates. Leadership style will therefore affect the likelihood of problem solving practice:

• matching up to the principles of TSI

● adhering to the process of TSI.

The implications of four leadership styles for TSI are explored briefly below.

● *Authoritarian leadership*. In authoritarian regimes dominating leaders discourage the contribution of others. People have to accept the leader's decisions. For TSI this means that the three activities, Creativity, Choice and Implementation, are not used in a meaningful way. The outcome of each phase will be decided by the leader. The systemic principle is violated. From a TSI perspective an authoritarian style is limiting and counterproductive.
● *Supervisory leadership*. Supervisory leadership stops short of the rigidity of autocratic control. Supervisory leaders will introduce topics for discussion and make clear their own view. They are influential although they are not dictators. For example, they set the agenda for how problems are to be solved, thus influencing without absolutely predetermining the outcome. This places limitations particularly on two of TSI's activities, Creativity and Choice. The systemic principle is threatened.
● Laissez faire *leadership*. A *laissez faire* leader refrains from structuring and controlling groups. Group members are expected to be self-directed. The leader listens but does not show approval or disapproval. The leader is overly careful not to inject his or her own thoughts into the process of management or problem solving. The group atmosphere is permissive so that creative thinking can in principle take place although other controls will take over. For example, without intervention, control of group processes and decision making is available to the most powerful people. This is equivalent to abandoning the question 'Why?' that represents one of the four main purposes of problem solving. It clearly violates the principle of human freedom and hence the other three as well.
● *Participative leadership*. Participative leaders encourage members to participate. Participation promotes creative thinking and choice of method, as well as boosting the relevance of change proposals generated through the use of the chosen method(s). Furthermore, group decisions are seen as group

achievements, which are also subject to continued involvement of group members so that they do not become insidified prescriptions. Group members more easily identify with decisions made in this way. In most respects this is TSI's preferred management style. This management style does, however, raise issues about facilitation style, the theme of the next pitfall.

Pitfall 3. Autocratic, supervisory and *laissez faire* leadership styles fail to match up to the needs of the problem solving system TSI in different ways. They prevent problem solving from meaningfully following the process of TSI and fully meeting its principles and main purposes.

Suggestion. Adopt a participative leadership style but take into account the following discussion on facilitation.

7.4 FACILITATION STYLE

Facilitation techniques have become increasingly important for problem solvers. In earlier times when methods merely addressed the question 'How should we do it?' there was need only for experts. The real issue for experts was facilitating the process of learning about 'How to do it'.

A significant limitation of 'How?' methods was slowly revealed. They all assume that knowing what needs to be done is unproblematic. In practice people discovered that often the main issue was precisely the question of 'What should be done?' This led to methods being developed that addressed the question 'What should we do?'

Methods that address the question 'What should we do?' not surprisingly encourage learning about what can be done. Learning of this sort is undertaken by participatory groups and so a new interest arose for facilitation. The new interest closed in on how the group processes can be made to work effectively. As a result, a new form of facilitation emerged, called process consultation, with the aim of improving group dynamics. The facilitator was urged to remain neutral in the process.

More recently process consultation has been criticised for

assuming good communication without the need to challenge assumptions and values underlying statements. Process consultation ignores the problem that communication may be found to be structured by people's power to influence. In that case group dynamics are power dynamics and the question of 'What should be done?' will be determined through those dynamics. Facilitation, then, will need to be interventionist to counterbalance the influence of power. The facilitator's role has to be active rather than neutral.

The point is that each of the three types of problem solving approach needs a different form of facilitation. The pitfall is that one approach to facilitation is adopted for all circumstances and so the problems just aired are walked straight into. If this were to happen within the process of TSI, then the principles of TSI would surely be violated and the value in the choice of method lost. Implementation using methods would be restricted by the accepted mode of facilitation.

Given below are the main ideas of three sorts of facilitation grouped under the heading of the type of method that they support. This will help you to employ a mode of facilitation most suitable to the type of method chosen for implementation. (Case 10.9, in Chapter 10, has facilitation as one of the main themes.)

'How?'

- Learning about 'How to do it'.
- The task is to identify the best way to achieve a given job.
- The role of the expert is to steer the process to achieve the given job.
- The expert's problem is how to achieve the set job efficiently and effectively.
- The main pitfall to avoid is trying to achieve a set task when significant disagreement about that set task is apparent.

'What?'

- Learning about what could be done.
- The task is to improve group dynamics to enhance learning about what can be done.

- The role of the facilitator is to steer the process to achieve the set task.
- The facilitator gets the process going and keeps it moving.
- The facilitator influences the situation to help to achieve the set task, which he or she can identify with as fair in the circumstances.
- The facilitator identifies with the task.
- The main pitfall to look out for is the group dynamic being political, preventing learning about what could be done from happening.

'Why?'

- Learning about whose interests are being supported in group dynamics, why and how they can be counterbalanced to permit equal participation.
- The facilitator actively introduces alternatives.
- The facilitator may be tactical, supporting positions that are not adequately aired.
- The facilitator can comment on content.
- The facilitator is a group member but has a responsibility to reveal his/her own values and assumptions by constantly appraising their own motives, thus setting an example to other group members.
- The main pitfalls to look out for include the following.
  - Observations by the facilitator can be disruptive and cause delays.
  - People may resist because the approach is confrontational.
  - The facilitator's position may be weakened because he or she is accepting challenges.
  - The question of whether the facilitator's intervention is ethically sound will never be completely certain, as indeed is the case in the other two forms of facilitation.

Pitfall 4. Inappropriate facilitation prevents effective problem solving.

Suggestion. Learn about and employ the three sorts of facilitation that support the three main types of problem solving approach. Also take into account the following discussion on personal style.

7.5 PERSONAL STYLE

People are individuals. People have personalities. There are endless characteristics of personalities. People's characteristics will to some extent, maybe to a great extent, determine the effectiveness of the parts of problem solving that involve interaction with other people. For example, a sensitive person who came across as too humble and non-assertive would be a disastrous facilitator in the mining community in Western Australia – generally a brash bunch of people who probably would laugh at and disregard such a person. On the other hand, a hard-nosed management style would go against the grain in a caring environment such as an agency dealing with homeless youngsters.

Pitfall 5. Personal style can be the root cause of a failed intervention.

Suggestion. Personal style must be considered when selecting a person for a consultancy or facilitation job. Personal style must match corporate or organisational culture where the work is to be done. Problem solving style dealt with next is related to personal style.

7.6 PROBLEM SOLVING STYLE

There are two main points to make about problem solving style.

● The style of methods in themselves.
● The style of operating method(s).

The points are not entirely separate.
    The style of methods in themselves may be important. There are three things to think about.

- Story telling, the use of metaphors, or other new and different methods, may make participants feel very uncomfortable and hence reduce the effectiveness of problem solving. This is not meant to provide an excuse for people to avoid these forms of problem solving, but does suggest that the use of new and different methods may have to be handled particularly carefully.
- Approaches work well with some people but not with others. For example, if a person understands ideas better through images rather than words, then metaphor will be the most effective form of creative thinking for them.
- Certain principles of methods may be damaging in the wrong circumstances. For example, a method proposing adversarial debate in a highly charged conflictual environment may accentuate rather than attenuate undesirable conflict.

The style of operating (a) method(s) is also of concern. Some people prefer to use a cookbook approach where methods are set out and literally followed. Other people like to operate in an open fashion, being guided by principles, whilst letting the method unfold as time goes by. To some extent this is determined by personality. This book provides both principles and cookbook methods and therefore allows you to choose the most suitable style according to your preference.

Pitfall 6. Adoption of an inappropriate problem solving style for any given circumstance may detrimentally affect intervention.

Suggestion. Taking into account circumstances, the following evaluation may be undertaken.

- Will the type of method being considered make participants feel uncomfortable?
- Are methods in use ineffective for the group of participants?
- Might the method that has been chosen have a negative or even a destabilising impact on group dynamics?
- What will be the most effective way of using a method; using a cookbook approach or being guided by principles?

7.7 TIME CONSTRAINTS

It is often assumed by managers that applying a problem solving system such as TSI, or indeed any method employed through TSI, is too time consuming. Because methods are 'too time consuming', managers feel unable to employ them effectively. Hopefully this book will help managers get to grips with the ideas more quickly than other sources permit. But this in itself is not sufficient for time-conscious people to be convinced that applying TSI is not excessively time-consuming. Such time-consuming concerns are false for two reasons.

- Time invested through an effective problem solving system today will save a greater amount of time later on. Planned management action is less time consuming in the long run than crisis management.
- All methods have different versions according to time available. With TSI there can be the following versions (and many more).
  - The five minute TSI.
  - The one hour TSI.
  - The one day TSI.
  - The one week TSI.
  - The one month TSI.
  - The three month TSI.
  - The six month TSI.
  - The one year TSI.
  Pitfall 7. Managers sometimes opt to ignore problem solving methods because they do not believe
- that they have sufficient time available to use them
- that the time invested repays in time saved in the long run.
  Suggestion. Learn several time versions of TSI and the methods that TSI employs. When the opportunity arises, evaluate as far as possible whether the time taken using each of the versions is less than the time ultimately saved.

7.8 AESTHETICS

Aesthetics of problem solving is normally neglected. Aesthetics are principles of appreciation. Problem solving can hardly be appreciated by problem solvers unless they enjoy it. If they do not enjoy it then problem solving is reduced to a means to an end and is less likely to be productive. The aesthetics of TSI are found in the notion of being creative and having fun.

Pitfall 8. There is a common perception among managers that problem solving is hard work, boring and is better avoided.

Suggestion. Make sure when possible that problem solving is fun and allowed to be funny. Make certain that creativity pervades the problem solving process as the recursive structure in the Problem Solving Mode of TSI wants.

7.9 MEASUREMENT

Measurement is crucial in problem solving. Measurement specifications are the basic parameters by which an intervention is guided. The choice of specification is therefore a crucial one. The tendency is to go for specifications that have obvious quantitative measures such as durability, reliability, accuracy and/or speed. These mainly relate to processes. In manufacturing and certain organisational-enterprises such as paper-based ones, measures of processes are relatively straightforward; they can be defined exactly, realised easily using well-designed instruments and are known to be good measures of the efficiency of the processes. The trouble for TSI is that these measures only cover the more technical elements of organisational processes, thus measuring a fragment of the characteristics of the four key dimensions of organisation. They do not measure less tangible aspects of organisation, for example assurance and empathy, the kinds of issue that are at the forefront of events whenever people are involved.

Pitfall 9. Traditional measurement methods cover only a fragment of the characteristics of TSI's four key dimensions of organisation.

Suggestion. Develop a system of measurement that covers all four key dimensions of organisation (e.g., see Case 10.6 in Chapter 10 and consult Further Reading).

7.10 TRAINING AND COMPETENCE

Implementing innovative change proposals, empowering the workforce, and so on, assume that people involved in the change process have the competence to manage themselves and their tasks in new conditions that will prevail. It is not always the case that there is sufficient competence. If it is not the case then implementation of changes is bound to be ineffective. This lesson was learnt a long time ago in Quality Management (QM), especially by the Japanese. Successful implementation of QM is normally supported by well-thought-out training programmes so that those involved are able to support and participate in the initiative. For example, the Japanese QM guru Ishikawa insists that, company-wide, people are trained to use the 'seven tools of QM' covered in Chapter 9. Another strand of QM called Supplier Development Strategy (also see Chapter 9) recognises that traditional organisational boundaries restrict what can be achieved, and so expands analysis to incorporate suppliers. Part of the 'new' way of working is to share expertise, which in some instances means transferring knowledge through joint training programmes. The view of organisation taken in this book suggests widening training and competence even further.

The mistake made too often, and especially during the world economic depression of the 1990s when expenditure has been carefully scrutinised, is to axe training programmes. Often the intention for commercial companies is to protect short-term profit margins, but the medium-term consequence is most likely to be a reversal of apparent financial viability as lack of competence in people takes its toll. Training must therefore be seen as an investment – in problem solving it is an investment into the effectiveness of change proposals to be implemented.

Pitfall 10. Organisational changes are sometimes made without considering the level of competence of those who will be involved and affected by the changes, resulting in ineffective implementation of change proposals.

Suggestion. Assess the level of competence of those likely to be affected by changes and design training packages for, or indeed with, them.

7.11 WHAT IS MEANT BY 'ORGANISATION'

This century, much thought has been applied to organisational analysis. Those readers who have studied management will have learnt about classical management theory through Frederick Taylor's scientific management, Max Weber's bureaucracy theory and Henry Fayol's administrative management theory. The aim of these theories was to put management on firm scientific grounds and to enhance this through rational thought. Following classical management theory came human relations theory, which deals with human needs and which classical theories neglect. The next school of thought was systems theory, which describes an organisation as if it were a distinct system that interacts with and adapts to its environment. Contingency theory was next, where ideal organisational processes are seen to be contingent on crucial factors, such as an organisation's size, the technology it uses and/or the nature of its environment. Alongside these developments, ideas were also developed about leadership and motivation and how these fit in with the different theories about organisation. Practically all textbooks on organisational analysis tell this story.

There are basic underlying models that help to describe the theories. The models are essentially twofold: mechanistic and organic. The classical ideas picture organisations as machines, whereas human relations theory and systems and contingency approaches treat organisations like organisms. What textbooks fail to report, however, is that these models have been found impoverished through critiques and alternative compositions. In particular, the systems-based contingency approach, which had taken pole position by the 1960s, has been overtaken during an assault that tested the thrust of systems-based analysis – the identification of causal relationships between organisation and environment. Furthermore, systems ideas were not geared specifically to addressing cultural and symbolic processes, macro-level power relations, or the interaction between theoretical innovation and social context. TSI practitioners clearly must avoid the pitfall that early systems thinkers did not, i.e., treating 'an organisation' as a separate social entity shaped by 'an environment'. Having said that, there is a point that I want to make to organisational analysts.

A wide array of new theories has been promulgated in academic circles by organisational analysts (refer to Reed and Hughes' book under Further Reading). This burgeoning of theories, however, has left organisational analysis with two new problematics: firstly, how to deal with a plurality of theories; and secondly, the 'so-what' criticism, i.e., all of this theory is fine only if the theorists also tell practitioners how they are supposed to proceed.

Whilst organisational analysts reworked the idea of organisation, a revolution was occurring in systems thinking itself. Some systems theorists, myself included, accepted the criticisms of its early formulations and the lessons brought forward by organisational analysts. A revolutionised systems theory subsequently has been developed called Critical Systems Thinking, which has demonstrated intellectual sensitivity, exploring the idea of organisation as cultural and symbolic processes and macro-level power relations (see Further Reading on Critical Systems Thinking).

An important application area of this 'new wave' systems thinking is problem solving. Systems-based problem solving has participated, on the one hand, in the intellectual debate just discussed and, on the other hand, in the need to translate these theories into practically useful forms. This book, for example, tries to generate an approach sensitive to a range of arguments in organisational analysis, an approach indeed where practitioners may be sensitive to the existence of many possibilities, out of which choice making has to proceed.

Solving Problem Solving is based on the argument that problem solving methods constructed from a plurality of theories hold strengths in some contexts, whilst having little to say about other ones, and that practitioners must take responsibility for choosing how to address problems. The book confirms that principles of some methods are geared up to managing organisational processes, some organisational design, whilst others deal better with organisational culture, or organisational politics. Practical application of problem solving methods along these lines has demonstrated the relevance of a range of methodological options. (Their commensurability, to some extent, can be found in the way they are able to confront practitioners with choice-making possibilities.) On the basis of these findings, systems thinkers have participated, and will continue to participate, in the debate about theoretical (in)commensurability, but this is beyond the scope of *Solving Problem Solving*.

It is reasonable to ask innovative organisational analysts now to reconsider the systems argument, which has surfaced from practical methodological work, in the same spirit that systems thinkers with a contemporary outlook took on board lessons presented to them from theory provided by organisational analysts.

Pitfall 11. It is easy to slip into a mode of thought where 'an organisation' is considered to be a separate organic social entity distinct from an environment that shapes it. This view of organisation has been routed because it is grossly impoverished. If used in problem solving it will diminish chances to achieve innovative change proposals.

Suggestion. When reading about organisation in this book, no matter how the term is written or introduced, remember that it is more realistic to appreciate (an) organisation(s) in terms of human relationships than as a separate organic social entity.

7.12 WHAT IS MEANT BY 'PROBLEM'

The common understanding of 'problem' is that it is an identifiable bad thing and that all forms of organisation experience them and must solve them so that they can maintain, or return to, normal organisational life. A crucial contention of TSI is that there is no such thing as a problem or a solution, nor is there such a condition as normal organisational life (and as said in the previous section, it is not useful to think in terms of 'an organisation' as a distinct, separate, organic social entity). These ideas are explored below.

In *Beyond TQM* (see Further Reading) my view that there is a problem with the common understanding of 'problems' was explained through a gremlin metaphor. I have chosen to provide an adaptation of the gremlin metaphor here for three reasons: firstly, it makes the point I want to get across; secondly, it reminds us that things can be done in a fun way (remember the importance of aesthetics in problem solving); and thirdly, it is an example of the use of a metaphor through a storyline, an approach to creativity explored in Chapter 9. The metaphor is that 'a gremlin in the works' is reminiscent of 'a problem'.

A gremlin is a creature often blamed for meddling with things and causing problems, but it is never seen or found. Gremlins are elusive. If something goes wrong, that is, a problem is thought to exist, we tend to blame an invisible gremlin. Problem solving, then, is akin to chasing, catching and exterminating gremlins.

Decision makers and problem solvers must be fully equipped to catch the gremlin, i.e., solve the problem. The necessary equipment is usually a five-stage problem solving method that identifies the problem and solves it. The equivalent for our metaphor is a net to catch the gremlin when it is tracked down and a desktop extermination chamber to destroy the gremlin once isolated and captured. Imagine the following problem solving scenario.

A factory manufacturing chemicals has a problem. Management believe that the problem must be identified and solved. They call in management consultants. The management consultants are briefed by the management team and then get stuck into the task at hand.

The management consultants start off by visiting Computer Services. The consultants know that the gremlin has been there because bugs in the software are found and the main computer keeps crashing. Computer Services has a problem. On further investigation the consultants find that the gremlin has just vanished up the air-conditioning, toward the Accounting Department.

After carrying out investigations in Accounting the evidence is clear enough. The gremlin has been through the books and now they will not balance. It has played tricks on the staff so that the bought ledger clerk has fallen out with the sales ledger clerk and the accounting manager has lost control. But, as usual, the gremlin has just slipped away, via the offices of senior management, this time to a pressure group's headquarters carrying a secret document found on the managing director's desk.

The consultants discover that a document has been leaked which provides a graphic account of a recent accidental release of toxic chemicals into the atmosphere. This is published in the local newspaper and covered on local radio. The managing director accepts an interview on television and requests for statistics for air emissions, and expenditure on pollution control, over the last year. Unfortunately the gremlin's legacy lives on.

Computer Services are approached for the statistics but, because of bugs in their software and the lack of information coming from the troubled Accounts Department, they provide incorrect information. The misinformation suggests that the factory has an appalling record, when actually it does not. The gremlin whispers into the ear of a keen member of staff from External Relations, suggesting that personal recognition may be gained if they send the information straight to the television studios. That evening the managing director is carved up live on television by an eager journalist. The next morning a large number of the public protest in anger outside the factory gates.

The managing director, incensed at the turn of events, calls in the consultants and demands a solution to his problem.

The consultants find that the gremlin has been everywhere although they never find it. The consultants are seen frantically rushing along corridors clutching the net designed to catch the gremlin. They dodge in and out of offices, giving rise to an air of confusion and expectancy. At the end of the day, late in the evening, the consultants are seen leaving through the reception area clasping the net, suggesting capture of the gremlin.

The next morning, at 9 o'clock dead as instructed, the consultants return to the factory looking cool and triumphant. They report the solution to the problem, i.e., how they caught and exterminated the wretched gremlin. They recount how it was done in five easy steps. The managing director is very impressed. The consultants leave with a cheque in hand at least the size of the story just strung.

Pitfall 12. Problems are believed to be real tangible things that can be identified and solved, thus enabling organisational life to be maintained or returned to normal.

Suggestion. Do not believe that problems can be identified and solved, nor that there is such a thing as normal organisational life. Recognise that problem solving is really a continuous process of managing interacting issues arising from four key dimensions of organisation (which are discussed in Chapter 3).

7.13 CHOOSING AND USING CONSULTANTS

There is a whole debate about issues relating to choosing and using consultants in problem solving. This debate raises concerns about the likelihood of meeting the principles of the problem solving system TSI when consultants are hired. The extent of this debate is such that it has been consolidated in a separate chapter (the next one).

Pitfall 13. Using consultants may prevent satisfactory achievement of the principles of the problem solving system TSI.

Suggestion. Learn about the issues that surround choosing and using consultants, and on the basis of these be critical when choosing them and remain critical when using them. Details that help this critical evaluation are given in the next chapter, to which we now turn our attention.

8
Choosing and Using Consultants

Pitfalls to avoid when problem solving with TSI are discussed in Chapter 7. Pitfalls to do with choosing and using consultants were briefly mentioned, recognised as being substantial and hence deferred for separate treatment in this chapter. The aim here is to provide advice on choosing and using consultants – the do's and don'ts relating to consultants.

The role of a consultant from a manager's point of view is to provide genuine advice. Advice might be necessary for one or more reasons. A number of obvious ones are set out below.

- When the problem solving process needs facilitation.
- When specialist knowledge has to be called in.
- When issues to be managed or ways forward are not transparent.
- When a second opinion is needed.
- When a fresh opinion is needed.

In principle, management have good reason to employ consultants. In practice, however, the truth about consultants set out below raises concern among managers and some guidance is often needed.

The scene for this chapter is set with the well-used idea of the world's three great lies, here in the context of consultants.

- The cheque is in the post.

- I'll love you in the morning.
- I'm a consultant and I'm here to help you.

Perhaps unfair to consultants? Let us take a more reasoned look.

There are two types of consultant, technical consultants and management consultants. The task of a technical consultant is relatively straightforward since the problems that they face are easy to define and improvements are simple to measure and to demonstrate.

Efficiency in the delivery system, productivity in the manufacturing processes and accuracy in paperwork are good examples where consultant's efforts can be measured and even translated into monetary terms. Consultants with a good and proven record can be chosen and used without too much bother. When it comes to management consultants, however, the reality is very different.

Management consultants most often are dealing with the human dimension of organisation. They are supporting management on matters far less tangible. There are no clear-cut solutions, nor are there easily identifiable problems. There is no obvious method or approach in any given circumstance as we discovered in Chapter 5. On the positive side, there is plenty of scope for management consultants to be inventive, although this must be watched. Where there is inventiveness there is bound to be some absolute nonsense, with dubious characters parading as management consultants pushing that nonsense, although their intentions may not be readily apparent. Not surprisingly, then, most of the guidance in this chapter targets choosing and using management rather than technical consultants.

The two types of consultant, technical and management, fall into two further categories, external and internal consultants. External consultants, broadly speaking, may be further categorised into two types, a profusion of commercial companies and the less prolific academic-based groups. Some consultants from each of these categories are very good, but there are pitfalls that have to be watched out for when choosing and using them. We will look for these, firstly assessing external and then internal consultants.

When employing an external commercial consultancy it is

worth asking what it is that motivates them. In my experience their main aim is to get a job done as quickly as possible and to build in follow-on work, thus maximising income to the consultancy in the short, medium, and long term. 'Well', you might ask, 'what is wrong with that? After all, even consultants must make a living just like anyone else.' True, but then there are consequences for their clients – i.e., you.

A cartoon in the '94 *Ivanhoe Career Guide to Management Consultants* says it all. The picture shows a managing director on the first floor window ledge outside his office about to jump. A management consultant stood on the street below hails the managing director, shouting 'I suggest you try a higher window ledge!'

To achieve their main aim consultants feel the need to please management by saying what management want to hear. Then management feel reassured and continue to employ them and consequently end up recycling their own ideas. This is a false reassurance. In doing this, consultants are not providing genuine advice. Consultants therefore contribute little to the wellbeing of whole organisations. In terms of our problem solving system, this is hardly creative.

One of my first experiences as a manager, in the sales-driven film business, provided a lesson of this sort. A part of our strategy was to implement a computer-based information system – an innovative idea for 1978. The staff involved carefully crafted a design relevant to local needs that also provided general support to the company's decision makers. The all-powerful sales director detected a danger in this to his *laissez faire* mode of leadership. Control information would become available and certain things would be in the open and revealed, such as 120-day accounts. He came up with an alternative idea not worth recounting here. This raised controversy. To resolve the controversy external commercial consultants were brought in. The consultant's report 'confirmed' that the sales director was more or less correct. This provided him with powerful ammunition that was hard to refute since it was external advice from a reputable consultancy. In the end no change was made and so the sales director got his own way. There was no innovation and no change.

Another grave concern about external consultants is their lack of commitment to the methods and ideas that they employ. Why do consultants employ them? The reason is simple. Consultants must have something to sell. The worry is that they must make it different and apparently better than what their competitor's can offer. They must forever be on the lookout for new things to package up. So, their first commitment is likely to target their product's novelty and saleability, with a secondary commitment to the matter of whether it actually works or not. All too easily managers can be persuaded to part with vast sums of money lured by gloss rather than being convinced by argument.

An example comes to mind. A very well-known company that I consulted for some time ago was sold the concept of TQM for US$2 million by a consulting company I have close links with. When I scanned the manual prepared for the company, I found that it amounted to a dozen or so snippets from Crosby, Deming, Juran, Shingo, Feigenbaum, Ishikawa, etc., poorly sown together. I could see the stitching very clearly, but then I had had the luxury of time to read these gurus' texts. Unfortunately, managers are too busy with day-to-day organisational matters to read so extensively. So they did not pick up that the material sold to the company was an incoherent, contradictory, confusing, glossed over but glitteringly packaged shambles. It was worthless to the company. Not surprisingly, a recent newspaper article reported that eight years after the first steps towards TQM in that company, there has been no perceptible improvement in the service provided. Again, there was no innovation and no change.

On another occasion I was helping a large London-based consultancy company to develop an appreciation of what they actually do. Given clarity of this sort they would be able to invest their resources more carefully. A whole evening was spent with six of their senior consultants, and very pleasant it was with flowing wine alongside prawns and avocado pears. In a very creative exercise, several metaphors were discussed to see whether they captured the essence of consulting practice. The most relevant metaphor chosen by the consultants themselves explained that their core mode of behaviour is parasitic! Is the task for consultants then to become more efficient parasites?

Academic-based groups offer an alternative to the parasitic, money-hungry, commercial companies. They are more likely to be committed to their ideas. The trouble is that many of them believe in their ideas but do not have the experience to believe themselves able to pull off those ideas in practice. Every job won is daunting to the academic, although it is valuable propaganda within their peer group. Relief of getting out of the job intact is followed by the true worth of the job to the academic. It provides the opportunity to talk and write for years about how his/her ideas were actually used (once?) in practice.

The confident academic can be worse. They are committed to their ideas and certain that they are right. They have published extensively telling everyone just this. In action they can be dogmatic and patronising and are capable of turning people off at a rapid pace.

In addition to these points, I fear that too many academics still remain out of touch with the manager's world. Some are too theoretical. Others wish to prevent precious theories from being sullied through the pollutive exercise of using them and evolving them in this way. In so doing they isolate themselves from management. Ask them how they would explain their ideas to a personnel manager and see them suddenly run out of words. There will be little interest or worry here, then, for management.

Perhaps a way around the difficulties posed by employing external consultants is to build in internal consultants? The internal consultant on paper is an adviser and intrapreneur. Unfortunately, internal consulting is plagued by its own faults. For a start, the consultants too easily become insular and lack dynamism. They cannot bring in the freshness of thought that external people are able to provide. Furthermore, issues brew that adversely affect and hence tangle up internal management. For example, internal consultants are often considered to be spies and are not trusted. Power issues surface where junior consulting staff are seen to be advising more senior ones in management. Innovative change proposals are not easy to achieve with internal consultants.

There are a few other general criticisms that management have pointed out to me (also see pages 322–324).

- Organisational problems are sometimes made to fit predesigned packages that consultants use.

- Consultants are known to accept jobs that they are not skilled to do.
- It is difficult for consultants to acquire the necessary technical, managerial and intimate knowledge necessary to make a useful contribution in organisational problem solving.

So, how should management choose and use consultants? I recommend the following.

When choosing consultants do not necessarily go for big firms. They are expensive and can get away with a lack of carefulness of approach, protected by their name and presumed reputation. Seriously consider employing smaller companies that are more likely to be committed to you and give personal and genuine advice. You could be adventurous and attempt to nurture an academic link. There is a lot of potential mileage in this if the right group is found. Most crucial of all, however, is that whatever reason you have for bringing in consultants, and whichever type you choose, remain highly critical of their services at all times. Have the confidence to make sure that they really know what they are talking about, but also that they are prepared to consider your input. Ask them why their approach will work better than any other one and then listen carefully to the response. Test them on some of their ideas; for example, with quality consultants advocating culture change, ask what they mean by culture and then ask them how this can be changed. If they cannot adequately answer these or other questions, then don't employ them. Be demanding. After all, you are footing the bill (and your time) and want value for money.

Part 4

TSI IN ACTION

9
How to Problem Solve – 'The Methods'

In Chapters 3, 4 and 5, the philosophy, principles and process, the three Ps of TSI, are presented. Respectively, the philosophy explains TSI's understanding of organisation for problem solving, principles propose kinds of action that we should take in that case and the process explains how to implement the principles. The task that remains for this part of the book is to construct a user's guide to some key methods that operationalise the process of TSI.

Chapter 5 explained that there are three modes to operate TSI: the Critical Review Mode, the Problem Solving Mode and the Critical Reflection Mode. Methods for each one are dealt with below in that order. They are presented and arranged as a set of guidelines with a commentary to aid understanding. The guidelines are illustrated where helpful with examples of organisational problem solving.

Before launching into the methods there is an important point that I would like to raise from Chapter 7. The style by which methods are operated is a real concern. Some people prefer to employ a cookbook approach where methods are set out and literally followed. Others like to work in an open fashion, being guided by principles whilst letting the method unfold as time goes by. This chapter provides both principles and methods so that you may choose your own style. If you prefer to be principle-driven, but have limited knowledge about a method you choose to use, then you can employ its cookbook version to kick-start the process and learn about and follow its principles by problem solving with the method.

Now, let us move on to the methods.

9.1 CRITICAL REVIEW MODE

As explained in Chapter 5, the Critical Review Mode critically reviews and categorises methods and their principles and incorporates them in the Problem Solving Mode of TSI. The principles of the Critical Review Mode are threefold.

- Assume to start with that each method under review advocates forms of creativity, choice and implementation.
- Assume to start with that each method under review tackles TSI's four key dimensions of organisation.
- Always assume that TSI can learn from the methods reviewed in terms of its own philosophy, principles, process and its own methods used to operationalise the three modes.

Methods are initially categorised according to the three phases of TSI. Categorisation is attained by asking first of all whether the method under review contributes to one or more of TSI's three phases. This is done by judging *if* the method usefully undertakes one or more of the following.

- Promotes creative thinking by
  - challenging preconceived ideas about problems
  - generating a new appreciation about problems.
- Explicitly asks the problem solver to choose between methods selecting the most suitable one for implementation in the circumstances.
- Generates and implements relevant innovative change proposals of any sort.

Bear in mind that early stages of categorisation are rather crude, but as the review continues an increasingly detailed and justified analysis unfolds.

The next step is to fill in details that justify or rework the first stab categorisation. This is done by changing the slant of the points given above. Using the same points, ask *how* the method under review achieves the purposes of the phases to which it has been categorised. The two slants on the points above, that is the *if* and *how* slants, focus respectively on categorisation and justifying the categorisation.

A second and equally important step in the review process focuses analysis on the constituents of the method under review that are categorised within the Implementation phase. The task is to ascertain which of the four key dimensions of organisation the constituents are able to tackle. The following questions aid this process.

- 'How can we design the most efficient organisational processes and arrange their implementation?'
- 'How can we achieve effective organisation?'
- 'What options should we decide upon?'
- 'Why should any design or any decision be adopted?'

There are other considerations to take into account. So far the review assumes that methods under review are dealt with separately from other methods. At some stage the method as categorised must be compared with and evaluated against other methods already incorporated in the Problem Solving Mode. The following three questions aid evaluation. Direct them at each phase in turn.

- Is the method under review as categorised more likely in all circumstances to achieve the given purpose of the phase than any other method already incorporated? If yes, then it supersedes those methods.
- Is the method as categorised complementary with other methods given the purpose of the phase? If yes, then it is incorporated with those methods.
- Is there a method in place that will better achieve the given purpose of the phase in all circumstances? If yes, then the method under review is discarded.

Ultimately the review process builds up a knowledge about

methods under review in terms of TSI's philosophy, principles, process and methods. It systematically builds up a knowledge about how the method can be employed through the process of TSI in intervention. In addition to this, every time the Critical Review Mode is operated it is crucial to ask whether TSI can learn anything from the method that has been reviewed in terms of its own philosophy, principles, process and its own methods.

The Critical Review Mode can be operated at any time to enrich TSI. But the Critical Review Mode has to be operated before the Problem Solving Mode can begin. The next section records my own use of the Critical Review Mode to develop a system of methods for the Problem Solving Mode. In fact it records only the essential methods that I use at the moment because of space limitations in this book. You may if you wish take my system of methods as a starter pack to help you begin problem solving without delay.

9.2 PROBLEM SOLVING MODE

The aim of the Problem Solving Mode is to help you to problem solve in line with the philosophy established in Chapter 3 and the principles set out in Chapter 4. To do this it uses the problem solving process explained in Chapter 5 to employ methods and their principles in TSI's three phases, Creativity, Choice, and Implementation. The methods put to work in the three phases have been incorporated following their evaluation through TSI's Critical Review Mode. This use of the Critical Review Mode has yielded a system of methods that is expressed in Figure 9.1. This system is briefly explained below for each of the three phases.

The Creativity phase employs the following two types of method that challenge preconceived ideas about problems and generate a new appreciation of problems.

- Idea generation and evaluation.
- Image generation and evaluation.

The two are shown in a cycle in Figure 9.1, underlining the

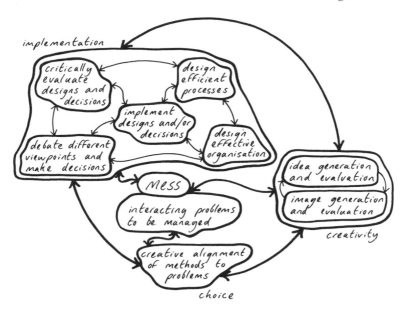

Figure 9.1 *System of methods employed in the Problem Solving Mode of TSI*

point that they can be used in a complementary way The outcome of the Creativity phase is an appreciation of the interacting problems, focusing on the core ones that urgently need
dealing with. This appreciation is passed on to the Choice phase
for further action.

The Choice phase takes as given the appreciation of the mess
in the form of interacting and core problems to be dealt with
provided by the Creativity phase. It critically evaluates which
method is the most suitable one to tackle those problems in the
circumstances. The chosen method is passed on to the
Implementation phase to generate innovative change proposals.

Implementation at any moment in time uses methods that
tackle one of the four key dimensions of organisation by
addressing one of the following four questions that reflect
those dimensions.

- 'How can we design the most efficient organisational pro-
  cesses and arrange their implementation?'
- 'How can we design and implement effective organisation?'
- 'What options should we decide upon, involving debate about

technical and human issues that arise in organisational activities leading to decisions about what to do?'
- 'Why should a design or a decision be adopted, involving debate about the interests of dominant and disadvantaged groups (disimprisoning them), and the desirability of balancing organisational and individual needs, taking into account physical, biological and social environments?'

Methods for designing focus on how to identify and implement the most efficient processes or the most effective organisation. Methods for debating explore and choose designs and/or decisions, or test competing alternatives if people's positions become polarised. The method for disimprisoning undertakes critical evaluation of designs and decisions assessing whose interests are served by them and the possible consequences of this and potential ways forward as alternative ways of developing designs or making decisions.

Methods for implementation have an immediate and given purpose as just indicated. A vital point to remember from the previous chapter is that methods can be used obliquely. This means that a method with an immediate and given purpose may be used indirectly to achieve one of the other main purposes of problem solving and its associated principles.

The system of methods for implementation is organised in a cycle in Figure 9.1, demonstrating that all methods for implementation are used in a complementary way in the Problem Solving Mode.

With an overview of the method component of the problem solving system now in place, the next task is to set out the methods, their principles and a commentary about their use. This is done for each of the phases, Creativity, Choice and Implementation, in that order. Note that the principles given for each method must be adhered to in the knowledge and wider guidance of TSI's four main principles that are explained in Chapter 4.

9.2.1 Creativity

- Creative thinking helps people to break out of preconceived assumptions that they hold about problems, creating innovative ways of appreciating problems and preparing the way for dealing with them.

- The aim of creative thinking in the Creativity phase is to
  - challenge preconceived ideas about problems
  - generate a new appreciation about problems
  - demonstrate the interacting nature of the problems and highlight the core ones.
- The expected output of creative thinking, therefore, is an appreciation of the interacting nature of problems with the core ones highlighted.
- There are three main principles of creative thinking.
  - Break out of assumptions that you are holding about the problems to be dealt with.
  - Make creative thinking a convention.
  - Creativity can be detected using the following criterion: an idea is creative if participants uncover an unexpected idea/image which they value.
- The methods used fall into two categories.
  - Idea generation and evaluation.
  - Image generation and evaluation.
- TSI has a recursive structure. The process of the Creativity phase works as follows.
  - Creativity – work toward the above-declared aim of creative thinking using the two categories of method listed above.
  - Choice – choose an appreciation of organisational problems according to how well competing appreciations capture organisational difficulties.
  - Implementation – pass on the chosen appreciation of the organisational problems to the next phase.

The value and basic principles of creative thinking will now be discussed. This paves the way for a meaningful presentation of methods a little later on.

Creative thinking is increasingly being valued as a vital force that drives change and progress. The management literature regularly features articles on creativity, discussing its importance in the domains of entrepreneurship, innovation and change. Creative thinking is recognised as invaluable for all three. The trick is to learn to use your mind to think in different ways and then employ unexpected insights that you value. There are, however, barriers that limit creative thinking and these are discussed below.

People manage masses of information in their everyday lives by employing well-established modes of thinking which help to make rapid sense of what is going on. This everyday thinking is essential to everyday living, enabling there to be speedy understanding and allowing many everyday events to be handled smoothly. Unfortunately, when it comes to management and problem solving, everyday assumptions can stop people from penetrating beneath surface events to get deep into organisational dynamics. They prevent analytical evaluation of what is happening, why and how the dynamics can be improved. Everyday thinking for these purposes is a trap. It is a conceptual trap.

Conceptual traps capture all of us most of the time. They are built on sets of assumptions that we hold. In management these might be assumptions about what in all circumstances is the best leadership style, the best way to motivate staff or the best form of organisation. For problem solving assumptions might be held about which is in all circumstances the best problem solving method, the best problem solving style or the best type of consultant. These assumptions normally are not challenged and tested. It is pretty certain that if such assumptions are not challenged or tested things will continue to be done in the same old way and so there will be impotence in efforts to introduce innovative change and progress.

Creative thinking recommends challenging assumptions. It certainly challenges the following assumptions.

- It is inevitable that things will be done in the same old way.
- If we hang around long enough innovative ideas will pop up.

Creative thinking recommends people to be active in the creation of new ideas and images which help to surface problems and hence solve them innovatively and effectively. Methods like those in this section can be taught and learnt and are likely to stimulate a creative process.

Active, creative thinking is not something that gets turned on occasionally when problems become troubling. It is supposed to become a habitual way of using your mind. Like learning a new language, you must keep practising and keep trying. Only in this way is it possible to become a fluent, creative thinker. Active, creative thinking must become convention.

The knack to breaking out of conceptual traps is to look at 'the same things' or 'the same situations' in different ways. The aim is to challenge assumptions, to provoke new thoughts and to generate alternative ways of thinking about the thing or situation. Even when promising new ways of thinking emerge, creative thinking needs to continue for as long as it helps to generate further alternatives. Each way of looking at things and appreciating problems is useful; none are unique or absolute, although one way will be chosen to proceed because it is most convincing to the participants.

Breaking out of conceptual traps sometimes generates alternative ways of thinking that seem funny. This is quite natural. After all a good joke is nothing more than thinking about something familiar suddenly in a different way that has a humorous value. A benefit is that joking makes problem solving fun. For example, pessimist managers have discovered a new theory of gravity – the world sucks!

Sometimes creative thinking generates alternatives that, rather than being funny, seem wrong or perverse and cause tension in our minds. A use of metaphor called synectics argues that it pays to suspend judgement in such cases. Wrongness and perverseness can be insightful because they come at a situation from a position that holds totally different assumptions. Although not immediately desirable, the challenge these assumptions put up at least raise questions about our own way of thinking.

Some alternatives that are uncovered turn out to be transient and are passed over. Other alternatives stick and become insightful. Insightfulness is achieved by working out the details of an alternative way of thinking about organisational problems.

Details of alternative ways of thinking are worked out by mixing divergent and convergent thinking. This distinction aids understanding of the creative process. Divergent thinking is about getting unstuck by appreciating situations from many different angles, uncovering a diversity of problems. Convergent thinking makes sense of the diversity of problems by demonstrating their interacting nature and highlighting the core ones.

Experience of using methods for creative thinking has led us to make another useful distinction, between those that spark off idea generation and those that evolve image generation. Idea generation stimulates an increase in individual thoughts about problems for further evaluation. Image generation helps to picture and vividly portray whole situations in different ways, which are evaluated as the images develop. The two forms of creative thinking are complementary. It is quite normal to interplay idea- and image-generating methods when problem solving.

At a general level, the process of creative thinking has been nicely captured by a colleague of mine, Russell Ackoff, who has come up with the following valuable three-stage summary.

- Identify the assumptions that constrain the set of alternatives that you consider.
- Deny the assumptions.
- Explore the consequences of denying the assumptions.

Exploring the consequences may lead to *unexpected ideas/images that are valued* – the essential output of creative thinking.

The methods presented below are about getting to grips with problems. Some of the methods can be used with a different focus to generate ideas and arguments about how to deal with the problems. That mode of use is reserved for the Implementation phase.

9.2.1.1 Idea generation and evaluation – The 'For what reason?' method

The 'For what reason?' method has one further principle to add to those in the general discussion on creativity.

- No idea, explanation or answer is sacrosanct.

The 'For what reason?' method is extremely simple to understand, less easy to practise, but can be very effective. The core principle is that no idea, explanation or answer is sacrosanct. They can be challenged by asking the question 'For what reason?' This is both divergent and convergent. It is divergent because it breaks out of current trains of thought. It is convergent because a break-out is a new idea possibly to be adopted and taken forward.

There are plenty of examples of the 'For what reason?' method in action. Children learn and understand things by asking 'Why?' It drives us, parents, mad, so why not turn this natural process of learning finally to our advantage? Edward De Bono employs the 'For what reason?' method in lateral thinking. Japanese quality management promotes the process of six 'For what reasons?', that is, for any idea, explanation or answer given, ask 'For what reason?', and then challenge the subsequent sequence of five answers with the same question, 'For what reason?', and see what you discover.

Answering the question 'For what reason?' can get bogged down at times and in that case requires critical and insightful reasoning. It is easy for the sequence of answers to become circular. To stop this happening demands new insight. When the sequence becomes circular the rule is to insist on a break-out from the circle. The break-out is your insight. If the process is not circular then it is progressive and likely to be insightful. (See Figure 9.2.)

Insights into problems are passed on to the Choice phase where (a) method(s) is/are chosen to tackle them.

Example. Assume that you have planned to implement ISO

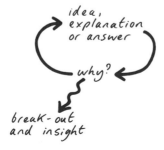

Figure 9.2   *Process of the 'For what reason?' method from the Creativity phase of TSI*

9000. This is an international quality assurance management system standard. The aim of the standard is to achieve consistency and hence quality in organisational processes. The 'For what reason?' method might lead to the following analysis. (The question 'For what reason?' is substituted below by 'Why?')

Why implement ISO 9000?
Because it will enhance our reputation.
Why will it enhance our reputation?
Because we will be accredited by a recognised authority.
Why will this accreditation enhance our reputation?
Because accreditation means achievement of consistency in organisational processes.
Why will consistency enhance our reputation?
Because our clients will receive the same standard product every time.
Why will standardisation enhance our reputation?
(And here is the break-out and the problem.)

Actually, it might not enhance our reputation because the product in the first place may not conform to the customer's requirements. Hence, ISO 9000 may lead to nothing more than consistently providing the client with a product that does not conform to their requirements. Another quality management approach such as Kaizen and its continuous improvement is needed to complement ISO 9000.

The 'For what reason?' method has led to this new insight about problems faced, which is passed on to the Choice phase.

9.2.1.2 *Idea generation and evaluation – Brainstorming*

The principles of brainstorming to be added to those given in the general discussion above on creativity are fourfold.

- Every idea potentially is a good idea.
- Every person potentially is a good idea generator.
- Every participant must contribute ideas.
- The best ideas are achieved by encouraging group talking and facilitating speech and debate.

Brainstorming is the most commonly used approach to creative thinking. It is relatively simple to use. The aim of brainstorming is to generate plenty of ideas that tease out problems. Brainstorming encourages many different ideas no matter how bland or indeed bizarre they may seem at first. The method takes steps to stop the normal inclination to criticise or reject ideas simply because they are different. Participants cannot criticise without coming up with an improved suggestion.

Divergence. First of all a summary of organisational problems is prepared and circulated to those who will participate in the brainstorming exercise. The summary is prepared by a facilitator based on a range of opinions gathered from the participants. The summary is very crude, but this does not matter because it is simply there to kick-start the idea-generating stage of brainstorming.

Participants gather at a designated time and place. The suitability of the location needs to be assessed. The environment must be conducive to creative thinking. Initially the facilitator introduces the event setting out the process to be followed and the rules. The main rules are

- no separate talking or conversations
- an idea can be discussed for clarification purposes only at the discretion of the facilitator
- no idea is thrown out in the divergent phase
- the divergent phase ends when ideas dry up.

The facilitator then begins the process. There are two ways that ideas can be generated. The first one is to allow participants to contribute ideas freely about the organisational problems at any time. The second way is to have a round robin. With a round robin, the facilitator starts by asking a participant to put forward one idea. Then the person sitting in the next seat to the left or the right is asked to put forward one idea. Other people are asked systematically following the chosen direction around the table. If a participant at any time does not wish to contribute an idea for whatever reason, then they say 'pass'. This cycle ideally keeps going until everyone in succession has passed twice.

As ideas about the problems are generated they are written-up on a flip chart for all to see. The formulation of words recorded on the sheets is given by the contributor. If more than one sheet is used, then full sheets are hung adjacent to each other on the wall. They must be clearly in view for all participants.

Convergence. The main rules are

- evaluation of ideas is initially through debate
- no one can criticise an idea unless they can improve on it
- if consensus/accommodation is not achieved through debate then a voting system will be used.

Convergence is a process of evaluating the ideas to choose the ones most representative of the problem. This involves further clarification and debate about the relative worth of the ideas. Each idea is numbered. They are systematically examined. The person who generated the idea explains it and answers questions of clarification about it. A formulation of words is finalised. The idea is then discussed. The idea is either carried forward for further debate or is dropped at that time. The idea is only dropped if all concerned agree on this.

Once all ideas have been clarified and debated a general discussion is held. The discussion initially focuses on clustering ideas that are closely related. Ideas are dropped, are absorbed, or are left clustered together. This reduces the number of different ideas to be dealt with making the process more time efficient.

Then the relative worth of each idea, or cluster of ideas, is discussed. The main thrust now is to choose the most pertinent ideas about the problems to be dealt with that will be taken forward to the Choice phase. The selection of idea(s) ideally occurs as a consensus/accommodation through debate. Debate leads to deletion of some ideas. It may also lead to the development of ideas or to the inclusion of new ones (divergence sneaking in again).

If a consensus/accommodation is not achieved then voting takes place. Before voting each person is given an opportunity to make out a case supporting their preferred idea(s). Voting takes place in several stages. The first vote allows everyone to vote for or against each one of the ideas. A cut-off point will have been predetermined for selection of ideas to go forward to the next vote. Examples of selection criteria are

• those with over 70% support
• the top 70%.

Time for discussion about the remaining ideas must be given after voting has taken place. Consensus/accommodation may be accelerated in this way. If not, further rounds of voting and debating take place until a final choice is made. This is taken forward to the Choice phase of TSI. If positions form around ideas and become polarised, it would be quite proper to draw in and adapt the method for Testing Polarised Viewpoints (TPV), otherwise operated in the Implementation phase.

Example. Given the relatively straightforward nature of brainstorming there is little value in using limited space on an example.

9.2.1.3 *Idea generation and evaluation – Nominal Group Technique*

There are four principles of Nominal Group Technique (NGT) that add to those given for creativity in the general discussion held earlier.

• Every idea potentially is a good idea.
• Every person potentially is a good idea generator.
• Every participant must contribute ideas.
• The best ideas are achieved through individual and group thinking, by facilitating sharing of ideas through the written form.

NGT shares the same aim as brainstorming, to generate an abundance of ideas about problems to improve the chances of coming up with well-informed solutions in the Implementation phase. It differs from brainstorming in that the idea generation does not happen through open or even structured spoken contributions. Idea generation comes from thinking, writing down thoughts and then sharing them in the written form. This has the benefit of preventing assertive, authoritative and articulate people, or groups, dominating the floor and controlling the process. Another advantage is that ideas remain anonymous, thus avoiding peer group pressure which restrains people from making out of the ordinary contributions. Conversely, it has the disadvantage of cutting out learning and understanding that occurs during speech. A consequent disadvantage is that it makes it more difficult to have fun.

Divergence. The preparation not surprisingly reflects the beginning part of brainstorming. A summary of the organisational problems is prepared and circulated to participants. The summary is prepared by the facilitator based on a range of opinions gathered from the participants. The summary is simply a trigger for the idea-generating stage of NGT.

As with brainstorming, participants gather at a designated time and place. Care must be given to ensure suitability of the location. The environment must be conducive to creative thinking. Initially the facilitator introduces the event, setting out the process to be followed and the rules. The main rule is

● no talking at all.

The facilitator needs a stack of cards approximately $5'' \times 3''$. Cards are handed out to the participants. Three cards are given to each person if fewer than eight people are participating, otherwise two cards are sufficient. The participants are then asked to write one idea on each card. About ten minutes should be sufficient time.

The cards are collected and shuffled. Volunteers are asked to transfer the ideas from the cards on to flip chart paper. Each volunteer writes up one sheet with six ideas per sheet thus leaving space for rewording later on. The sheet has a clear left-hand margin and each idea is distinguished with a bullet set in that margin.

The remaining participants read to themselves the entries as they are written up. The volunteers return to their seats when their writing job is complete and also read the entries. At this stage participants

- look for ideas which are out of the ordinary
- use ideas to trigger off new ideas in their thoughts
- record new ideas that they value for use later on.

Convergence. NGT now turns to convergence. The aim is to choose the best ideas about organisational problems from the collection of ideas on the flip chart sheets. If many participants have generated many, many ideas, then the best way to start is to use the divergence method from brainstorming to get the number of ideas down to a manageable size. Twenty is a good target. As with brainstorming this entails clarification, clustering and then voting.

The facilitator gives out five cards to each of the participants. The cards have a # in the top left and a circle in the bottom right large enough for a number to be written in. Participants choose the five most valuable ideas in their opinion. The number of each idea is entered on to its own card to the right of the #. The ideas are now ranked in order of preference. The most preferred idea is given a weighting of 5 which is entered into the circle on the bottom right of the card. The least preferred idea is weighted with a 1. The other ideas are weighted in sequence. All five cards of each participant now have recorded the idea number on the top left and the weighting value on the bottom right.

The participants' cards are collected and sorted out by the facilitator into idea number. Participants usually have a break at this stage. The aim is to record how many votes each idea received and the total weighting. For example, an idea might have received ten votes of which three were weighted 5, four were weighted 4, two were weighted 3, one was weighted 2 and none were weighted 1. The total weighting is the sum of weightings from each card which in this case amounts to 39. The result is written as ten votes with a weighting of 39, or 10/39.

The consensus/accommodation is declared to be the ideas with the highest weighting. The top ten ideas are ranked in this way. Draws are resolved where possible by promoting the idea that had the greatest number of votes. On occasions there may be an obvious break in the ranking where a group of ideas clearly score much more highly than the remainder. This can be used as another means of converging on the most preferred idea(s) about problems to take forward to the Choice phase.

Example. Given the relatively straightforward nature of NGT there is little value in using limited space on an example.

9.2.1.4 Image generation and evaluation – Metaphors

The main principles for metaphor analysis to attach to the general principles already given above are twofold.

- Create whole images of organisation, not just collections of ideas.
- Generate insight into the problems by applying many different descriptive forms to problems faced that are not literally applicable.

One way that people make sense of things is through analogies and metaphors. The processes are similar but can be distinguished. A definition of each one makes the distinction and helps us to understand how metaphor can be used in the process of creative thinking and uncovering problems to be dealt with.

- An analogy is a process of reasoning from parallel cases.
- A metaphor is the application of a descriptive form to an object or action to which it is not literally applicable.

Analogies and metaphors are discussed below in that order.

Science is a knowledge-generating process. Knowledge can be generated by reasoning between parallel cases, i.e., through analogies. Physics is a scientific discipline that has used analogies to make sense of particular phenomena. One phenomenon understood in this way is light. At one time light was a little-understood phenomenon. Physicists brought forward an explanation of light by drawing parallels between the behaviour of light and the behaviour of water waves. From this parallel came the wave theory of light. This parallel, however, provided only a partial explanation. Some properties of light do not conform to the theory of water waves. A second parallel was drawn between light and particles. Some of the behaviour of light not explained by the wave theory was explained by the moving particle theory. So two analogies had been drawn. The first analogy reasoned that light behaved like waves. The second analogy reasoned that light behaved like moving particles. Niels Bohr called this dual analogy 'the wavicle theory of light' and from this was born the idea of complementarity between theories.

Problem solving also is concerned with generating knowledge, specifically about organisational problems. Metaphors have been put forward as a more adequate way of doing this than analogies, which are more closely associated with the scientific endeavour. The main reason for choosing metaphors is that they are prevalent in everyday thought and language. Even more to the point, managers use metaphors continuously to describe the work situation even though most do not know it. There are many examples of this (the metaphor is highlighted with italics).

- This new product is our *springboard* to the future.
- Office politics operate according to *the law of the jungle*.
- Trouble begins with those *dinosaurs* at HQ.
- The hazards have arisen because *organisational evolution* occurs in an *ad hoc* manner.
- I don't want to *shepherd a disorganised department*, I want to be *driving an efficient machine*.
- Let's not rush into this decision. I don't think we have thought it through thoroughly enough. It would be better if we took *a helicopter view* first of all.

There are lots of problems that can be represented by these metaphors. Try and think of some metaphors that you have heard recently at work. What problems do they bring to mind?

The aim of image generation using metaphors is twofold.

- To make managers aware that they use metaphors in everyday management thinking (that has just been done).
- To harness the potential value of the normally invisible and jumbled use of metaphors by developing a formal method that makes the process an explicit and organised part of creative thinking about organisational problems (the next task).

The method given below asks you to employ metaphors to help generate creative thinking about organisational problems. It can feel strange at first and often early efforts fail to come up with metaphors that provoke insight. What you need to do, at least in the first instance, is to try out metaphors that are meaningful to you and discover what images they help to create. Types of metaphor you can use include the following.

- The following five main metaphors have been used as models in management and organisation theory:
  - *mechanistic* operations
  - adapting, growing, evolving, etc.; the *organic* organisation
  - *organic but intelligent*, conscious of and planning for the future
  - behaving according to social rules and practices – *the corporate culture*
  - events dominated by *a political dynamic.*
- Storylines from films, plays, lyrics, operas or books.
- Pictures, drawings, cartoons or photographs.
- Things that are going on in current affairs.
- Accounts of events from history books.
- Memories and anecdotes from your own life such as family sagas, a holiday experience, some specific event that happened with your children or your parents, an occurrence at work, a deep friendship, etc.
- Something that you own like a pinball machine, egg-laying hens, a CD disc, a collection of old books, an encyclopaedia, an atlas, a board game, a mobile phone, a springboard, training equipment, a photo album, a pair of binoculars, etc.
- Somewhere that has captured your imagination like a rain forest, a jungle, a mountain range, the Arctic, volcanic Iceland, an ornamental garden, a forest glade, a dungeon, a cathedral, a wine cellar, a city centre, a place where you go to reflect and wind down, etc.

There is one further tip. Do some preliminary work once you have chosen a metaphor. Work out its attributes, characteristics, the dynamic it represents and the stakeholders the metaphor embraces. Then use those details to make sense of the situation you are facing.

Also remember that if one metaphor does not work, then move on and try another. Never get bogged down. Furthermore, even if you hit upon a metaphor that is insightful, especially if this is early on in the process, do not assume that you have been creative enough. Keep trying new images out for a reasonable period of time.

Image generation using metaphors has a divergent and a convergent phase. Metaphors are used initially to understand organisational images already in play. Then new ones are introduced to create alternative images and understanding. Analysis of the images is then undertaken in a convergent phase to assess which of the images brings forward a most plausible explanation of the problems faced. The process starts with the divergent phase.

Divergence. To start the process of image generation, try to find out which metaphors are already in play. Talk informally to people as individuals and in groups. Extract from the conversations organisational image(s) that people hold about the problems and bring these into focus.

A good way of guiding your early thinking is to use the five main metaphors that have been used as models in management and organisation theory which are provided above (under the first bullet point of metaphors). This will help to explain the corporate culture and prevalent attitude toward management and organisation, which is valuable information that is bound to be helpful as the problem solving process progresses. Assess from this thinking what problems exist.

As well as undertaking explorations with the main management models, unearth other dominant metaphors that people are using. If you get stuck, reflect on the alternative types of metaphor provided earlier. Extract any findings or problems that you uncover.

Continue the process of image generation by introducing new metaphors. What additional metaphors induce meaningful insight? What new findings or problems are uncovered?

Convergence. Each metaphor generates in a more or less useful form partial understanding about organisational problems. This is divergent thinking. The process now moves on to a convergent phase. Using the images and insights generated decide

- what you think is happening
- why you think this is happening
- what you believe is the most plausible opinion about the problems to be dealt with.

To help this process undertake the following critical evaluation.

- Ask if the insights generated by each metaphor are equally helpful.
- Ask how successfully the metaphors reconcile information.
- Ask what problems each metaphor surfaces and whether tackling these would be the most effective way of managing the organisation.

Ultimately you must choose a most plausible opinion about the problems to be managed to pass on to the Choice phase.

Example. Summarised below is a case study that we give to participants on our training seminars. The original piece was written by my friend Chow Kok Fong, then Chief Executive in Singapore of the Construction Industry Development Board. An episode using the case provides one example of the image-generating method just described.

I had set the case study. Several groups were thrashing out ideas, but I noticed in one group a demure lady, Sharon Wong, working on her own as usual. I carefully tracked her progress. I asked her to present her thinking to the group as a whole. The group were stunned as this otherwise retiring young person burst into life with her most meaningful metaphor. Thankfully Sharon's presentation was recorded and an edited version of it appears after the summary of the case below. Interestingly, the image-creating process was a fun experience for Sharon and brought out a dimension to her character that the other components of the seminar failed to touch. Her presentation triggered off a rush of further thinking among seminar participants.

The case study works as follows. Groups are asked to use the image-generating method to come up with a most plausible explanation of the following situation (abstracted from the original case).

Chow Kok Fong is Chief Executive of the Construction Industry Development Board (CIDB) in Singapore. The CIDB is a government agency. Its main aim is to improve the competitiveness and quality delivery capability of the construction sector and to support the export of the country's construction services.

The CIDB is staffed with young, ambitious people who are the cream of the graduates in architecture, building, engineering and economics. The board's success depends largely on how well these ambitious officers can be brought together as a team. It is essential that each one feels that they have a stake in the board's mission.

The board's policy proposals had to be tested against the interests of various parties. Interest groups in the construction sector included contractors, developers, other public sector procurement agencies, the professional bodies representing architects, engineers and the unions. Also to be taken into account was the political impact of decisions on civilian satisfaction as well as the concerns of governments of neighbouring countries, such as Malaysia and Thailand, from where cheap labour can be imported.

Singapore is a small island. It has an open economy. It is open to competition from across the world. It is vulnerable to changes in the international economy. Singapore faces challenges posed by continuous external challenges.

The creative response from Sharon using a well-known story line went as follows.

There are two main things that I would like to tell you about after having experienced the process of image generation focusing on the Construction Industry Development Board (CIDB) case study – the metaphor and the process. That is, first I would like to tell you about the metaphor I used that led to a most plausible explanation of the CIDB case. Then I would like to comment generally on how the process worked for me.

The metaphor that provided me with the most plausible explanation was the story about King Arthur and the Knights of the Round Table. Even if you do not know this story yourself, the use of the metaphor I am about to describe will impart the basic storyline.

I will give you an idea about the stakeholders and the situation first.

- You have got Chow Kok Fong as King Arthur.
- You have got his whole flurry of graduate officers as the Knights of the Round Table.
- The Singapore government is Merlin, the wizard assisting Arthur.
- The Kingdom of Camelot is Singapore.
- Enemies inside the Kingdom include other interested parties.
- Enemies outside the Kingdom include competitors and governments in the region.

The dynamic is along the following lines.

King Arthur is the only one able to extract the magic sword from the stone. This provided evidence of a true leader. King Arthur has the required special quality to pull the sword out of the stone. Chow Kok Fong is able to pull together the opposing forces and hence to confirm his leadership.

King Arthur formed strategic allies. He has to gather support in the Kingdom for his major proposals. These are aimed at dealing with internal and external enemies to benefit the people. Strategic allies have been established by marrying off princes to princesses (i.e., building up permanent relationships).

Arthur is assisted by Merlin but has to be particularly careful not to alienate this wizard. Merlin holds far reaching powers over the people, the exact nature of which is not fully known. Merlin's support gives King Arthur clout.

King Arthur also has to be careful with the Knights of the Round Table. He must maintain their loyalty, otherwise they may join some other competing army. The Round Table can only be strong if all the Knights show solidarity. Each Knight is like a splinter of the table. A splintered table has no strength but put together as a solid whole the table represents great strength.

The Kingdom needs order. Rules and regulations are set to achieve this. Order means stability and more chances to protect the Kingdom.

Warfare is inevitable. Battles are monitored by setting missions and assessing how well those are achieved. Missions are like conquering and gaining prizes in victory.

For me the story of King Arthur captures well the stakeholders and the dynamic present in the CIDB case study. It suggests that the main task for the CIDB to help to improve the competitiveness and quality delivery capability of the construction sector is to manage the interested parties and not, as might be mistakenly assumed, to put in place more efficient construction methods. Now I would like to tell you about the process and how I found it.

The process in action is not as systematic as the method we were asked to try out would suggest. In some senses the process can be described as a set of experiences that gave rise to different images of the situation. For me the process amounted to using metaphors to create experiences, undergoing those experiences, and through this developing enhanced knowledge about the situation.

Initially there was no rush of ideas, no adrenaline and therefore no image generation. Nothing clicked as our group explored various metaphors. I was trying to understand the situation through one metaphor after another, but none captured the essence of the dynamic. The experiences were not very rich. Almost as soon as I used the King Arthur metaphor, however, a flood of thoughts rushed through my mind as if a dam had suddenly burst. It became a whole experience that portrayed Chow Kok Fong and the CIDB in the setting of the story. I saw stakeholders as characters and the political dynamic as the storyline. It was fun, insightful and very exciting to see the situation in such a fundamentally different way as happened with this metaphor.

My recommendation to you if you get stuck is to keep going, keep exploring new alternatives because you do not know what experience may happen with the next image that you create.

The most plausible opinion about the problems faced by Chow Kok Fong, given by Sharon Wong, our creative Singaporean, focuses on maintaining relationships between interested parties. In a problem solving situation this finding would be passed on to the Choice phase.

We will now move on to the Choice phase.

9.2.2 Choice

- The Choice phase is useful
  - when it is not clear cut which method(s) would be the most suitable one(s) to tackle the problems surfaced in the Creativity phase, in the circumstances
  - to reflect critically on a choice that by all accounts in the Creativity phase appears clear cut.
- The aim of the Choice phase is to choose (a) method(s) that will best tackle the appreciation of the problems brought forward from the Creativity phase.
- The expected output of the Choice phase, therefore, is choice of the most suitable method(s) in the circumstances.
- There are five main principles of the Choice phase.
  - There is/are (a) most suitable method(s) to tackle the problems surfaced in the Creativity phase, in the circumstances.
  - All methods have an immediate and given purpose.
  - All methods can be used obliquely to achieve some purpose other than their immediate and given purpose.
  - The four main types of method accord with the four key dimensions of organisation set out in TSI's philosophy.
  - Choice is a process of critical evaluation of the alternative options to achieve the most suitable decision in the circum-

stances and must never be treated like a pigeon-holing exercise.
- The method used is a complementarist framework for choice based on the following four key dimensions of organisation set out in TSI's philosophy.
  - Efficient organisational processes.
  - Effective organisational design.
  - Organisational culture.
  - Organisational politics.
  It has two stages.
  - Choose type of method.
  - Choose actual method.
- TSI has a recursive structure. The process of the Choice phase is as follows.
  - Creativity – challenge the usual way of problem solving by considering alternative methods according the complementarist framework for choice.
  - Choice – work toward the above-declared purpose using the complementarist framework.
  - Implementation – pass on the chosen method(s) to the Implementation phase.

Choose type of method. Begin by asking which of the following four key dimensions highlights the most pressing organisational problems to be dealt with according to the findings of the Creativity phase. The answer will be a choice of one or more of the key dimensions, which are repeated below for convenience.

- Organisational processes – flows and controls over flows.
- Organisational design – functions, their organisation, co-ordination and control.
- Organisational culture – mediation of behaviour in terms of people's relationship to social rules and practices.
- Organisational politics – power and potency to influence the flow of events.

Confirm your choice by checking whether problems faced are addressed by methods aligned to the chosen key dimension(s). The following reasoning will help.

- *Organisational processes.* It has been decided what needs to be done and the issues concerning why it is to be done and for whom have been properly addressed – the question therefore remains, 'Is the task now a matter of designing the most efficient processes?' Methods aligned in *Solving Problem Solving* to designing efficient processes are Quality Management (QM) and Business Process Reengineering (BPR).

- *Organisational design*. It has been decided what needs to be done and the issues concerning why it is to be done and for whom have been properly addressed – the question therefore remains, 'Is the task now a matter of designing the most effective organisation?' The method aligned to designing effective organisation is called Diagnosis for Effective Organisation (DEO).
- *Organisational culture*. Deciding what needs to be done, why and for whom are problematic – there is not a shared or common understanding – the question therefore remains, 'What do we want to do?' Methods aligned to organisational culture are Exploring and Choosing Designs (ECD), Exploring and Making Decisions (EMD) and Testing Polarised Viewpoints (TPV).
- *Organisational politics*. It has been decided what to do and how to do it – the question therefore remains, 'Whose interests are being served by the design and/or the decision?' The follow-on questions are 'Why should a design or decision be adopted, what should be done and/or why should this decision on what is to be done be accepted?' Furthermore, 'Why should the design be implemented, whose interests would be served and what would be the consequences of this?' It is also important to explore organisational biases (e.g., race, gender, management structure) and to assess the impact of this on designs and decisions. The method aligned to organisational politics is called Critically Evaluating Designs and Decisions (CEDD).

Choose actual method. Continue by asking which method(s) in the key dimension chosen as the one(s) containing the most pressing problems has/have a purpose directly relevant to the problems that must be dealt with. Each method in each of the key dimensions has an immediate and given purpose that can be used to this end; (a) method(s) is/are chosen that has/have an immediate and given purpose which tackles head-on core organisational problems. A summary of immediate and given purposes of the methods incorporated in the problem solving system in this book is given below (please also take into account the ideas in Chapter 6 on 'What is happening when you problem solve').

- Designing processes.
  - Continuous improvement – Quality Management (QM). The aim is to meet customer's agreed requirements, formal and informal, at lowest cost, first time every time.
  - Radical change – Business Process Reengineering (BPR). The aim is to defunctionalise the business and rebuild it on a relatively small number of core business processes each thought to be breakthroughs.
- Designing organisation.
  - Diagnosis for Effective Organisation (DEO). The aim is to identify through diagnosis what is causing organisational ineffectiveness and to think through alternative and more effective organisational designs.
- Implementing Designs and Decisions (IDD). The aim is to implement efficiently and effectively new designs and/or decisions.
- Debating.
  - Exploring and Choosing Designs (ECD). The aim is to debate and come up with an idealised design free from all constraints except technical feasibility and viability.
  - Exploring and Making Decisions (EMD). The aim is to explore different perceptions about problems faced and to come up with a decision about what to do.
  - Testing Polarised Viewpoints (TPV). The aim is to uncover strengths and weaknesses in competing designs and/or decisions and from this to agree upon an improved strategy.
- Disimprisoning.
  - Critically Evaluating Designs and Decisions (CEDD). The aim is to ensure that even the most disadvantaged people have been explicitly accommodated.

If there is not a method in this book or your own system of methods that is suitable for the job then further research needs to be done. Relevant extant methods in the problem solving literature must be searched for. The Critical Review Mode will need to be brought into action if new methods are to be incorporated in your system of methods.

If there are no extant methods then a new method must be developed to be incorporated within your system of methods. This must go through the Critical Review Mode. The following questions must be asked of the method whilst it is being developed.

- When will this method be useful?
- What is the main aim of the method?
- What will be the output of the method?
- What are the principles of the method?
- What are the mechanisms or guidelines of the method?
- What does the method not do which are issues to be taken into account during the process?

Special attention should be paid to the method in action in its early uses through the Critical Reflection Mode – asking penetrating questions about the adequacy of the method. (Note that the problem solving system TSI is clearly a learning and adaptive system.)

If you wish to use a method obliquely then Choice is a little more complicated. It involves translating the principles of a method so that they match up to the oblique purpose of its use. It also means gearing up the mechanisms of the method to achieve the oblique purpose. The following example provides a helpful illustration of an oblique use of principles of human freedom through ECD.

Example. The example is taken from a piece by Jason Magidson (see Further Reading) that describes some very interesting examples of the use of a method described later in this chapter called Exploring and Choosing Designs (ECD). ECD is an approach that has as its given and immediate purpose the task of coming up with an idealised design free from all constraints except technical feasibility and viability. It is a method that stimulates debate with the essential principles of learning and understanding. Magidson's use of ECD, however, is clearly carried out with principles of human freedom at the fore as we shall soon see. The case deals with problems in communities in inner-city Philadelphia. Typical inner-city problems plagued communities, such as homicide, rape, robbery, aggravated assault, burglary, larceny, auto thefts and arson. Some community volunteers decided to do something about their problems. They started a grassroots movement consisting of people frustrated with the efforts of government but determined to do something about it. The government were 'reluctant' so the grassroots movement decided to grasp their own problems and make improvements. INTERACT, the organisation employing Magidson, were enlisted to participate in the process of improvement.

The process began using a part of Implementing Designs and Decisions (IDD) that undertakes *obstruction analysis* (described on page 173). Four interacting categories in which progress is necessary if society is to develop were considered: the political–economic (scarcity of resources), the scientific (lack of knowledge), the ethical–moral (areas of conflict) and the aesthetic (vision of a desirable state and belief in the possibility of its realisation). This exercise was conducted firstly so that solutions developed could be tested to determine whether they would remove the obstructions. This means that the outcome of the whole ECD exercise was subject to principles of human freedom. Let us pick up on one obstruction and follow it through the intervention to demonstrate how principles of human freedom prevailed.

The obstruction in the political–economic category was a maldistribution of wealth that reduced the quality of various services supplied to the citizens of Philadelphia. Many of Philadelphia's services are budget-based and funding comes from decision makers whose objectives are frequently in conflict with those who need and use the services.

The current funding structure for providers of youth services (e.g., community and recreation centres) obstructs development. Much of the centre's efforts had been spent in fundraising. Their success depended on whether they met requirements of decision makers, for example in government agencies. The requirements of these decision makers frequently do not match the requirements for successful community development. If proposals do not match the interests of decision makers who allocate funds, they are likely to be rejected.

ECD was used to come up with an idealised design. The community volunteers assumed that their neighbourhoods had been destroyed the night before and that they were designing the ideal neighbourhoods with which they would replace them today (i.e., there were no obstructions assumed except technical feasibility and viability). The participants specified characteristics that they felt ought to exist ideally in their neighbourhoods. After the group specified the (56 idealised) characteristics, they developed two means of more closely approximating their ideals. 'Pride Coupons' was one of them.

The Pride Coupon Program was designed to promote a variety of quality activities through which youths could develop their talents, be recognised for doing so and derive satisfaction in the process. Also, it was intended to eliminate the obstruction of the current funding system that had resulted in poor services to youths and to address the scarcity of meaningful, legitimate, after-school activities. The principles of human freedom in the form of a process-generating potency to address social asymmetry were therefore prevalent at this stage.

The essence of the idea was to turn the funding structure on its head so that the service providers depend on demand. This can be accomplished by 'subsidising' the users of services and allowing them to choose which service providers to buy from. Each provider's income therefore depends on how many youths purchase from them. Preference is indicated through choice. This arrangement dramatically increases the quality and variety of services and reduces waste. Youths spend vouchers called 'Pride Coupons' at a youth activity organisation of their choice. Providers are reimbursed by submitting the coupons they collect to a fund established by donations from foundations, corporations, government agencies and private individuals. Services put in place through political interest but which do not raise the youths' interest receive no demand and become financially and socially defunct.

This example clearly demonstrates the oblique use of principles of human freedom not called for in the given and immediate purpose of ECD, the main method employed. It could be argued, however, that this case shows that ECD is already capable of tackling issues of coercion. TSI explains to the contrary that ECD and other similar methods have not demonstrated their specific relevance for dealing with coercion. It is hence not good enough to assume that these types of issue can be accommodated for, or that they are catered for in principle by anything other than a method explicitly created to evaluate critically decisions and designs with human freedom being the main guiding principle. There has to be direct evidence that the question of 'Whose interests are being served?' is genuinely worked over and the results harvested and made use of. Oblique use of a method means using it in a way that transcends the immediate and given purpose for which it is best suited – thus obliquely introducing an agenda not normally or explicitly served by the method.

9.2.3 Implementation

- Implementation of relevant innovative change proposals is needed when an organisation has problems to be dealt with.
- The aim of the Implementation phase is to employ (a) method(s) to generate and implement relevant innovative change proposals that will tackle the core problems whilst dealing with as many other problems as possible.
- There are four main principles of the Implementation phase.
  - Always hold TSI's four main principles in mind when generating and implementing innovative change proposals.
  - Use the principles of the chosen method(s) to guide development of change proposals.
  - Use the immediate and given purpose of the chosen method(s) to evaluate the relevance of proposals for change.
  - If an oblique use of a method is intended then use the principles and purpose of that method to evaluate the relevance of proposals for change.
- The expected output of the Implementation phase is, therefore, implementation of relevant innovative change proposals.
- The methods used tackle one of TSI's four key dimensions of organisation.
  - Efficient organisational processes.
  - Effective organisational design.

- Organisational culture.
- Organisational politics.
• TSI has a recursive structure. The process of the Implementation phase is as follows.
  - Creativity. The process of creativity is found within the method itself, but is influenced by the problem solving style adopted.
  - Choice. Assess how well the proposals for change directly tackle the problems and choose the most appropriate ones in the circumstances.
  - Implementation. Work toward the above aim of the Implementation phase using the incorporated methods that as a whole tackle TSI's four key dimensions of organisation.

Methods to tackle each of the four key dimensions of organisation are presented below.

9.2.3.1 *Process design – Continuous improvement: Quality Management*

• Quality Management (QM) is useful when the Creativity phase shows that
  - there is variation and a lack of consistency in processes
  - there is unnecessary waste in the processes
  - the customers' needs are not being satisfied (the customer is anyone, internal or external, who is provided with a product, service or information).
• The immediate and given purpose is to meet customers' agreed requirements, formal and informal, at lowest cost, first time every time. (Achieving agreement may involve the use of other methods, especially those that encourage debate.)
• The output will be efficient design of processes that satisfies customers' needs; but what is happening when you problem solve with this method is explained in detail in Chapter 6.
• There are two main principles that drive QM.
  - Efficiency can be achieved by continuously redesigning the processes in line with customers' requirements.
  - The key to good management is to ensure that customers are satisfied.

- The method has two main stages.
  - Set up and operationalise a steering group that: sets the organisational mission, designs or chooses QM educational modules and sets up quality action teams.
  - Set up and operationalise quality action teams that: set the local mission, implement QM educational modules, undertake customer analysis, identify projects, choose projects and implement projects.

  The first stage is necessary only when QM is to be implemented company-wide, say in a Total Quality Management programme.

A number of foundational ideas are found in the aim of QM given above. These are briefly reviewed below. Each of these points must be taken into account when QM is used.

- QM extends the traditional idea that customers are people external to the organisation who buy or utilise its products, services or information; to include people within and outside an organisation to whom we supply or from whom we receive products, services or information. It therefore closely conforms to TSI's view of organisation.
- Customers have requirements that must be met. Requirements are measurable specifications. The choice of specification is critical. Measurable specifications are discussed briefly in Chapter 7 under the heading Measurement.
- Requirements must be agreed by all parties concerned. External customers are one party with one set of needs. These needs may not mirror totally organisational or members' needs. Requirements therefore cannot be totally dictated by external customers, whose viewpoints in any case are likely to diverge. They must be negotiated and ways forward thought through before working agreements are made. TSI's philosophy states that all needs must be taken into account and balanced.
- With QM both formal and informal procedures are of concern. Formal procedures are those which are established and commonly understood among organisational members and are often recorded in procedures manuals. Informal procedures

are those that come about through people interacting. These too must be assessed and managed.

- At lowest cost means that there is no unnecessary loss or waste in time, effort or material in the production and delivery of a product, service or information. At lowest cost therefore means 'do it efficiently'. The cost of not doing it efficiently is known as failure cost.
- First time every time is a policy that withholds licences to fail. Things do go wrong, but the root cause of the error must be considered and dealt with so that it does not recur.

Implementation of QM can be organisation-wide, within divisions or in some smaller whole unit. The ideal of Total Quality Management is to implement QM organisation-wide, but this is not always practically feasible or strategically desirable. If QM is being implemented in a relatively small unit requiring only one or a few quality action teams, then the first stage of implementation can be absorbed by those teams. It will be assumed below that implementation is organisation-wide and so both stages are explained.

QM method begins by *setting up a steering group*. A group of people is formed to steer the process of implementation. The group comprises about six people representing different organisational functions and levels. This reflects TSI's systemic principle. The group is co-ordinated by a leader, but this person is not necessarily the senior person. The group has to set an organisational mission, design or choose QM educational modules and set up quality action teams. The group co-ordinates progress and generally assists in the implementation process.

Set organisational mission. The steering group initially sets an organisational mission. This is a mission for the whole activity undergoing the QM programme. A simple set of questions given in the method for Exploring and Choosing Designs (ECD) is used here.

Design or choose QM educational modules. The steering group may feel the need to design special QM modules themselves, or could approach competent external consultants or management education bodies for help (see Chapter 8 on choosing and using consultants). Whichever, the steering group must task itself with initial selection of QM educational modules that are most likely to raise quality awareness and provide members of the quality action team with working knowledge of the 'seven quality tools'. The seven tools are essential QM techniques understandable and usable by anyone. They help to identify inconsistencies in processes. The seven tools are reviewed at the end of this chapter.

Set up quality action teams. The steering group sets up a coalition of quality action teams to carry out continuous improvement to process design. The teams must provide seamless coverage of the processes of the whole organisation. Each one will be apportioned a task area and will take responsibility for its procedures. Together the groups will cover the entire system of organisational procedures in breadth and depth. The method named Diagnosis for Effective Organisation (DEO) with its Viable System Model (VSM) may suggest ways of organising quality action teams.

Quality action teams set local mission. When the steering group has prepared the way for quality to be implemented, the main tasks then shift to quality action teams. They straightaway set their own mission using the six mission-setting questions mentioned earlier. The overall mission must be taken as given but interpreted to maintain the identity of the whole that must be reflected throughout the organisation.

In some cases QM will be implemented in one area of the organisation. The need for a steering group is greatly reduced. The tasks and duties of the steering group can easily be absorbed by the quality action teams through a co-ordinator. This may involve one person as a co-ordinator and only one or a few quality action teams. In that case the teams will take into account the organisational mission as it stands and progress from there.

Undertake customer analysis. The emphasis with QM is on the customer. Quality action teams must direct their attention to customer-centred problems. Customers' requirements must be determined and agreed. Once these basic parameters have been set performance can be monitored. Performance analysis exposes weaknesses in processes where improvements must be made. Projects are then set up to improve weak areas. Customer analysis can be undertaken in five steps.

- Name the customers.
- Determine and agree customers' requirements.
- Assess performance against the requirements.
- Identify weaknesses in the processes where improvements can be made that will help to meet the requirements.
- Identify projects to make improvements.

Identifying projects to make improvements involves putting together well-thought-out and informed proposals. There are seven guidelines that help proposal formation.

- Problems to be tackled by a project must be clearly identified so that all causes and symptoms are understood.
- Ends must be clearly stated so that a set of requirements to be met can be established and a measurable means of showing this stated. This includes setting major milestones and their expected time of completion.
- Resource requirements must be stated.
- Large projects must be broken down, or decomposed, into subprojects that are distinct but interdependent. They must be measurable against the aims of the subproject and the project overall.
- Ownership of projects and subprojects must be clearly established so that accountability for the success of the project is unambiguous.
- Rigorous measurement procedures must be highlighted which allow for failure analysis, so that the degree of failure being tackled can be compared to other proposed projects when projects are being chosen and can be used to show improvements during implementation.
- The project must be compared to other projects and their relative worth assessed prior to choice of project to be implemented.

Choose projects to be implemented. Choice of project has to be made from the set identified during customer analysis. The quality guru Juran has helped this process considerably. He reckons that there are two types of project.

- The vital few
- The useful many.

The Pareto principle is used to argue that 80% of failure cost can be dealt with by 20% of the projects – these being the vital few. The idea is to focus on exceptional projects first so that maximum improvement can be made in the short term. The remaining 20% of failure cost is cleared up with the other 80% of the projects – the useful many. The useful many are important to QM as it strives for continuous improvement.

Criteria for grouping into the two categories are given below.

- Rank the projects according to failure cost.
- Assess the extent to which the project will impact on customer satisfaction.
- Assess the extent to which the project focuses on improvement of either internal or external customer interface.
- Assess the extent to which the project is relevant in terms of meeting the local mission.
- Compare projects and assess which ones are logically dependent and/or supportive and which ones are not.
- Carefully think about a project not considered to be logically dependent or supportive with other projects to see if it can be considered vital in some other way.
- Rank the projects taking into account the preceding criteria.

The choice of an initial project is a critical one. There is a great need for success in the early stages since failure can cause permanent damage to the QM initiative, with people becoming despondent and demotivated. Projects are all about making a positive impact, but if projects go wrong then they can backfire. The effects of a backfire can be disastrous. There is no point taking risks in the early stages of implementation. The following points provide additional tactical guidelines for choosing projects at the start of the process.

- Select a project that will be visible and will not be considered trivial.
- Select a project that can easily be made more visible because it has clear objectives that are measurable and hence they can be shown to have been met.
- Select a project where results are expected to be visible relatively quickly.
- Select a project that offers relatively easy possibilities for improvement.
- Select a project that is easily controlled.

Implement projects. Detailed implementation planning is vital. A version of the method for Implementing Designs and Decisions (IDD) would be appropriate here. In any case, all those involved must be well organised so that it is known exactly who is going to do what, when it is to be done by and which sort of measurement will be used to monitor progress. Resource scheduling must be calculated.

Each project must be monitored and controlled. There must be a reporting system that achieves the following.

- Assesses whether the quality initiative is realising expected benefits.
- Assesses the overall success of projects.
- Co-ordinates efforts and avoids duplication.
- Spreads news about successes and lessons to all quality action teams.
- Maximises the benefit to the business overall.
- Monitors overall costs and savings.

The project is implemented when it has been evaluated as suggested above and is considered to be completely ready. After implementation a report must be made for the record and for possible future reference. The report must contain the following information.

- A record of the benefits achieved and the costs incurred.
- Details of any deviations from the initial plan.
- How improvements have been consolidated and maintained.
- Whether there are ideas that have wider applicability.

- How the project contributed to other projects.
- What lessons were learned and how these can be built upon.
- What are the key achievements that deserve recognition.

There are four further issues to take into account when implementing QM. Each one has (a) recommended method(s).

- Does the process redesign sufficiently take into account the issue of whose interests are being served and why? Use the method for Critically Evaluating Designs and Decisions (CEDD).
- Are there competing designs that people are aligning themselves to? Use the method for Testing Polarised Viewpoints (TPV).
- Which tools and techniques are available that can be used in projects to improve process design? See the section 'Other Problem Solving Methods' at the end of this chapter for guidance.
- How can the design be implemented. Use the method for Implementing Designs and Decisions (IDD).

Example. (A pseudonym is used for the company discussed in this case study to maintain confidentiality as requested). The following case is provided by Lew Yue Wah who reports on efforts to improve and standardise bunker transfer practices in Singapore on chartered vessels using Quality Management (QM). I am grateful to Lew Yue Wah for permitting me to report his intervention in *Solving Problem Solving*. The case utilises part of the QM method and some useful support techniques, looking at the work of a quality action team as they began to 'undertake customer analysis' (after all other stages were completed). A quick introduction to bunker transfer sets the background.

Bunker transfer happens at ports where barges deliver fuel oil to ships. The process begins with a surveyor boarding the ship to gauge the ship's bunker tanks prior to and on completion of a bunker transfer operation. This is done alongside the ship's chief engineer. The surveyor also confirms the required fuel type and draws representative samples from the ship's manifold during transfer operations and submits them for grading. Tanks are then opened and the level of oil is accurately measured with an approved measuring tape. Clarification about safety procedures is made. Then the bunker transfer operation commences. On completion of the bunker transfer a final measure is taken by the surveyor and the bunkers are closed. The amount supplied is calculated. The same procedures are followed on the barge so that there is a cross-check measure. The surveyor then compares the two quantities and obtains a bunker variance percentage. Documentation is completed.

To start with, internal and external customers were named from the point of view of an anonymous chartered supplier featured in this case. The main ones are given below.

- Internal.
  - Cost analysis and charter hire manager who is responsible for payment to the owner of the chartered ship.
  - Bunker Purchasing Department which monitors the on-board quantity of the bunkers from their departure port, stores and integrates the data with stability and tank capacities of ships, and uses this in a computer-assisted planning system enabling computerised loading without having manually to calculate the ship's stability.
  - Management staff who oversee the bunkering department and seek out opportunities to minimise cost and reduce waste.
  - Chartering Department which liaises with ship owners and brokers to ensure that the bunker cost of the ship is duly agreed by joint surveys when delivering or redelivering the ship.
- External.
  - Bunker suppliers including the firms, traders, brokers and physical suppliers.
  - Chief engineer and master of ship who supervise the chartered suppliers during bunker operations.
  - Surveyor who provides an independent survey to check and supervise delivery and generally protect the interests of the chartered suppliers.
  - Ship owner whose concerns include cost as well as making certain that fuel is supplied to specification, thus preventing harm to the ship's engines.
  - Port agent who liaises closely with chartered suppliers,

arranging among other things proper documentation for speedy delivery of bunkers to the ships.

Internal customers were consulted informally about their needs and performance against requirements. This entailed casual conversation and interviews, but also included declared needs and gauged satisfaction at claims meetings and from records of previous correspondence.

External customers were much more difficult to access. A formal approach was adopted. A questionnaire was developed that was open-ended thus catering for significant differences in their needs. Questionnaires were sent out to surveyors, ship masters, bunker suppliers, surveyors and port agents. Some telephone surveys were conducted.

Of all the needs identified, four stood out after Pareto Analysis as absolutely crucial but containing significant weaknesses where improvements could be made. The top four needs were as follows.

- Availability and accuracy of berthing times, locations and cancellation of berthings.
- Co-operation between the ship's command and the contracted supplier.
- Agreed procedures for drawing samples and conforming to International Standards.
- Reducing bunker variance.

Of the four needs 'reducing bunker variance' was chosen as most pressing and the first project to be undertaken. Of the criteria mentioned earlier, the project scored highly on the following.

- There was a significant failure cost. Typically a disagreement of plus or minus 0.5% is not disputed. On a 1,000-ton delivery it is possible for a chief engineer to claim only, say, 995 tons was delivered without being challenged, thus leaving five tons of fuel 'in his pocket'.
- The project will impact significantly on customer satisfaction if it eradicates a perpetual source of disagreement between chartered suppliers and ship owners.

- The project therefore focuses on improvement of internal and external customer interface.
- The project is relevant because it helps the chartered supplier to move toward its quality mission of minimising cost and unnecessary waste.

The baseline performance was set at current performance. In the previous four months the number of unacceptable bunker variances was ten, seven, ten and eight respectively. A target of three per month was set. The target of three was unavoidably arbitrary since no known application of QM to bunkering could be found as a benchmark. Perfection was impossible to achieve because factors exist that cannot be controlled. Three of these factors are given below.

- The weather hampers accuracy in measurement and causes variance to occur (see scatter diagram later in the case study — Figure 9.5).
- Fluctuations of temperature in tanks cause erroneous spot readings which affect the volume of oil calculated.
- New barges require a period of time when curve/constant error of the bunker tanks is ascertained.

Identifying weaknesses where improvements were possible was achieved using a number of Ishikawa's 'seven tools' of QM. The main ones employed in this case were fishbone diagrams, control charts, and scatter diagrams. Each is briefly discussed below.

A fishbone diagram was used to identify the causes down to their roots at an actionable level (see Figure 9.3). A representative team met to help construct the Fishbone. The fishhead states the problem. The four main bones looking for causes were Equipment, Environment, Procedures and People. Brainstorming sessions using the round-robin techniques generated ideas for the root cause of the problem. The fishbone diagram was constructed from the range of ideas using a version of the convergence step of Brainstorming described in the Creativity phase of TSI earlier in the book.

From the diagram 16 actionable root causes were obtained (they are circled). Further research was undertaken into each

126

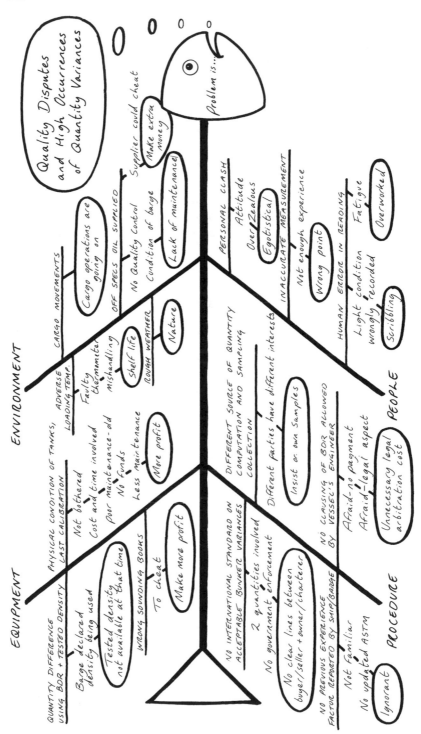

Figure 9.3 Fishbone diagram for the Quality Management (QM) case

one. The results of the research showed only four of the brain-stormed root causes could be verified. The four are listed below.

• Barge declared density affecting quantity measurements.
• Sea and weather state affecting variances.
• Dates of barge tank calibration and age of barges affecting accuracy of measurements.
• The number of samples collected by various parties from bunker surveys.

The remainder of the causes could not be verified because they largely involved problems of a human nature. Much discussion was held around this issue. It was finally decided to go ahead with minimising the problems of the four verifiable root causes which were largely technical in the belief that this would also reduce obliquely some of the human problems. The main hope here rested on the belief that there would be improved trust and understanding when chances of error and dishonesty had been substantially reduced. Some of the verification techniques are now discussed.

Control charts were used to help verify root causes. A control chart is a graph that plots sample measurements over time. Control limits are set. The task is to follow the progress of a measured variable over time to ensure that it remains under control (i.e., within control limits). Signs that the variable is not under control are all forms of inconsistency. Inconsistency comes in several forms.

• An upward or downward trend in the measure.
• A sudden jump in the average measure.
• When the measure oscillates.

In this case a control chart was used to look for inconsistency in the density of delivered oil. Density and volume are related. Inconsistency in density may therefore reflect inconsistency in volume.

A barge supplier always provides a declared density for the buyer at the time of physical delivery. This is declared in a Bunker Delivery Receipt and is the density measured at the terminal. Error can occur in the declared density in production such as in the blending process.

Four months of tested density was compared to declared density supplied by the barge at the time of the bunkering operation. The difference was plotted on a control chart (see Figure 9.4). Upper and Lower Control Limits and Action Limits were taken from standards accepted by the Marine Bunker Surveying Market. The standard is 40 points of density variation for the upper and lower limit. Acceptable variation in Upper and Lower Action Limits is set at 60 points. Action Limits are those limits where action has to be seriously considered.

There are four measures in the chart outside of the Action Limits. The suppliers were contacted and agreed that the error existed in the declared density. Overall, however, these four measures represented 12% out of control which was accepted as tolerable since this ratio would not cause unacceptable bunker variances. The graph was also checked for trends, jumps and oscillations, although none were found.

A third tool used to help identify causes of variation was scatter diagrams. The congenial relationship between sea state and bunker variance was assessed. A four-month survey was undertaken. The results showed that the higher the swell

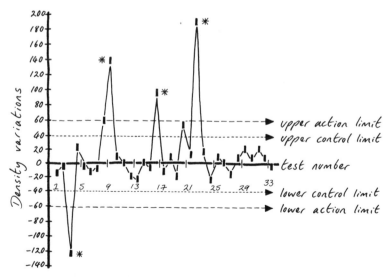

Figure 9.4   *Sample variations from Bunker Delivery Receipts showing limits used in the Quality Management (QM) case*

reported, the higher the bunker variance reported (see Figure 9.5). The swell causes the ship to pitch and range therefore making measurement far more problematic. This suggests that most, if not all, inaccuracies are genuine errors in measurement rather than purposely misreported.

Other forms of technique were used to identify causes of variance including Pareto Charts and Check Lists.

Brainstorming was then used to come up with a range of solutions to help minimise variance in the root causes. Practical methods for each solution had to be given for the proposed solution to be taken forward. The results were organised on a solutions matrix (see Figure 9.6). The matrix included judgements on feasibility and effectiveness ranking on a scale from 1 to 5. The more feasible or the more effective, the larger the number given. These scores were multiplied and the overall results were compared so that the best solutions could be selected. The favoured solutions (the choices) are indicated on Figure 9.6 with a Y for yes, whilst those rejected are given N for no.

The quality action team carried out detailed analysis of the 15 solutions. As seen, only ten were considered to be feasible and effective. The solutions addressed verified and unverified root causes and were consistent with the goal of meeting cus-

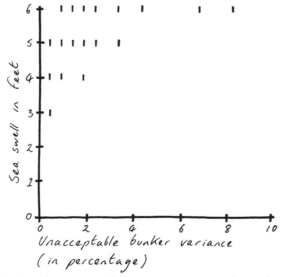

Figure 9.5 *Scatter diagram used to demonstrate correlation between bunker variance and sea swell in the Quality Management (QM) case*

130

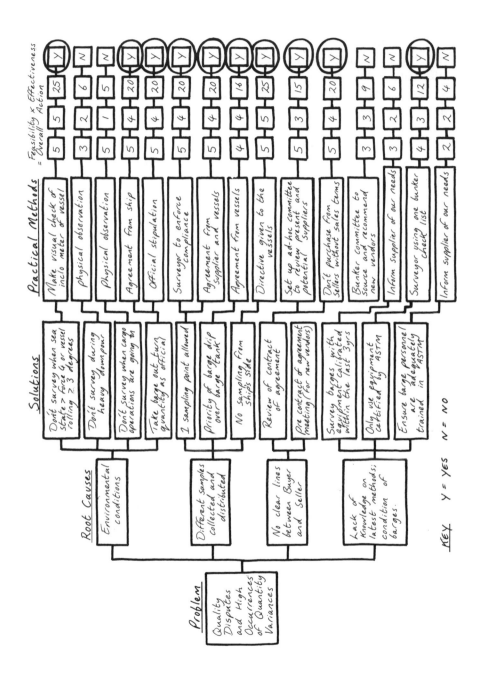

KEY   Y = YES   N = NO

tomer's needs. An action plan was drawn up. For each point of action three things had to be determined.

- What to do?
- How to do it?
- Evidence of completion.

For example, one action was to put in place a procedure that ensured the surveyor's approved equipment was used for the transfer. This was achieved in two ways. The surveyor had to bring the equipment along, which had to be recorded in the survey bunker report. An instruction had to be sent to the surveyor which was documented using a copy of the letter. A comprehensive monitoring plan was also installed.

The process of QM implementation proceeded along these lines and substantial improvements were made.

9.2.3.2 *Process design – Radical Change: Business Process Reengineering*

- Business Process Reengineering (BPR) is useful when the Creativity phase suggests that
  - radical organisational change to the design of its processes is needed to enhance effectiveness or to survive
  - there is parity in competitiveness in the organisational-enterprise's business.
- The immediate and given purpose is to defunctionalise the business and rebuild it on a relatively small number of core business processes.
- The output will be a radically changed operation that is leveraged into the market-place; but what is happening when you problem solve with this method is explained in detail in Chapter 6.
- There are four main principles that guide BPR.
  - BPR is proactive and radical.
  - Changing processes means radical improvement rather than continuous improvement.
  - Manage processes rather than functions on a company-wide basis – i.e., defunctionalise organisation.

Figure 9.6 *Solutions matrix used in the Quality Management (QM) case*

- Operational strategies drive business strategies – listen to the customer but hear the processes – leverage the processes into the market-place.
- The method has three stages.
  - Breakthrough.
  - Redesign.
  - Realisation.

BPR aims to leverage operations into the market-place following radical change. This achieves an operational lead. It focuses on what organisations can do beyond what must be done. BPR adds this extra competitive dimension to Quality Management (QM). QM only focuses on what organisations must do to give customers what they want, to attain a lead in customer satisfaction. Earlier stages in the drive toward competitiveness saw QM go beyond competitiveness with respect to productivity that gave a cost lead; and productivity stepped past product characteristics that yielded a marketing lead.

BPR wants efficiency in processes. Most processes meander through the organisation, worn into place like a cowpath in a field. The routes are followed day after day and eventually take on a historical importance along with the functional organisation, but are inefficient.

The focal point of BPR is to improve and to manage these processes. The old functional scheme is smashed as if breaking the china. BPR puts the china back together again in the form of about five to eight core business processes made lean and nimble. The core processes with perceived increased value are leveraged into the market-place.

Operational strategies are used to drive business strategies. Core business processes are set up to achieve operational strategies. The core processes are broad in coverage, streamlining the whole business from suppliers through to consumers. Process management is very wide, cutting across all organisational activities.

There are three types of BPR.

- Cost improvement.
- Achieving parity with the best competitors.
- Breakpoint improvement.

The first two are achievable using tools of QM. Tools of QM are employed to help develop an understanding of the flows of processes and the efficiency of processes. QM is an enabler for BPR because it discovers and eliminates waste and establishes how things are done. As explained earlier, QM produces cost advantages and increased customer satisfaction, but these can be matched by other organisational-enterprises all playing the same game, for example through benchmarking. Ultimately these approaches to quality management are limited in a competitive environment where parity can be achieved. Only breakthroughs which have a recognisable advantage in the marketplace and which set the rules are competitive enough. Breakthroughs are the unique element of BPR and the subject of further discussion below.

Breakthroughs occur from a breakpoint. A breakpoint is defined for a commercial company as achievement of excellence in one or more value metric where the market-place clearly recognises the advantage and where the ensuing result is a disproportionate and sustained increase in market share. A generalised version of this would embrace other types of organisation.

The value metrics used are fourfold.

- *Quality.* The principles of quality management including
  - continuous improvement
  - meeting customer's agreed requirements
  - eliminating variation in processes
  - eliminating unnecessary waste.
- *Cost.* The principles of cost management in areas such as
  - design and engineering
  - administration
  - purchasing
  - inventory
  - distribution.
- *Service.* The basic principles of good service such as
  - customer support
  - product or service support.
- *Cycle time.* The basic principles of speedy performance including
  - time to market

- response to market
- lead time.

A metric map is created. This map costs activities, normally using activity-based costing standards such as cost against lead time. The mapping highlights activities that hold opportunities for cost saving through streamlining.

In addition to this, market research is carried out listening to the customers'

- understanding of the market-place
- description of what is competitive parity
- feelings on how in future to maintain competitive parity.

Taking into account the results of the metric map and market research, a new vision is created about what would support a surge into the market-place. Competing visions can be tested against two essential BPR questions and the answer must be positive for the go-ahead.

- Would the market-place consider this vision a breakthrough?
- Will what is delivered create a disproportionate reaction in the market-place?

Research and experiments that address these questions must be carried out.

Breakthrough is not only the unique idea of BPR, it is also the core component of the first stage of BPR. There are three stages in total.

- Breakthrough.
- Redesign.
- Realisation.

Breakthrough as explained is about creating strategic vision for dominance or renewed competitiveness and achieving this in the market-place. It is about discovering what can be done to the processes to achieve the strategy. Strategic vision is set. Core business processes are then chosen to take the strategy to the market-place using process mapping.

Process mapping is the essential tool of the business process reengineer. A process map charts sequences of events using standard symbols. The process is mapped and then measures are applied such as costs incurred or time taken. This enables a comparison to be made on efficiency of competing alternative process designs. Processes can be physical, paper-based, computer-based or be a sequence of activities, all ideally ordered in a logical manner. The most commonly used type of map is activity-based which is illustrated in the example presented a little later.

Process mapping can be simple or very detailed. To start with in the Breakthrough stage a 'quickmap' is produced. A quickmap is a first attempt to represent organisational processes. It includes the perceived core business processes not forgetting other connections. Details can be added to this later although if the final representation is complex then the whole effort must be classed as a failure. The point is to streamline and simplify!

Redesign adds detail and planning. The aim is to work out what the chosen core processes will look like after reengineering. The focus is on supplier relations, customer relations and operational processes. Rigorous process mapping is undertaken to design the most efficient core processes, normally using an activity-based approach.

The conceptual design is then translated into an engineered design that must capture and control markets. Techniques for creative thinking focusing on the generation of ideas for the engineered design are essential and must be drawn in here. The result is a relatively simple process that can be taken forward and realised.

Realisation is undertaken using tools from organisational management such as the method for Implementing Designs and Decisions (IDD) included in the system of methods in this chapter. To be consistent with the principles of BPR the implementation must be a company-wide effort.

There are three further issues to take into account when redesigning business processes. Each one has a recommended method.

- Does the process redesign sufficiently take into account the issue of whose interests are being served and why? Use the method for Critically Evaluating Designs and Decisions (CEDD).

- Are there competing designs that people are aligning themselves to? Use the method for Testing Polarised Viewpoints (TPV).
- How can the design be implemented. Use the method for Implementing Designs and Decisions (IDD).

Example. The following case is provided by Mark Rowan, a Senior Manager with Advance Bank in Australia, who explains how they employed Business Process Reengineering (BPR) to take a lead in personal loans and other products. I am grateful to Mark and Advance Bank for permitting me to include an account of their reengineering of personal loans in *Solving Problem Solving*.

Advance Bank is Australia's sixth largest Stock Exchange-listed bank. It was formed in 1985 and has grown from a New South Wales-based home lender with total assets of Aus\$2.1 billion and 168 branches to a banking group with assets of Aus\$10 billion and 245 branches, with representation in all mainland states of Australia plus Hong Kong.

Advance Bank is committed to providing a high level of customer service to their personal banking clients. Advance Bank applies all the principles of Quality Management (QM) to its processes. Processes are viewed as the essence of the bank's business. Not only does most work get done through processes, be they manual or automated, but a great deal of what differentiates banks from each other is inherent in their individual work processes. Process is therefore considered one of the most important factors contributing to competitive advantage.

Recently, the bank took a careful look at its process design and recognised that reengineering was essential to maintain and improve its position in the market-place. A number of core business processes were identified, which in effect were those that supported the main products which the bank wanted to promote. One of these products was personal loans.

The personal loans product was of great concern to Advance Bank because the product had never reached a critical mass in terms of loanbook size. An activity-based process map was drawn up as shown in Figure 9.7 (also showing typical symbols

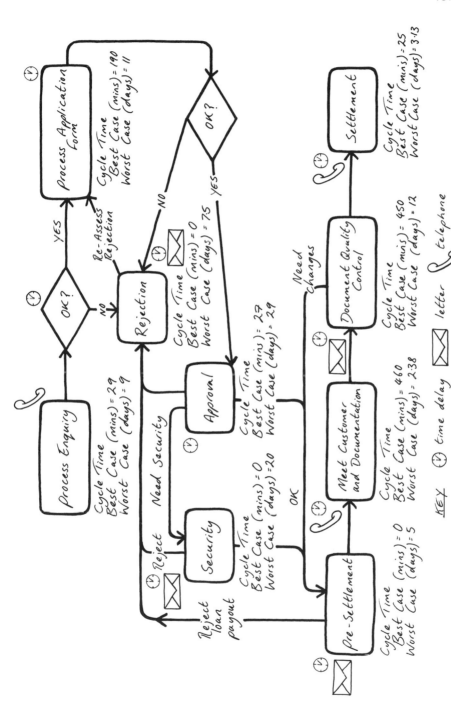

Figure 9.7 Activity-based process map used in the Business Process Reengineering (BPR) case

used). It was discovered that it was taking far too long to process a loan even when everything was in order. The best-case turnaround of 2.6 days from enquiry to settlement meant the lender having to move mountains. Twenty weeks was the worst-case turnaround from enquiry to settlement.

From the process map an activity-based costing was calculated. It was discovered that approximately an Aus$1 million loss per annum was being incurred when overhead and other costs were allocated. This could no longer be sustained. Furthermore, it was believed that the process, approach and marketing may well have been discouraging borrowers that the bank wanted.

It was acknowledged that radical change was required. A complete overhaul of the processes would make personal loans more efficient. All possible ways of reducing time and cost were considered. For example, reengineers assessed whether checks could be made whilst the borrower was on the line, e.g., getting income and employment details early in the collection process whilst another person would check these details in a form of parallel processing. Areas most likely to provide leverage in the market-place were identified and most effort was put into these with the expectation that they would provide the biggest benefit (a kind of Pareto analysis).

A vastly improved process design was achieved and implemented. At the same time this overcame the problems of inefficiency and unsatisfactory marketing, since the new efficient process became the marketing tool – operations were leveraged in the market-place.

The major initiatives achieved through reengineering of personal loans processing are set out below.

- All personal loans are centralised in a Telebanking Centre.
- The introduction of a score card has automated the approval process which is now done statistically on a portfolio approach.
- Downloading of contracts through an Image LAN (Local Area Network) to the customer's nominated branch for signing.
- All lending is unsecured. This removes the security process.
- Approval time reduced to one hour from the time of initial telephone contact.

- A top-value customer is now able to have a personal loan approved and advanced in 30 minutes.

Marketing was enhanced and made more efficient too.

- Marketing is now better focused on important target groups including students, computers and travel.
- The cost of processing and rejecting 'poor' applications was reduced and in some cases eliminated by focused strategic marketing.
- Better borrowers receive good service and are therefore attracted to Advance Bank's improving the quality of the portfolio.
- Personal loans are used to attract new customers to Advance Bank who then become valued customers rather than being disenfranchised.
- There is an increased focus on providing better quality service to existing customers, increasing their value to Advance Bank and increasing profitability through the use of these higher margin products.
- There are increased cross-selling opportunities.

Although we cannot show the new personal loans processes in map form, for commercial reasons, enough samples of the tasks and achievements of Advance Bank's reengineering of process design have been given to demonstrate the great value that BPR can offer in the right circumstances.

9.2.3.3 Organisational design – Diagnosis for Effective Organisation

- Diagnosis for Effective Organisation (DEO) is useful when the Creativity phase confirms that the main problem is poor or ineffective organisation of activities characterised by
  - a breakdown in communications
  - people being out of touch with events
  - redundancy in or duplication of activities
  - slow response to change
  - people's jobs being meddled with by 'higher authorities'

  – an authoritarian regime
  – centralisation of administration and management
  – too many committees
  – etc.
- The immediate and given purpose is to identify through diagnosis what is leading to organisational ineffectiveness and to think through alternative organisational designs.
- The output will be more effective organisation; but what is happening when you problem solve with this method is explained in detail in Chapter 6.
- The main principles include the following.
  – Concentrate on organisation rather than structure.
  – Concentrate on management functions rather than departments.
  – An organisation must have vision and direction. Vision and direction are not permanent.
  – Organisation is understood to contain both vertical and horizontal interdependent activities.
  – There must be a balance between internal and external needs.
  – Place a strong emphasis on the interaction between organisation and environment (a special case where this kind of thinking is found useful).
  – Organisation must be responsive to internal and external changes.
  – Each activity is given autonomy to achieve set tasks. This supports self-organisation and local decision making whilst maintaining accountability. There need be only as much coordination and control over activities as is necessary to maintain integrity and viability of the whole organisation.
- The method presented below operationalises a unique model of organisation. The model guides the process of thinking about organisation in terms of the principles set out above. The model, however, should not be used literally as a blueprint for organisation, just as a guide to promote thinking about organisation.

The model that has inspired the method in this section is known as the Viable System Model (VSM) (see Further Reading). The model brings together five main management functions and

organises them according to a carefully worked-out series of
information flows (see Figure 9.8). The functions are

- operations
- co-ordination
- control
- intelligence
- policy.

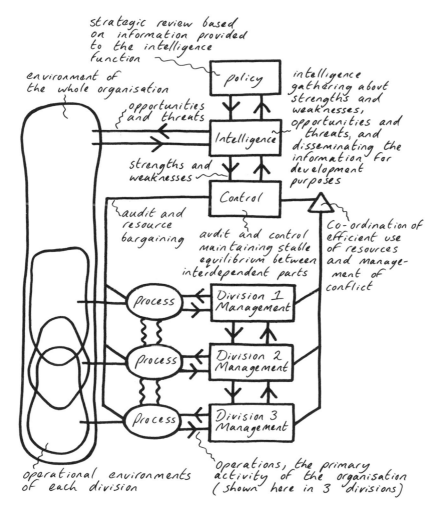

Figure 9.8 *The Viable System Model (VSM) used in Diagnosis for Effective Organisation (DEO)*

The types of flow are

- lines of command and control
- audit channels
- vital information about problems faced in the operations
- vital information about opportunities and threats in the environment.

The functions and flows are explained below (refer to Figure 9.8). The symbols in the figure are easy to pick up. A circle means processes of the division. A square means management of a division. Management and the processes are linked. An amoeba shape represents operational environment of a division. Processes and the operational environments are interlinked.

Broadly speaking, the model separates out the main operations and specifies the relationship between the operations and the management functions that serve them. The operations comprise a number of divisions with their operational managers. Operations with their own management are the primary activity. Each division is considered to be a viable entity in its own right. Viability here means that the division holds a guarantee of continuity. The divisions are serviced through four management functions; these are co-ordination, control, intelligence and policy.

Co-ordination ensures that there is an efficient and stable use of resources achieved in a harmonious fashion, i.e., it also, or even primarily, manages conflict. It receives vital information about short-term problems faced in operations. Control is an audit and control function that maintains relatively stable equilibrium between the interdependent parts. It does this in various ways. Control deals with vital information about problems in operations that co-ordination is not able to cope with. Control manages resource bargaining. Control also audits the divisions in a regular and routine manner. These include operational, quality and financial audits, such as budget reviews. Control action is taken when audits show up operational problems that have not or cannot be dealt with through co-ordination.

The intelligence and development function captures information about the total environment. This comprises internal and external environments. Intelligence is gathered about strengths and weaknesses of internal processes and opportunities and threats in the external environment. Vital information about strengths, weaknesses, opportunities and threats are disseminated throughout the organisation to those who benefit from it. Policy deals with strategic decisions and issues of management style. It receives all relevant information about strengths, weaknesses, opportunities and threats, and on the basis of this information reviews and modifies policy.

We will now turn our attention to the method that operationalises the model just described. The method has two main parts, diagnosis and redesign. They are presented in that order.

Diagnosis uses the model to build up a picture of organisation as it is and highlights organisational problems. Diagnosis begins by asking 'What is the primary activity of the organisation?' The primary activity is what the organisation 'is in business to do', i.e., what operations are. Some types of organisation and suggested primary activities are given below.

- A steel manufacturing company is in business to manufacture steel.
- An airline transports passengers and freight.
- A business school educates managers.
- A winery makes wine.
- A hotel provides accommodation and other facilities for guests.
- Etc.

The primary activity in terms of the model we are employing is organisational operations. Operations in the model are split into coherent activities called divisions. The next step of the method, then, is to split activities of operations into divisions. Divisions will rarely, if ever, be departments. You can split the activities up using one or more of the following criteria.

- Geographical.
- Client type.
- Activity type.
- Core business process (identified in Business Process Reengineering, BPR).
- Product type.

- Service type.
- Etc.

It is important to double check that divisions represent operations and not management functions that provide a service to them. For example, the primary activity of a steel manufacturer is to manufacture types of steel from raw products; whereas personnel, finance, marketing, strategic management, etc., are there to provide a service that enables the manufacturing process to operate effectively and efficiently overall. These and other service functions must not be taken as divisions – they support divisions.

The next thing to do is to compare divisions and evaluate whether any of them can be lumped together. The number of divisions rarely needs to exceed seven. It is often the case when around seven or more divisions have been identified that some are closely related and are best combined into one division. For example, an Asian airline's management team reassessing its organisation for effectiveness might choose transportation as its primary activity. A number of divisions could then be identified as follows.

- Livestock carriage.
- National passenger destinations.
- Parcel and post conveyance.
- Regional passenger destinations.
- European passenger destinations.
- Container transportation.
- North American passenger destinations.

It is possible to lump these into two divisions – freight and passenger.

- Freight (livestock, parcel and post, containers).
- Passenger (national, regional, European, North American).

Reorganising thinking about the organisational operations in this way improves clarity of understanding about the activities. Always remember, though, that other ways of splitting up the primary activities into divisions might produce better clarity of understanding and should be explored.

Attention so far has focused on lumping divisions. It is also worth considering splitting up divisions. Splitting divisions provides another opportunity to appraise alternative ways of organising the activities.

Another good reason to explore alternative ways of splitting up the operations is that it improves confidence in any chosen set of divisions. Normally it is possible to think up two or three different ways of dividing up operations. For example, operations of a rapidly growing entertainment group can be split according to service type.

- Hotels.
- Restaurants.
- Bars.

An alternative is to split the operations according to maturity.

- Established business.
- New business.
- Proposed businesses.

Yet another option is to split operations up geographically.

- Town A.
- Town B.
- Town C.

The aim is to uncover a grouping of divisions which provides the best understanding of how things work and where problems are found. This is taken forward to the next step in the method.

The next step, for each division, is to divide it up further into its own divisions. Assume that three main divisions are chosen: established, new and proposed businesses. The next level of analysis could then divide each one into: hotels, restaurants and bars. Each of these divisions is split up yet further so that a third level is created. The three levels of analysis mirror the systemic philosophy of TSI set out in Chapter 3.

Do not get stuck if the options on divisions that you come up with to represent the organisation are not readily agreeable. Run with one, any one, and assess it by trying it out. If you have two favoured options then develop them both. To help you to assess possible ways of splitting up the operations, evaluate each attempt in the following way. Ask if the proposed splitting up

- draws a problem area into focus
- is logical
- is coherent
- provides clarity
- is relatively simple
- is relatively informative.

('Relatively' means relative to other ways of splitting up activities.)

The most important criterion given above is to split things up so that the bulk of problems is centred in one division. This is what is meant by 'drawing a problem area into focus'. If this can be achieved then the remainder of diagnosis is simplified because diagnosis can be narrowed down to a particular area.

It is perfectly possible to carry on splitting divisions up into four, five or even more levels. However, the aim of the method, as already mentioned, is to focus diagnosis on one division where most of the problems appear to reside. The division is positioned at level 2 in a three-level schema. It is useful to sum-marise these three levels in a diagrammatic form. Figure 9.9, drawing upon the VSM, shows the recommended diagrammatic form using the entertainment example. Established business is assumed to be the division where the problems are mainly found. Existing business is therefore positioned at level 2.

The three levels shown in Figure 9.9 are a good example of bringing into action the systemic principle argued for in Chap-ter 4. Let me explain this further. DEO is likely to lead to pro-posals for change. It is crucial that change proposals take into account the impact they will have on other divisions and their own subdivisions. At level 1 in Figure 9.9 it is easy to see that changing established business will have an impact on new and proposed businesses. Just as important is the need to work out

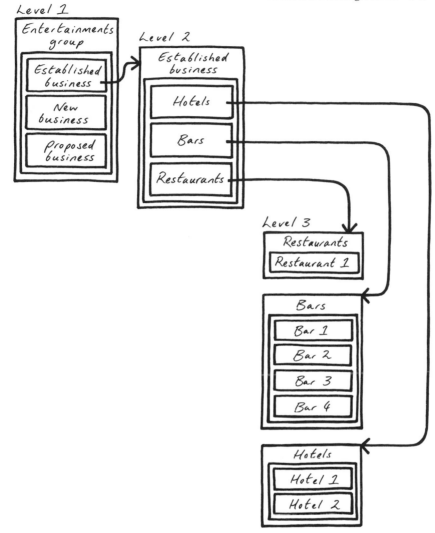

Figure 9.9 *Three-level representation of an entertainments group used in Diagnosis for Effective Organisation (DEO)*

details of implementation at levels 2 and 3 for the two hotels, two restaurants and four bars. If, and only if, all three levels (the total functional organisation) are dealt with as one system can we expect to establish effective organisational design.

Diagnosis continues, but the emphasis now switches away from operations to the management functions that serve operations. These as already mentioned are co-ordination, control, intelligence and policy functions. The aim is to check if management functions are operating and to assess how effectively they operate together to serve primary activities, i.e., is there effective organisation? In other words, is the organisation designed to manage its operations and change?

Management functions exist to deal with change. All forms of organisation experience and need to respond to change. For example, changes occur inside organisational-enterprises and in 'their business environment'. The internal operational environment is subject to change and must be reviewed in terms of its strengths and weaknesses, i.e., how well its tasks are being met. 'The business environment' is also changing. Opportunities and threats come and go. Examples of opportunities are

- new training approaches
- advances in technology
- competitor's blunders
- niches to diversify into
- supplier development programmes
- etc.

Examples of threats include

- shortage of spare parts
- increase in the number and capabilities of competitors
- effects of poor weather on a winery
- a spate of hijacks curtailing demand for international flights
- bad press about the value of consultants threatening consulting practice
- etc.

Co-ordination is normally the first management function to be analysed. Co-ordination of the divisions is necessary in the short term when the divisions are unable on their own to handle changes but are able to do so if their operations are co-ordinated with those of other divisions. This means co-ordinating conflict and all forms of existing resources that divisions have so that each one is able to meet its tasks effectively and harmoniously, whilst short-term problems are managed.

For example, let us assume a touring company in Africa specialising in safaris has three divisions identified at level 1. These are

- walk-in business
- group bookings
- lodge-based tours.

Walk-in business is where people walk into the booking office to book up on scheduled safaris running in the next week or so; group bookings are bookings made for large groups at least six months in advance; lodge-based tours are mainly for rich people on business who have only a spare day or two and want to fly straight to the lodge to save time. Occasions will arise when the three divisions must be co-ordinated. The following scenario provides one example of this.

Assume group bookings made last year increased substantially. Large deposits have been taken confirming the business. Business increased to the extent that this division is stretched for drivers and vehicles. An international incident like the Gulf War has just happened. This has hit tourism generally. American and Japanese business travel has plummeted for fear of terrorism. Walk-in business and lodge-based tours have suddenly experienced a sharp decline in demand. Co-ordination is now required to move vehicles and drivers from declining business to support the confirmed group bookings.

Effectiveness of co-ordination in any organisation can be assessed in the following way.

Ask, 'Are the divisions co-ordinated?' If the answer is 'no' then obviously a significant problem has been identified. If the answer is 'yes', then continue with the following questions.

Ask questions about the effectiveness of the co-ordination function.

- Is co-ordination reliable and responsive enough? Does co-ordination respond with reasonable speed?
- Is there clear responsibility for implementing co-ordination procedures?
- Do all the main management processes practise co-ordination? The three possibilities are
  - none does (there is a problem)

- some do (there is a problem)
- all do (things are OK).

If there is a problem then check the management processes to identify the offending areas, e.g.,
- personnel and training
- sales and marketing
- finance
- management information systems
- legal matters
- etc.

- Are the procedures for co-ordination agreed and understood by all divisions?
- Is co-ordination too centralised? Are there co-ordination procedures carried out at level 1 that would be more effectively handled at level 2 or level 3?
- Are the co-ordinators adequately skilled and qualified to carry out their tasks?
- Are there procedures in place to take control action where procedures for co-ordination are unable to manage significant changes?
- People in the co-ordination function should *facilitate* the co-ordination of activities. Ask if co-ordination is facilitated or if it interferes in activities. If co-ordination is facilitated then that is fine. If not, then find out in which ways co-ordination interferes; e.g.,
  - management style is threatening
  - resources are moved around without any obvious need
  - procedures are established which limit flexibility of co-ordination so that, even when co-ordination is needed, procedures exist that rule against this (in some senses co-ordination assumes the role of control).

At this stage it is useful to represent your findings diagrammatically. The operations and their co-ordination are represented using the model described earlier. Figure 9.10 is a development of the division shown in Figure 9.9, labelled 'Established Business'.

Three divisions have been identified for 'Established Business'. These are connected on the right of the diagram by a co-ordination function. Figure 9.10 has been annotated with some

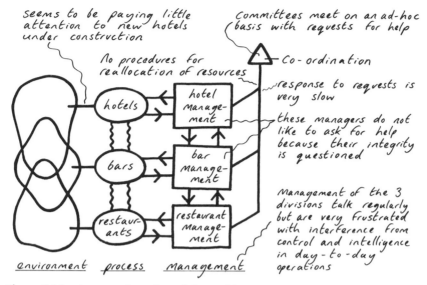

Figure 9.10 Annotated version of the Viable System Model (VSM) focusing on co-ordination used in the case of an entertainments group

hypothetical findings as if the line of questioning above had been followed. This example will be carried throughout the remaining presentation.

Carrying out the above investigation will surface problems. These are dealt with after the full diagnosis is completed, i.e., after the remaining management functions, control, intelligence and policy, have been analysed.

It is usual for control to be the next management function to be diagnosed. Control is needed when co-ordination can no longer manage the changing situation. For example, extending the African touring company illustration from above, it could be that all resources possible are reallocated from walk-in business, but group tours still cannot meet the increased demand. Non-budgeted resources are then needed. This is a control decision.

Control's responsibility over resource allocation includes annual resource bargaining and setting budgets. Control also interprets and implements policy (we will return to policy). It audits divisions maintaining a clear overall picture of divisions and sustaining accountability. The effectiveness of control can be judged using the line of questioning given below.

Ask, 'Are the divisions controlled?' If the answer is 'no', then a very serious flaw has been identified. If, as is more likely, the answer is 'yes', then the following line of questioning must be followed.

- Is control taking over as it should do when co-ordination procedures are not able to manage significant changes?
- Is control reliable and responsive enough? Does control respond with reasonable speed and maintain stability?
- Is control allocating resources?
- Is control auditing processes of divisions?
- Is control interpreting and implementing policy?
- Who carries out control procedures?
- Do all the main management processes practice control? The three possibilities are
  - none does (there is a problem)
  - some do (there is a problem)
  - all do (things are OK).
- If there is a problem then check which management processes are part of that problem, e.g.,
  - personnel and training
  - sales and marketing
  - finance
  - management information systems
  - legal matters
  - etc.
- People involved in the control function should ensure that policy is implemented and stability maintained in a *supportive* way. Ask if control is supportive or if it dictates. If control is supportive then that is fine. If not, then find out why control is perceived to be a dictator; e.g.,
  - auditing is like policing giving rise to management by fear
  - policy is implemented by sending memos
  - no explanation is given about the outcome of resource bargaining
  - decision making is centralised in a separate building or location
  - people in control are not accountable or open to any form of criticism from the divisions
  - control procedures are not understood in the divisions

- control procedures are rigid, like red tape, and are subject to excessive bureaucratic control
- control decisions are made by committees who are not really in touch with matters they are controlling
- etc.

The diagram shown in Figure 9.10 based on the model presented earlier is now developed further. Figure 9.11 includes the control function. It is positioned in the diagram to show that it takes over when co-ordination procedures can no longer cope. The diagram shows that this information flows up the right-hand side. To the left-hand side of the diagram control is shown to audit processes and to deal with resource bargaining. Figure 9.11 has been annotated with hypothetical findings as if diagnosis of control had been undertaken.

As with the earlier parts of diagnosis, scrutinising the control function along the lines suggested above is likely to surface further problems. These are tackled later on in the redesign

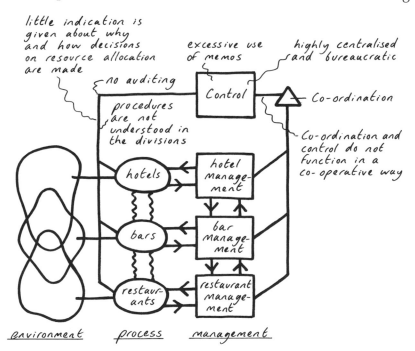

Figure 9.11 *Annotated version of the Viable System Model (VSM) focusing on control used in the case of an entertainments group*

stage of this method. The next management function to be diagnosed for effective organisation is the intelligence function.

The service given to the primary activity by the management functions must include an intelligent component. Without an intelligent component it would not be possible to operate efficiently and effectively the primary activities and the whole organisation in its surroundings, all at the same time. Intelligence is needed to assess *the strengths and weaknesses of the internal operations,* including primary activities, co-ordination and control; and to be in touch with external organisational events, *'the business context' in terms of opportunities and threats.* In this sense the intelligence function is a SWOT function, bringing together information about all aspects of the organisation. This enables effective policy to be made and updated. The effectiveness of an organisational intelligence can be assessed as follows.

Ask, 'Is there an adequate intelligence function?' If the answer is 'no' then the main organisational activities are vulnerable to change. Even if the answer is 'yes' then treat it as contestable and ask the following questions.

- Is intelligence assessing the strengths and weaknesses of the primary activities and the co-ordination and control functions?
- Is intelligence in touch with the opportunities and threats in the external environment, i.e., 'the business context'?
- Is intelligence ensuring that information generated is disseminated to all relevant divisions and management functions?
- Do all the main management processes benefit from intelligence? The three possibilities are
  - none does (there is a problem)
  - some do (there is a problem)
  - all do (things are OK).
- If there is a problem then check which management processes are involved, e.g.,
  - personnel and training
  - sales and marketing
  - finance
  - management information systems
  - legal matters
  - etc.

- Is intelligence looking into the future?
- Is intelligence picking up and following trends?
- Is intelligence open to novel ideas?
- Is intelligence integrating information into a useful form for policy making?
- Who carries out intelligence gathering and ensures that information gets to all people who would benefit from it?
- People involved in intelligence gathering should have an *open policy*. They should disseminate information to all those who would benefit from it. Ask if intelligence information is dealt with in an open manner. If it is, then that is fine. If not, then find out the reasons why information is not getting into the hands of people who need it. Ask if
  - there are adequate procedures that ensure information is shared
  - procedures are commonly understood
  - information is being controlled to serve certain people's interests.

The diagram in Figure 9.11 has been updated in Figure 9.12 to include the intelligence function. Notice the position of intelligence. It is in touch internally with operations through the control and co-ordination functions. It also has a direct link to the organisational environment shown as a large amoeba shape to the left of the diagram, incorporating all of local divisional environments. Again, a few annotations have been included on the diagram, continuing the hypothetical example, this time expressing concerns about intelligence. Problems unearthed during diagnosis of the intelligence function are dealt with at the end of the full diagnosis.

The final step in the diagnostic process puts the spotlight on policy. Policy is a management function that sets vision, direction and objectives to be met. The policy function comes into play when objectives are not being met, or when vision and direction no longer seem to be relevant given discoveries by intelligence about opportunities and/or threats in the organisational environment. The effectiveness of policy can be assessed as set out below.

Ask, 'Is there a policy function?' If the answer is 'no' then there is serious trouble which must be attended to most

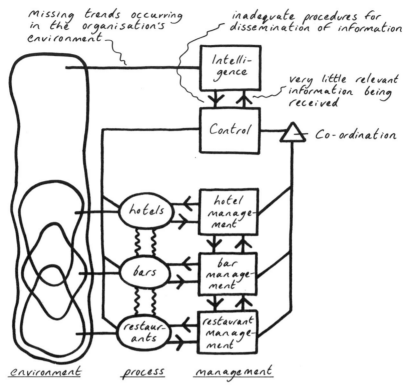

missing trends occurring in the organisation's environment

inadequate procedures for dissemination of information

Intelligence

very little relevant information being received

Control

Co-ordination

hotels — hotel management

bars — bar management

restaurants — restaurant management

environment　　process　　management

Figure 9.12　*Annotated version of the Viable System Model (VSM) focusing on intelligence used in the case of an entertainments group*

urgently. If the answer is 'yes' then the degree of effectiveness should be explored further.

Ask the following questions to test the effectiveness of policy making.

- Is there a clear vision and a definite direction? Are there measurable objectives to be met?
- Are there procedures to bring policy into play when new opportunities and/or threats are recognised?
- Are there procedures to alert policy when tasks to be performed can no longer be co-ordinated and controlled to meet agreed objectives?
- People on the policy-making board should *represent* the divisions and the main management functions, as well as other interested and consultative bodies. Only in this way can

policy be made that organisational members will be committed to. Also, without a wide range of perspectives coming into play it is less likely that innovative and effective policy will be made. Find out who is involved in policy making, who is not, and ask why? The following questions will help.

- Who is on the board and how does it make decisions on policy? Is there representation and participation?
- Are the vision and direction set suitable for the division in focus?
- Are the vision, direction and set objectives being implemented as desired?
- Is policy being overridden by any of the management functions?
- In particular, do the primary activities of the division concur with agreed vision, direction and objectives?
- Is policy taking into account all the information supplied by the intelligence function?

A complete diagrammatic representation can now be achieved. The policy function has been added in Figure 9.13. The policy function feeds and is fed by the intelligence function.

Diagnosis is now complete. Problems have been identified such as those recorded as annotations on the last four figures. It is time to switch attention to how things can be improved. It is time to move on to redesign.

Redesign is based on the model introduced earlier in this section. A version of the VSM is drawn that shows what role people are actually playing and the command and control flows that actually exist. These are the lines on the diagram. If flows are in place as recommended by the model then draw in lines to represent this. If flows exist that are weak, show them with a dotted line. If command or control flows are found that should not exist, they must be drawn in. The resultant record of findings provides a strong visual image of organisational problems in design. Figure 9.14 provides an example based on information accumulated in the hypothetical example summarised in Figures 9.10 to 9.13. (People are not included in Figure 9.14 because none were featured in the example presented above.)

Figure 9.14 shows how ineffective the organisation is that we have been following. Many of the lines of command and control

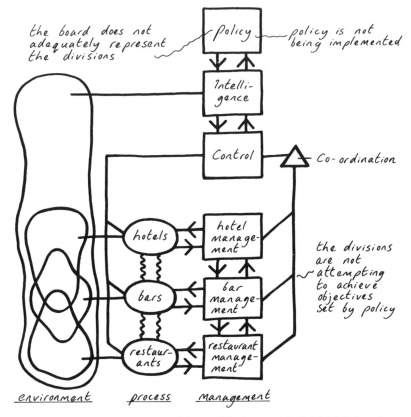

the board does not adequately represent the divisions

Policy

policy is not being implemented

Intelli-gence

Control

Co-ordination

hotels

hotel manage-ment

the divisions are not attempting to achieve objectives set by policy

bars

bar manage-ment

restaur-ants

restaurant manage-ment

environment   *process*   *management*

Figure 9.13 *Annotated version of the Viable System Model (VSM) focusing on policy used in the case of an entertainments group*

are weak or missing completely. Management functions are ineffective, in some cases barely operating, and intelligence and control are interfering in the running of divisions. The organis-ation is not effectively in touch with its external environment, particularly at the level of the whole organisation.

The next thing to do is to group problems surfaced. Common themes or core problems must be searched for. All other prob-lems must be listed. The analysis complements the diagram-matic representation in Figure 9.14. Together they provide as clearly as possible insight and evidence to support the need for change. Summarising the annotations from Figures 9.10 to 9.13 permits me to illustrate this point.

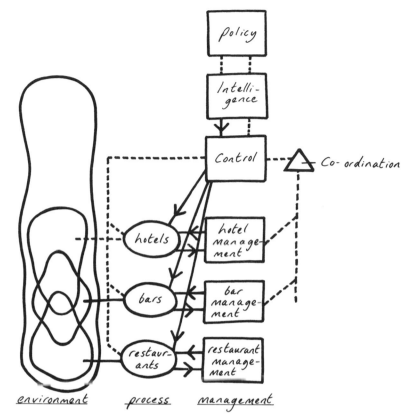

Figure 9.14 *Viable System Model (VSM) example of an entertainments group showing ineffectiveness in organisation*

- The hotel managers seem to be paying little attention to the new hotels under construction.
- Management of the three divisions talk regularly but are very frustrated with interference from control and intelligence.
- Bars seem to be run with separate identities.
- Managers don't like to ask for help because their integrity is questioned.
- Co-ordination's response to requests from divisional managers is very slow.
- Co-ordination committees meet on an *ad hoc* basis to deal with requests for help from divisional managers.
- There are no co-ordination procedures for the dissemination of information.
- Co-ordination and control do not function in co-operation.

- Control is highly centralised and bureaucratic.
- Control makes excessive use of memos.
- There is no auditing.
- Little explanation is given about reasons for resource allocation.
- Very little relevant information is collected and disseminated about strengths and weaknesses of the operations of divisions, co-ordination and control.
- Intelligence is missing trends in 'the business context'.
- The board does not adequately represent the divisions.
- Policy is not being implemented – the divisions are not attempting to achieve objectives set by policy.

Common themes that emerge from the grouped problems include the following.

- There is an overall lack of procedures.
- The control function dominates and acts in an authoritative and interventionist manner.
- Organisational responsiveness is poor.

Before any further work is done on redesign, an agreed purpose for the division in focus, and for each of the divisions it is split up into, must be defined. A method for setting missions contained in the method for Exploring and Choosing Designs (ECD) is used here. The remaining task is to construct a version of Figure 9.14 that allocates or reallocates people to functions and puts the desired information flows back in place, in line with agreed purposes. Procedures that actually put flows of information in place must be fixed. The procedures must be clear and comprehensive. There must be procedures for operations and each management function. The procedures must interrelate in a logical and coherent way. Procedures for management functions must be written that guarantee service to operations. All the main management processes must be covered. These procedures must not interfere or get in the way of autonomy in operations or procedures in other management functions. There also must be procedures for the following activities in the organisation.

- Resource bargaining.

- Accountability.
- Review of performance.
- Corporate and legal requirements.
- Quality control.
- Forecasting.
- Management of external environmental changes.

There are three further issues to take into account when formulating an idealised design. Each one has a recommended method.

- Has the design sufficiently taken into account the issue of whose interests are being served and why? Use the method for Critically Evaluating Designs and Decisions (CEDD).
- Are there competing designs that people are aligning themselves to? Use the method for Testing Polarised Viewpoints (TPV).
- How can the design be implemented? Use the method for Implementing Designs and Decisions (IDD).

The diagnosis and further analysis described above provide a complete and penetrative tool that gets directly at the problem of designing effective organisation. A full-blown application of this method is now given that will add yet further detail and understanding about achieving effective organisation.

Example. (A pseudonym is used for the company in this case study to maintain confidentiality as requested.) This example details a consultancy carried out by my colleague John Beckford, to whom I am very grateful for letting me share the results of his efforts with readers of *Solving Problem Solving*.

CARCO was a long-established motor dealership in the UK being managed at the time of the intervention by the third generation of its family owners. At the outset of the intervention the company employed 50 people, many of them with long service. The directors realised that their business was in a state of terminal crisis, being virtually insolvent and, in management terms, out of control.

The VSM was used as the main tool to tackle the problems. It was evident to all concerned that crisis point had been reached because of CARCO's ineffective organisation. A method for operationalising the VSM paralleling the one described above was used to guide implementation and deal with problems of ineffective organisation. The account is written in the mould of this book's version of the method.

What is the primary activity of the organisational-enterprise? CARCO was a 'full-service one-stop' motor retailer. Its primary activity was that of a motor trader. A suitable description of what the organisational-enterprise was in business to do is:

> To provide a comprehensive sales and support system aimed at satisfying customer expectations by the sale of new and used vehicles, servicing, repairs, parts, fuel and vehicle hire services.

Split the activities of the primary task into divisions. It was found in this case most fruitful to use an activity-based split. This reflected the traditional type of divisions in the industry and CARCO was more or less organised in this way. Alternative ways of splitting added nothing to diagnosis and so were not taken up. The divisions chosen were

- New Vehicle Sales
- Used Vehicle Sales
- Vehicle Servicing
- Body Repairs
- Parts Sales
- Forecourt Services
- Vehicle Hire.

Each of these is an activity within the primary organisational purpose. None are management functions existing as a service to the primary activity.

Compare the divisions and evaluate whether they can be grouped. In this case a number of alternative groupings would have been possible. For example, the Service, Parts and Body Repair divisions could have been lumped together as a division called

After Sales. Similarly, new and used sales could have been lumped together forming a division called Sales.

The decision not to lump divisions in this way reflected the needs of the business at the time. Firstly, the management and control of CARCO was in such a poor state that any unnecessary change to the basic design would have been self-defeating. The real need in this case was greater clarity about the management of the operations such as measurable accountability. Another crucial 'reason of the moment' concerned uncertainty about financial performance and viability of the enterprise as a whole and each of the extant divisions. Grouping at this stage would arguably have made the task of identifying poor performers more difficult. A third reason further alleviating the need to lump concerned the actual management staff. Management staff were deployed according to the chosen set of divisions.

Consider splitting up the divisions. This option was also considered. A number of possibilities were explored, for example dividing business divisions between personal and commercial customers, or between new and existing customers. These would again have moved away from the established organisational design that was ultimately held on to. There was no obvious diagnostic or organisational gain. This analysis did, however, prepare the way for the next stage.

Divide each division into its own divisions. CARCO was a relatively small company making identification of the next layer of divisions straightforward (see Figure 9.15). New and Used Vehicle Sales each split into three divisions, having three separate salesmen. Service broke down into Servicing Work and Breakdown Recovery. Body Repairs divided into Painting Work and Panel Work. Parts divided into Trade Sales, Counter Sales and Internal Sales. The Forecourt division divided into four operating shifts. Finally, Vehicle Hire was divided into three Sales Agents.

Again, a number of options were considered for these divisions but none brought with them genuine advantages to the diagnosis.

Evaluate the split. The divisions are organised in a logical way.

164

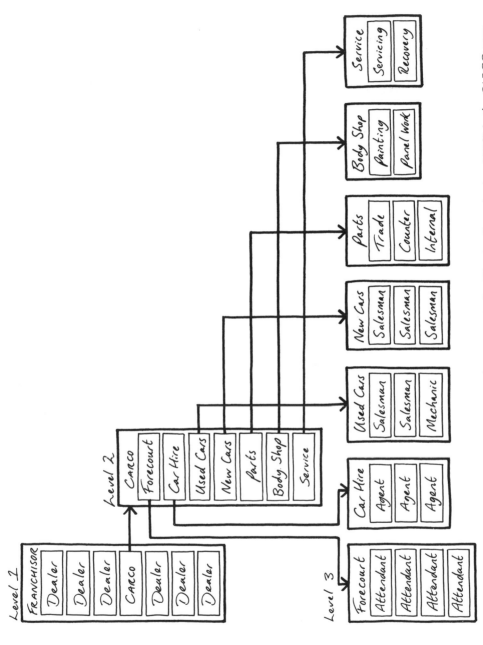

Figure 9.15 Three-level representation used in Diagnosis for Effective Organisation (DEO) in the CARGO case

Within each division, the splits into subdivisions reflect the primary activity. The divisions of the primary activity could in principle be operated as a separate company. Divisions are coherent in their reflection of perceptions about the business; they are clear, relatively simple and they are informative about organisational workings.

Identify the local environment for each division and appraise how well it is tuned in to that environment. New Sales environment at the time of the study consisted of three principal elements. Firstly, there had been a significant decline in total market size due to an economic downturn in the UK. Despite this the manufacturer was demanding increasing sales volumes. Whilst these were necessary for long-term financial viability, a decline of some 30% in the market is not easy to overcome in the short term. The New Sales division was aware of the decline and made attempts to overcome it through advertising and other promotional activities.

The second element was the attitude of business user customers. Again, driven by the decline in the economy, coupled with its subsequent impact on company-owned vehicles, customers in this area were less willing to purchase cars but more demanding when they did so, for example seeking more competitive pricing. CARCO was losing out to competitors despite its attempts to contest against low pricing and higher quality.

The third element was private buyers. Economic uncertainty such as concern over job security significantly curtailed buying. Private buyers held on to their cars for longer.

Whilst the division staff were well aware of these three factors, they were unable to exert control over the market-place. Buyer behaviour could not be influenced.

Used Sales ran up against a proliferation of other high-quality used vehicle outlets in CARCO's region. They were the first to specialise in nearly new vehicles but their initiative was taken over by better-funded competitors. Even worse, CARCO was running short on funds to support the operation. Staff were also undertaking private transactions at the expense of CARCO. These staff did not have the interests of the company at heart.

Vehicle servicing was reasonably well tuned to its environment although greater efforts should have been made to satisfy demand. The manufacturer's vehicles registered in the area considerably exceeded the number of manufacturer's vehicles sold in the area. This meant that the servicing workshop consistently outperformed expectations. Unfortunately, complacent attitudes led to failure in fully developing the market.

Body Repairs was threatened by reorganisation of the insurance industry, the source of funds for the bulk of the work. Insurance companies now like to work with approved repairers. CARCO had neglected to obtain approved repairer status from the major insurers. Insurers were no longer interested in discussing repair work with CARCO. This opportunity was lost.

Parts Sales had historically enjoyed high sales volume arising from its earlier status as a distribution centre. Perhaps again due to complacency, no research of the business environment or promotional activity had been undertaken.

Forecourt ran on inertia. The layout and location of the premises were powerful determinants of sales volume. Again, minimal promotional activity was engaged in and zero response was made to counter emerging competitors.

Vehicle Hire when established had also been unique in the area. It was at one time the only internationally branded vehicle hire outlet. Its success attracted new competitors but, yet again, no effective response had been made.

We will now turn our attention to the management functions.

Co-ordination. CARCO was an unusual company needing only a simple co-ordination function. This partly arose because of the discrete identity and services offered to customers that rarely gave rise to conflict between divisions. Most co-ordination should have been adequately covered by uncomplicated procedures. For example, when a customer ordered a new or used vehicle, Sales had only to ensure that the Service Department had time to prepare the vehicle for delivery. Despite this, alignment between divisions was weak and regular crises occurred leading to unnecessary overtime and late delivery of vehicles.

At the corporate level sources of conflict came from major issues like allocation of resources, values and expectations, ethical standards, etc. In this respect there was virtually no co-ordination with each division setting their own ethos, none of which reflected CARCO's needs as a whole.

Whilst the co-ordination function exists as a service to operations, certain senior management messages also may be conveyed by this route in the interest of organisational cohesion. In CARCO this simply did not happen. All in all the co-ordination function lacked adequate articulation.

Control. CARCO had as its control unit a managing director, sales director, plus a senior accountant supported by an Accounts Department. The two directors came from the third and fourth generations of the family owners.

Control was not taking over from the co-ordination function. Control was not reliable or responsive. There were no budgets, standards or expectations, in fact no accountability for allocated resources. Those responsible for control responded to requests for information in any way they wanted. Operational managers therefore referred queries to people in control who would return with the answer they wanted. Furthermore, there was no clear reporting structure. There were no control procedures at all. Control was therefore reactive and piecemeal, dictating emergency action to one division and then another, without in addition considering the impact on other divisions.

There was no auditing of operational activities other than the legally required financial audit. Employees in control were not accountable to anyone nor were they open to criticism. Poor communication emanating from control and a lack of coherence in its responses meant that control just could not be understood within the divisions.

Intelligence. No continuous intelligence function operated. There had been sporadic intelligence activities leading to the establishment of the Vehicle Hire and Used Vehicle divisions. The intelligence function sprang into action when the external threats were belatedly acknowledged; they could no longer be ignored. For example, both the bankers and the manufacturers threatened CARCO with closure. Sadly, this was a case of environmental information being forced into CARCO rather than being gathered intelligently. Even during the course of the intervention there was a marked reluctance to disseminate the new flow of information to those divisions which so desperately needed it.

Policy. There was no policy function. CARCO was really in a mess. The managing director who purported to fulfil this role did not have the ability or inclination to do so. Consequently there was no vision, no objectives and no procedures for resolving policy questions. Questions were bounced back into the maelstrom of ideas and problems swirling around the intelligence, control, co-ordination and operational functions (see Figure 9.16).

CARCO was effectively closed; closed to outside events, to new ideas and to all concept of good management practice. The only sense in which it was open was as a generous family money box. The company was in a crisis.

Redesign. CARCO had ineffective organisation. It needed effective organisational design to improve radically the following faults.

- Communication was ineffective throughout CARCO.
- No budgets or performance standards existed.
- Divisions were not co-ordinated.
- Communication with the environment was minimal.
- There was no evidence of corporate planning or policy.
- There was no shared culture, no shared values (a cultural problem).
- Control when exerted was autocratic (a political problem).

These problems were addressed in the following way. The first objective agreed was survival. This became the guiding principle. Any decision to be made was measured against the following criteria – 'Will the proposed action contribute to or detract from the chances of survival?' The actions taken are summarised below (also see Figure 9.17).

- Vehicle Hire and Used Car divisions were closed down. The financial constraints under which CARCO was operating at this stage made relaunch of those divisions out of the question.
- Members of staff who could not come to terms with the requirements of the dash for survival were encouraged to seek alternative employment. The sales director left to pursue alternative career interests.

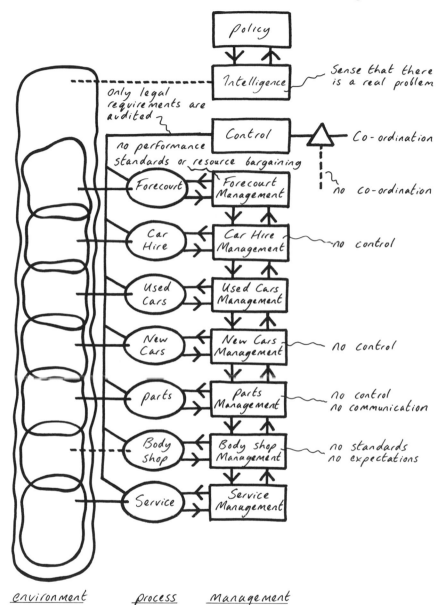

Figure 9.16 *Viable System Model (VSM) representation showing ineffectiveness in organisation in the CARCO case*

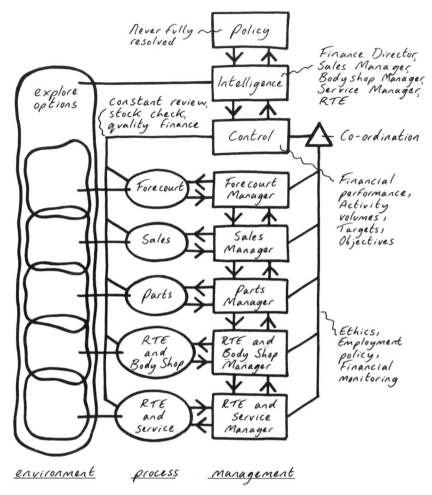

Figure 9.17   *Minimal reorganisation of CARCO using the Viable System Model (VSM)*

- Procedures were developed for co-ordination.
- A budgeting system was set up incorporating procedures for approving capital expenditure.
- The manager of Servicing division took over responsibility for Body Shop as well. The divisions remained separate, the manager was shared.
- Audits were instigated for issues such as quality, stock levels and finance.
- Intelligence and control functions were redesigned incorporat-

ing managers of the operating divisions, enhancing communication and changing management philosophy. Managers took an active interest in matters of intelligence in their own technical areas and for the organisation as a whole.

- Policy was never satisfactorily resolved. The managing director adopted a *laissez faire* management style most of the time (see Chapter 7 on leadership style), allowing groups performing control and intelligence to formulate policy. Occasionally he felt compelled to demonstrate that he held ultimate power causing a breakdown in continuity.

The result of the intervention makes only partially happy reading. There was overall significant improvement in the performance of CARCO throughout the period of intervention. For example, operating losses were halved in the first 12 months and sales performance improved. The company gained some value. Unfortunately commercial realities dictated that survival was not to be. The bankers and the manufacturers lost patience despite improvements mentioned. They were just not big or quick enough.

9.2.3.4 *Implementing Designs and Decisions*

- Implementing Designs and Decisions (IDD) is useful when methods in the Implementation phase have been used to come up with new designs and/or decisions that need to be efficiently and effectively implemented.
- The immediate and given purpose is to implement efficiently and effectively new designs and/or decisions.
- The output is the implementation; but what is happening when you problem solve with this method is explained in detail in Chapter 6.
- The main principle is to find a most efficient and effective means to implement a decision or design.
- There are three stages to the method.
  - Identify the future that the organisation is already in.
  - Compare the design or decision to that future and identify the gap.
  - Find the most effective and efficient way of closing the gap.

The method below is described as if it were being used to implement changes to the whole organisation. In some cases, such as with projects in Quality Management (QM), only parts of organisations will be affected. In such cases the method needs to be suitably adapted.

Incidentally, this first stage can be carried out before exploring and choosing alternative designs or making decisions. It may yield information that is useful in the debate process.

The future that the organisation is already in is determined in three steps.

- Systems analysis. What the organisation is, how it operates and its current state.
- Obstruction analysis. Which internal and external conditions, policies and practices obstruct organisational development.
- Reference projections. What will happen if there are no significant changes in the management of the organisation or in the organisational environment.

Systems analysis wants you to develop a description of the current situation. You must detail the following organisational details.

- The nature of the organisation. This means distinguishing the primary task of the organisation from other activities. Establish the following.
  - What the products or services are.
  - What the processes are that create the products and services.
  - What the products or services are for.
  - Who the products or services are for.
- Organisational performance past and present. The meaning of and criteria for performance actually in use must be agreed upon (which may mean using the method for Exploring and Making Decisions (EMD)). Evaluation against the criteria is then undertaken.
- Operations. Prepare a set of flow charts that shows sources of information, instruction, money and material for each division (process mapping from Business Process Reengineering (BPR) could help here).

- Structure of the organisation. The organisational chart show-
  ing the structure of authority and responsibility.
- The 'business' environment. There are many matters to take
  into account here including the following.
  - Stakeholders and their interests.
  - Details about competitors.
  - Special interest groups.
  - Regulations, laws and taxes.
  - How organisational activities are affecting the physical, bio-
    logical, and social environment.
- Management style. Following on from structure, management
  style is established. The following questions can be asked.
  - How are problems identified, decisions made, implemented
    and controlled?
  - What types of decision are centralised?
  - Do those with responsibility who are accountable have the
    necessary authority?
  - Is management autocratic or participative?
  - How well does information flow to those who need it?
- Organisational culture. This is characterised by the implicit or
  explicit rules and practices that mediate behaviour in the
  organisation.
- Personnel policies and practices. The following practices are
  described: recruitment, hiring, orientation of new employees,
  assignment, reassignment, compensation, training and education, promotion, firing, resigning, retirement, etc.

Obstruction analysis identifies internally and externally imposed
constraints that obstruct the development of the organisation.

- Internal obstructions are of two sorts.
  - Internal discrepancies between what is actually practised
    and what is assumed or declared to be practised (either
    Brainstorming or Nominal Group Technique (NGT) can be
    used to help here, with a focus on ideas rather than
    problems).
  - Internal conflicts such as conflicts between individuals,
    individuals and the organisation, between divisions, within
    divisions, within the organisation as a whole, etc.
- External obstructions are mainly conflicts with parties such as

stakeholders, the government, communities, suppliers, unions, customers, special interest groups, etc.

Reference projections are extrapolations of the criteria for performance, agreed upon earlier, into the future assuming no significant changes occur. They are created in the knowledge of the description of the current organisation and the obstructions to change. They are not forecasts in the traditional planning sense. They are 'What ifs?' A most plausible reference scenario is generated. The following procedure can be used.

- Set a time horizon.
- Prepare a summary of the main performance criteria.
- Extrapolate trends for each performance indicator. Ask what will happen if no changes occur.
- Prepare a table to summarise these projections, with a column for a statement on whether the trend will have a positive or negative effect on the organisation.
- Prepare a description of the organisation at the end of the time horizon with an analysis of how it got there.

Comparing the design or decision to the reference scenario is the next step. A design or decision to be implemented is brought forward. It is compared to the performance criteria and reference scenario now established. Comparison will yield a set of differences that constitute gaps between what would happen if things were allowed to continue and what organisational members would most like. Where criteria are not shared there exists a gap between what is expected to happen and what is desired to happen. These gaps can be translated into goals, objectives and ideals ready for determining the most effective and efficient way of closing them.

The procedure for *closing gaps* can be summarised along the following lines.

- Declare goals and objectives to be met. These are brought forward from the previous comparison stage.
- Identify the means to achieve the goals and objectives. Generate plans, policies and proposals and examine them to decide whether they are capable of helping to fill the gap between

the desired future and that captured in the reference scenario. Do not necessarily go for obvious means. Use creativity-enhancing techniques from the Creativity phase to explore ways of closing the gap and achieving the desired future. Evaluate the process in the following way.

- State the anticipated effects of the means and when they are expected to happen.
- Draw out the critical assumptions on which these expectations are based.
- Set out the critical information used in selecting the means.
- Provide a brief description of how the means were selected and by whom.
- Assess whose interests are being served by the chosen means (use the method for Critically Evaluating Designs and Decisions (CEDD)).

Resource planning determines what resources are required, when, where and sorts out how otherwise unavailable resources are to be generated or acquired. There are five types of resource that must be considered.

- Inputs such as materials, supplies, energy and services.
- Facilities and equipment.
- Personnel.
- Information.
- Money.

The following questions must be asked about each resource.

- How much will be required? When and where will it be required?
- How much will be available at each location at each relevant point in time, assuming no changes in current resource plans or policies?
- What are the gaps between requirements and availability?
- How can these gaps be filled; by developing or generating them internally or by acquisition from an external source, and how much will this cost?

The concluding stage of closing the gap is actual implementation and control. Decisions must be made about who is to be responsible for doing what and by when. Planning decisions are translated into assignments and schedules. A detailed approach such as Project Planning can be used to put together schedules (see Further Reading). Assignments are specified in the following way.

- Define the nature of the task to be carried out.
- Define the goals and objectives.
- State who is responsible for carrying out the task.
- Declare the steps to be taken.
- State who is responsible for each step.
- Set the timing for each step.
- Allocate funds to each step.
- Declare the critical assumptions on which implementation is based.
- State the expected effects on performance and when they are expected.
- Declare the assumptions on which the expectations are based.

Control is maintained by comparing planned progress to actual progress. Comparison is made for all crucial elements of the task. A comprehensive list of what is to be monitored, by whom and when is constructed. Deviations are noted and corrective action taken.

There are two further issues to take into account with IDD. Each one has a recommended method.

- Has the implementation sufficiently taken into account the issue of whose interests are being served and why? Use the method for Critically Evaluating Designs and Decisions (CEDD).
- Are there competing ideas about the best way to implement the design and/or decision that people are aligning themselves to? Use the method for Testing Polarised Viewpoints (TPV).

Example. Given the relatively straightforward nature of IDD there is little value in using limited space on an example. However, Case Study 10.7 in Chapter 10 does provide a reasonably detailed account of IDD.

9.2.3.5 Debating – Exploring and Choosing Designs

- Exploring and Choosing Designs (ECD) is useful in planning when the Creativity phase demonstrates a need to explore creatively idealised designs as optional ways to tackle problems faced, overcoming hidden assumptions that normally hold progress back.
- The immediate and given purpose is to debate and come up with an idealised design free from all constraints except technical feasibility and viability.
- The output will be an idealised design; but what is happening when you problem solve with this method is explained in detail in Chapter 6.
- The principles are twofold.
  - Suspend judgement held by stakeholders about what is possible.
  - Work out an idealised design that stakeholders would have now if they could have any design they wanted.
- The method has three stages.
  - Select a mission.
  - Specify the desired properties of the design.
  - Idealised design of the system.

Idealised design assumes that conceptual traps in problem solving arise mainly from a concern with what is feasible. Idealised design overcomes this by removing all constraints except those relating to technical feasibility and viability. Idealised design therefore has the following rules.

- Anything is possible except science fiction.
- The design must be capable of surviving if it were brought into existence.
- The design must be capable of rapid and effective learning and adaptation.

Idealised design suspends judgement about assumptions held

by stakeholders. Judgements only serve to get in the way of progressive creative thinking and change. In place of this, idealised design works out the design that stakeholders would have now if they could have any design they wanted taking into account the three rules. It is a method that generates debate by asking people to consider alternative idealised designs. There are three stages to idealised design.

- Select a mission.
- Specify the desired properties of the design.
- Idealised design of the system.

Selecting the mission. The mission is the overriding purpose that unifies and mobilises all parts of the organisation that are planned for. The process of forming a mission must be challenging, exciting and fun to the stakeholders. It provides a focus for the idealised design process that follows. The mission must specify the main organisation purpose that the stakeholders would like even if this deviates significantly from the current purpose. Selecting the mission can be undertaken using any or all of the methods for creative thinking, focusing on ideas for the future. A suggested set of questions that generates extensive debate about organisational mission setting is given below.

- What do we think we do?
- Are we doing what we think we do?
- Why are we doing it?
- Are we doing the right thing?
- What else could we do?
- What would be the benefit of doing something else?

These questions ask what it is that organisational members want to achieve. The aim is to formulate a succinct statement which captures overall purpose and philosophy.

Specify the desired properties of the design. The desired properties of the design planned for can be formulated using Idea Generation and Evaluation methods. Idealised design imposes its own rules on these processes so that, for example, ideas are not dismissed on the grounds of feasibility. The properties must be those that the stakeholders believe the organisation planned for should, ideally, have now.

Important aspects of the organisation must be addressed in the following way.

- *Culture*. What should be the values, expectations and attitudes – the social rules, practices and ways of conceiving these?
- *Inputs*. Consider the following five main resource types – equipment and buildings, information, materials, money and people. Ask the following of each one.
  - What is required?
  - Should it be acquired from an internal or external source?
  - For those resources to be acquired, from what sources should they be acquired and how?
- *Organisational processes*.
  - Who should own the organisation and what should their role be?
  - Which functions necessary for organisational activity should be provided by the organisation itself and which should be acquired from external sources?
  - What policies and practices should apply to personnel with respect to recruiting, hiring, orientation, compensation and incentives, benefits, promotions, career development, retirement and severance?
  - How should the processes be designed and organised?
- The design.
  - How should the processes be organised?
  - How should the organisation be structured and managed?
- Products and services.
  - What products or services should the organisation offer and what special characteristics, if any, should they have?
  - How should internal development of products or services be organised and carried out?
  - How should acquisition be organised and carried out?
- Markets and customers.
  - What types of customer should the organisation seek?
  - In which market areas?
  - How should the organisation's products or services be distributed and sold?

- How should the organisation's products and services be
  marketed and serviced?
- The environment.
  - How should the organisation relate to its stakeholders and
    the communities in which it operates?
  - How should information on stakeholders' perceptions of
    the organisation be obtained and used?
  - How should the organisation relate to environmental, con-
    sumer and other special interest groups?

Idealised design of the system. Idealised design must produce a
design that stakeholders would replace the existing design with
if they were free to replace it with any system they wanted,
subject to the rules of idealised design. There are three guidelines that help the process.
- If there is no objective basis for making a decision on idealised
  design, then design the system experimentally so that the best
  alternative can be chosen in the circumstances. The design is
  a learning system.
- Design the system so that the features incorporated in the
  design can be continuously evaluated. Again, the design is a
  learning system.
- Since the design incorporates assumptions about the future,
  the design must incorporate a function that can monitor
  assumptions and the ability to make modifications if an
  assumption turns out to be false. The design is an adaptive
  system.

Prepare two detailed designs in this way. The first design must
accept constraints imposed by some wider containing system
that the design will be a part of. The second design must be
unconstrained by any aspect of the containing system. The two
designs can be compared and contrasted, thus highlighting
potential constraining factors and the effect that they may have
on the idealised design. It enables the designers to think
through ways in which the constraints of the containing system
can be overcome.

There are four further issues to take into account when formulating an idealised design. Each one has a recommended
method.

- Has the process sufficiently taken into account the issue of whose interests are being served and why? Use the method for Critically Evaluating Designs and Decisions (CEDD).
- Are there competing designs that people are aligning themselves to? Use the method for Testing Polarised Viewpoints (TPV).
- Is the design viable? Use the method Diagnosis for Effective Organisation (DEO).
- How can the design be implemented? Use the method for Implementing Designs and Decisions (IDD).

Example. This example presents an idealised design of the USA healthcare system produced by the INTERACT Healthcare Consortium. I am grateful to the consortium for agreeing to my sharing their idealised design with the readers of *Solving Problem Solving*.

The effort began in May 1992 with the aim of satisfying the user of American healthcare services, free of political considerations. A full report has been produced including two detailed case studies (see Further Reading). The account herein is an abridged version of the report, concentrating on the main features of the design as an example of what can be achieved by suspending judgement about assumptions held.

The main concern of the report is anxiety with proposed reforms to healthcare in the USA that seem only to reform the financing of the system. The proposed change is to the way medical care is paid for by its users. The reforms do promise to cover persons currently not insured which is considered to be a good thing, but overall the reforms are questionable because they do not take into account all aspects of healthcare together as a whole. Tinkering with parts does not guarantee improvements on the whole and may even harm it. Design must be systemic. (This is also argued in the philosophy of TSI, given in Chapter 3.) There is little value in changing the way healthcare is paid for if the system paid for leaves much to be desired.

The consortium began the process of idealised design assuming that the current healthcare system was destroyed the night before, but the overall context remained untouched. The consortium then proceeded to design a replacement system which it would implement if it were free to do so without constraints. This meant taking a fresh and creative look at healthcare, not trying to repair the current system but designing a completely new and better one.

The idealised design not surprisingly affects the behaviour of all the system's stakeholders. Representatives of all stakeholder groups were therefore involved. The stakeholders were named as

- individual and institutional healthcare providers
- users of the system
- communities in which healthcare is provided
- employers
- insurance companies
- suppliers to the healthcare industry
- the government of the USA.

The consortium was unhappy with certain aspects of the popular Quality Management (QM) approach that could have been chosen. In particular it was concerned that continuous improvement consisted only of identifying problems, prioritising them and attempting to solve the most important ones separately. The consortium sought to dissolve all problems by redesigning the current system so that the problems are eliminated, not merely solved. It did this with uncommon innovativeness by shifting the focus from treatment of illness and disabilities to the maintenance of wellness. This is, in effect, the first stage of idealised design – *setting the mission*.

The *desired properties* are extensively laid out in the consortium's report but are summarised here. Overall the objectives of the new system are to reduce healthcare costs, increase quality of service and expand access to all residents of the USA. Furthermore, the design must follow three rules: it must be technologically feasible, capable of surviving if it were brought into existence today and capable of learning and adapting. In the knowledge of the mission, its objectives and these rules, the following desired properties were specified.

- The design should provide essential healthcare services to every legal resident of the USA. It should provide cover to all employed illegal residents at a cost to the employers. This is expected to discourage employment of illegal residents and their immigration (a problem in the USA).

- Services should be funded by annual healthcare tax paid by individuals. Tax reflects income, age, number of dependants, lifestyle, health status and the environment. Those with low or no income would pay no tax.
- Employers should pay a healthcare tax proportional to the hazards of their employment conditions.
- The Inland Revenue Service (IRS) should collect the taxes and issue annual healthcare vouchers and wellness stamps to each individual. The value of the voucher would reflect the health-related characteristics of the individual.
- Individuals should be free to select any primary-care provider who has elected to practise within the system and pay them with vouchers. The primary-care providers would receive monthly payments from the IRS in line with the vouchers submitted. Out of this the providers must pay for the essential healthcare services they prescribe. Therefore, the better the health of the patients the more profitable it would be for the primary-care providers and the lower the tax rate for the individual.
- Individuals can choose primary-care providers outside the system but continue to pay healthcare tax.
- Monetary incentives should be given for services like prenatal care and immunisation of children. This encourages people who do not currently use such services therefore decreasing costs in the long run.
- Healthcare programmes should be administered by Community Healthcare Boards. These boards must define essential healthcare services, certify healthcare providers and monitor the quality of their services. This would reduce the number of malpractice suits. In addition, the boards must maintain a medical information system that is part of a national network and establish courts to adjudicate complaints. A federal body should set medical record and other informational standards. The IRS would provide a budget to each Community Healthcare Board.
- The system must include the following checks and balances to assure patients receive as much service as they need.

- The value of an individual's voucher increases with each annual reregistration with the same primary-care provider.
- Individuals can change primary-care providers once a year with no penalty and more often with a penalty.
- Individuals can obtain a second opinion. Individuals pay if this agrees with those of the primary-care providers. Primary-care providers pay if the second opinion disagrees.
- The Community Healthcare Board arranges for audits of provider performance and revokes certification or demands further education of those who do not meet standards.
- The Community Healthcare Information System provides information regarding the best practices and the quality of services provided by those operating both within and outside the system.
- Primary-care providers can insure themselves against adverse selection of patients which reduces their income below what is considered to be a minimum.
- The Federal Government provides scholarships to medical students who agree to serve for a specified time as a primary-care provider in currently underserved rural or urban areas.

The main effects of the design are forecasted to be as follows.

- A total estimated saving of US$300 billion per year.
- Extension of cover to all residents of the USA.
- Significant reduction in the role of the Federal Government.
- Employers, after the first year, cover the cost of work-related healthcare only.
- Incentives and disincentives encourage preferred behaviour of participants.
- More healthcare providers will provide primary care.
- Integrated healthcare systems will develop.
- It promotes health at least as much as treating illnesses and disabilities, reducing costs such as absence from work.

Detailed design would continue from here.

The idealised design is not a variant of managed competition. The market it creates is free. It allows unconstrained but monitored competition. The government could assess risks and establish the value of vouchers and tax rates, but it would not pay for services. In essence, this design goes beyond reform into a radical transformation of healthcare. It differs from other proposals because it places control in the hands of the users, not the subsidisers.

9.2.3.6 Debating – Exploring and Making Decisions

- Exploring and Making Decisions (EMD) is useful when the only problem surfaced in the Creativity phase is that there is no clear or agreeable appreciation of what the problems are that must be dealt with.
- The immediate and given purpose is to explore different perceptions about problems faced to come up with a decision about what to do.
- The output will be a decision about what to do; but what is happening when you problem solve with this method is explained in detail in Chapter 6.
- There are three main principles that drive the process of EMD.
  - The method is a learning system.
  - Decisions are made in terms of relevance to those involved, systemic rules that must not be violated and feasibility as determined by cultural rules and practices.
  - There are two distinct modes of thought, logic-based inquiry and cultural inquiry, which are used comparatively to generate meaningful debate about what can be done.
- The method has four stages.
  - Undertake further creative thinking about the problem situation.
  - Identify relevant themes for debate.
  - Explore the most relevant themes.
  - Make a decision about what to do.

One possible outcome of the Creativity phase is that the only problem surfaced is no clear or agreeable appreciation of what the problems are that must be dealt with. In that case it is necessary to choose a method that will directly explore this problem and come up with a decision about what to do. EMD is not used to identify problems since this has already been done and a result achieved. The clear aim is to explore different perceptions about what to do. The method therefore develops a rich appreciation about the problem situation, identifies themes about the problem situation from this, explores those themes with the aim of uncovering options about what to do and then makes a decision about what to do.

Undertake further creative thinking about the problem situation. The results of the Creativity phase are brought forward to start the process of EMD. This information is used in conjunction with additional information gathered to develop an appreciation of the problem situation. Additional information will include any of the following that have not been taken into account in the Creativity phase.

- Secondary data such as minutes of committee meetings, company brochures and internal reports.
- Results of formal interviews.
- Results of informal interviews.

The information is then summarised in diagrammatic form called a rich picture (see Figure 9.18 for an example of what one looks like). A rich picture is a cartoon-like expression which, as cartoons do, accentuates key features of the subject matter. In rich pictures the key features include: who is involved, what is happening, why things are happening, what conflicts exist and other crucial issues. A rich picture portrays all of this on one sheet with annotations enabling problem solvers to see the problem situation as a whole, as a whole set of interacting problems. The information can be processed in parallel which is analytically efficient, aiding problem solvers to pick out relevant themes to be explored. This is, in fact, a part of the cultural inquiry mentioned under the principles of EMD.

The following are annotations to the rich picture.

- Managers are not clear about the corporate mission.
- Managers do not manage, they are too involved in day-to-day operational activities.
- Research and development is weak.
- Budgetary control is weak.
- Staff appraisal is weak.

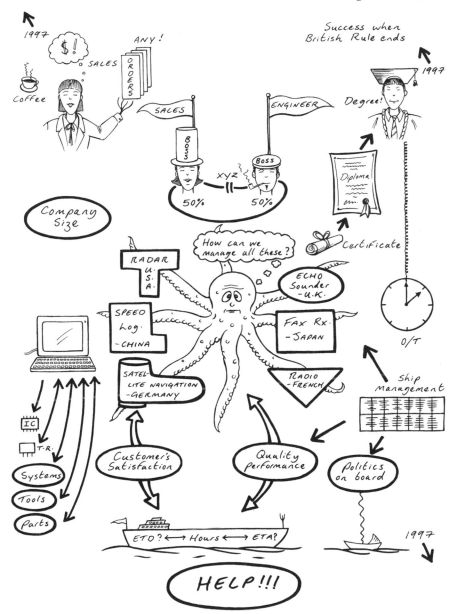

Figure 9.18 *Example of a rich picture used in Exploring and Making Decisions (EMD) – shipping problems in Hong Kong*

- There is ineffective communication and rising conflict between Sales and Service Departments.
- Customer complaints are on the increase.
- There is increasing competition.

Identify relevant themes for debate. Creating a rich picture involves entering into a further process of learning about the problem situation. The rich picture captures knowledge about the actual situation and by accentuating key features of it suggests themes to be further explored. The most relevant themes as perceived by participants are drawn out, recorded and then explored. A useful way of identifying themes is to name relevant systems, that is, to come up with systems that will generate plenty of relevant and meaningful debate about the problem situation that is thought about in relevant systems terms. Debate is where learning happens in relation to decision making and moves the process on to logic-based inquiry.

An example will help here. Referring to Figure 9.18 and the annotations, the following themes might be extracted for further debate. (This and the linked example below are based on work done by Loo Wing Chuen.)

- A customer satisfaction system.
- A human resource development system.
- A creative business idea-generating system.
- A conflict management system.
- A communication and control system.

Explore the most relevant systems. Any one of the relevant systems can be explored. There is no rule that tells you which one is most relevant, that is a matter of judgement. Judgements are tested out through exploration. Exploration of any relevant system is initially a logic-based inquiry that develops an ideal version of that system given the business context.

The ideal system is constructed around six elements that together power-up systemic thought. They 'force' problem solvers to think about the whole and not to be confined to particular parts. The six categories with their unique definitions, which must be accurately employed, are given below.

- *Customers*. Who are the customers in this ideal system, that is, who will benefit from or be a victim of the purposeful activity of the ideal system?

- *Actors.* Who are the actors in this ideal system, that is, who will carry out the activities?
- *Transformation process.* What is the transformation process of this ideal system, that is, what is the purposeful activity that transforms inputs of the system into outputs of the system, and what exactly are those inputs and outputs?
- *World view.* What is the view of the organisation represented here as an ideal system that makes the transformation identified above a meaningful one?
- *Owners.* Who are the owners of this system, that is, who in the whole scheme of things have or may have the inclination and capacity to stop the activity?
- *Environmental constraints.* What are the constraints in the environment of this ideal system that have to be taken as given, that is, what factors exist that are neither controlled nor influenced by this ideal system?

This is known as CATWOE, a mnemonic. The ideal system is identified using these six categories to generate a logic-based knowledge about it. The knowledge generated must be stored. This is normally done either by writing a single, comprehensive statement about the ideal system or by noting against each category the considered opinion of the participants.

There are a few extra tips worth noting. Constructing an ideal system is most logically done starting with what is being transformed and why. In other words, identify the core transformation first and then put in place the world view that attaches a purpose to the transformation. Once this has been done it is much easier to identify the customers, actors, owners and environmental constraints. Also, when choosing the transformation of the ideal system, make sure that the output is without question a direct transformation of the input (people cannot literally be converted into money; information cannot literally be transformed into rolled steel; people's social needs cannot literally be transformed into a work's swimming pool!). One other point, do not choose themes and relevant systems which are primary activities like the ones discussed for the DEO method. Much more insight is gained if themes with controversial issues are explored reflecting the nature of the problem. (This last point represents an important distinction between EMD and DEO.)

An example is provided here that explores a 'creative business idea-generating system' from the earlier example. Both a comprehensive statement and noting against categories are illustrated. The statement is:

> An employee and management-owned and operated system, seeking to identify new business opportunities by accruing knowledge about technology, company resources and market needs.

The categories are explained as follows.

- Customer is the management and its clients.
- Actors are the Research and Development group and management.
- Transformation is ideas into business opportunities.
- World view is that business opportunities come from rigorous and continuous evaluation of the market-place.
- Owners are the management.
- Environmental constraints includes relevant legislation.

The next thing to do in the logic-based component of EMD is to construct a systems diagram of the ideal system. The diagram shows the logical flows and controls between the main activities of the ideal system. The diagram will be compared to knowledge about the actual situation captured in the rich picture, but firstly it has to be constructed.

The systems model must be built directly from the relevant system and its theme under exploration, and from nothing else. It is an account of the transformation and other activities of the ideal system. It is constructed by drawing out the minimum number of verbs, around six to eight, necessary to describe the transformation and activities. Verbs are used because they are doing-words and only doing-words can represent activities.

The verbs are logically ordered according to how they depend on each other and how they would work together if they were part of a real system. A commonly used approach and a reasonable starting point is to cluster verbs into key subsystems. Key subsystems include operations, monitor and control over internal activities, monitor and control of the business environment, strategic planning and business policy (note the similarities between these and the VSM used in DEO which at this stage can provide guidance about systemic design logic). If useful, any subsystem can be blown up to provide much more detail about how it must operate.

The ideal systems model shown in Figure 9.19 continues the example above.

The method now moves on to comparison. The ideal systems model is compared to the rich picture of the actual situation with the aim of generating debate about possible decisions that could be taken leading to improvements in the problem situation. This is where the logic-based inquiry and cultural inquiry are used in comparative mode to engender meaningful debate about what can be done.

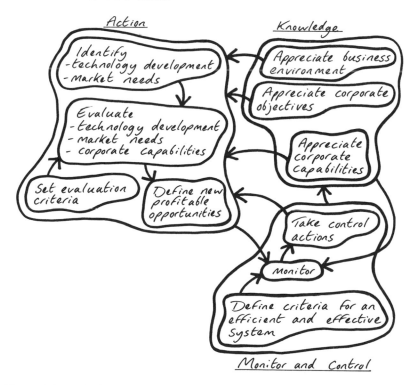

Figure 9.19 *Ideal systems model of a 'creative business idea-generating system'*

There are three suggested means of comparison.

- Take a number of ideal systems models, compare them to the actual situation captured in the rich picture and note any differences that stand out between the two.
- Take a most relevant ideal systems model and compare its activities to the activities of the actual situation captured in the rich picture. This can be done by asking the following questions.
  - Does this activity exist in the actual situation?
  - How well is this activity done in the actual situation?
- Use the ideal system to simulate qualitatively the consequences of its existence in the actual situation and assess whether this is a better scenario than the predicted future scenario extrapolated from the actual situation.

Make a decision about what to do. Comparison inevitably leads to consideration of possible changes that must be decided upon. The kind of decisions made are rarely black-and-white ones. They are normally the result of further debate where participants discuss potential improvements. The debate aims to confirm which changes are most relevant, systemically desirable, culturally feasible and likely to bring about changes that as many people as possible will consider to be improvements.

There are three further issues to take into account during the process of EMD. Each one has a recommended method.

- Has the process sufficiently taken into account the issue of whose interests are being served and why? Use the method for Critically Evaluating Designs and Decisions (CEDD).
- Is the decision about organisational design? Use the method Diagnosis for Effective Organisation (DEO).
- How can the decision be implemented. Use the method for Implementing Designs and Decisions (IDD).

Example. (A pseudonym is used for the factory featured in this case study to maintain confidentiality as requested.) The holding company of the factory featured in this case study has been in existence in Europe for a large part of this century. The factory in the spotlight, called HARDCO, has been manufacturing hardware products for about 40 years. It has experienced rapid growth, doubling its turnover twice over in the last ten years. The products, however, are now on the decline in the market-place. A range of about six new products is being launched over the next few years. The factory is organised along conventional, functional departmental lines. There are regular monthly meetings of senior management, who focus decision making mainly on investment, layout and production capabilities. Decisions are disseminated by distribution of minutes of the meetings.

The bulk of people's time is spent on production, including material and product quality, rejects, reliability, productivity and meeting schedules. A standard performance system has been implemented based on work study analysis. This details the number of operators required, how they should be deployed, how many hours of production are needed, shift patterns, and so on. These details are passed on to production supervisors who must ensure that set targets are met. If they are not met then 'penalties' are incurred by the supervisor and their team in the form of costing over targets.

Supervisors are rushed off their feet trying to ensure that production targets are met. They are responsible for up to 50 operators and several production lines. Supervisors never have enough time for their work and practically no time at all to reflect on the way things are done and to look for ways of improvement. On the very rare occasions when time is spent analysing problems, discussion normally fizzles out because problem definition and ownership are impossible to work out. The reason is that only managers and supervisors are responsible and accountable and so there is little workforce co-operation. Furthermore, the workforce is fragmented into many tiny specialised units making traceability nearly impossible. When one unit appears to be a culprit in, say, poor quality creeping into a product, it simply and easily diverts blame to some other task.

Attitude and morale of staff not surprisingly are less than desirable. Staff are not motivated. This is accentuated by appraisal systems used where employees are graded according to competence and results. The idea was to introduce fairness, but the result was to cause resentment and to discourage employees from achieving beyond the basic requirements of their grading. The lower grades accepted their label and so staff development became a joke.

There were many other key features of the situation that could be elaborated on here, but it must be clear by now that one of the main difficulties faced was low participation of employees in all respects of their work, leading to great difficulty in problem definition and progressive improvement. The situation is represented in the rich picture shown in Figure 9.20.

Exploring and Making Decisions (EMD) was used to open up the communication channels between all levels and all functions, to help learning and understanding between those people and to generate a way forward that was meaningful to them all. The process began with representatives exploring the situation and coming up with several rich pictures that illustrated their concerns, one of which is shown in Figure 9.20. From this a number of different ways of thinking about the problems faced were discussed. When using EMD these themes are consolidated in a list of relevant systems.

The main themes identified by representatives in HARDCO were as follows.

- An employee satisfaction system.
- A work organisation system.
- A system for internal participation.
- A product development system.
- A reengineering system.
- A market response system.
- Etc.

Each of these were discussed, considering the ways in which the current situation could be improved in the light of the insights that each one generated. A work organisation system was chosen for further explanation, not because it was right but because it led to greater insight in debate than the others. It was a theme that all people were able to relate to. It was a theme that in discussion embraced some of the concerns hit by other relevant systems, like the employee participation system.

The kind of thinking generated through this theme is as follows. Organisational design is created by people. In HARDCO the design had been created by senior managers who enter-

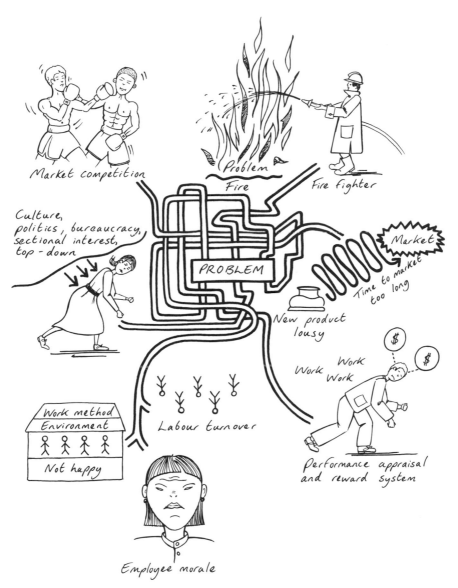

Figure 9.20 *Rich picture used in Exploring and Making Decisions (EMD) – HARDCO*

tained only the factory's objectives and needs. They did not consider the needs of departments or individuals. The design of the organisation therefore dictates a style of work rather than a style of work influencing organisational design. The way forward then is to reorganise but this must involve people participating in the redesign of their own work and consequently allowing people to influence the way the organisation is designed.

EMD was therefore used to identify a process to bring about change in the organisation. It did not generate a solution to the work organisation problem. It did generate ideas about how the problem could be tackled. An ideal system representation of a work organisation system was developed, first in the form of a comprehensive definition. This reinforced the ideas about the process to be followed.

The definition was constructed using the CATWOE mnemonic as follows.

- *Customers*. Who are the customers in this ideal system, that is, who will benefit from or be a victim of the purposeful activity of the ideal system? An improved work organisation system built through the participation of employees would benefit the employees, but would also benefit all those who have a direct or indirect relationship with the organisation such as suppliers and consumers, shareholders, employees' families, and so on. Benefits clearly are wide ranging which reinforces the relevance of this way forward. The only likely victims are HARDCO's competitors.
- *Actors*. Who are the actors in this ideal system, that is, who will carry out the activities? Those involved in the process include all employees. There are other perceived beneficiaries such as suppliers and consumers whose involvement should be encouraged.
- *Transformation process*. What is the transformation process of this ideal system, that is, what is the purposeful activity that transforms inputs of the system into outputs of the system, and what exactly are those inputs and outputs? The transformation will be from a current work organisation that is inefficient and ineffective and alienates the workforce, to one

that is both efficient and effective, but is also responsive and enjoys the support of employees.

- *World view*. What is the view of the organisation represented here as an ideal system that makes the transformation identified above a meaningful one? Ultimately a work organisation that accommodates for employees' needs and interests, whilst meeting organisational requirements, is the only sustainable way forward.

- *Owners*. Who are the owners of this system, that is, who in the whole scheme of things has or may have the inclination and capacity to stop the activity? The owners will be the participants. Employees are the essential stakeholders who can stop the activity.

- *Environmental constraints*. What are the constraints in the environment of this ideal system that have to be taken as given, that is, what factors exist that are neither controlled nor influenced by this ideal system? Although not absolutely unchangeable, it has to be recognised that years of operating in a traditional way have conditioned long-term employees and have established a culture of resentment against management. Overcoming this constraint will be extremely problematic, but hopefully it will be possible to influence this way of thinking, thus rendering the issue not a constraint. Obvious environmental constraints include legislation, technological feasibility, budget restrictions, and so on.

Verbs were identified that describe the process of changing work organisation and were themselves organised as a basic process in the form of an idealised systems model. This model is shown in Figure 9.21. The process was implemented with some success, but that is another story. This case, although grossly simplified, has demonstrated how EMD can lead to decision making where the main output of the exercise comes from the process itself rather than the solution, i.e., the learning and understanding that ensue.

9.2.3.7 Debating – Testing Polarised Viewpoints

- Testing Polarised Viewpoints (TPV) is useful when views

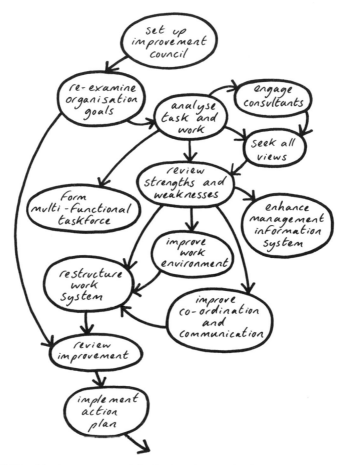

Figure 9.21 *Ideal systems model of a 'work organisation system' – HARDCO*

about alternative designs or decisions become polarised and the problem solving process becomes stuck. (A warning must be given here. TPV encourages a process of adversarial debate and should not be used if the atmosphere is strongly negatively conflictual.)

- The immediate and given purpose is to uncover strengths and weaknesses in competing designs and/or decisions and from this to agree upon improvements.
- The output will be a reformulated strategy that ideally all parties agree to; but what is happening when you problem solve with this method is explained in detail in Chapter 6.

• There are two principles to follow when testing polarised opinions about alternative designs and decisions.
  – Debate is adversarial in the belief that oppositional thinking will surface important strengths and weaknesses of the alternatives.
  – Debate is synthetic because it brings into the same frame competing designs or decisions, compares and contrasts their strengths and weaknesses and produces a plan for action.
• The method has four stages.
  – Group formation.
  – Assumption surfacing.
  – Investigative debate.
  – Synthesis.

The core idea of the method is that designs and decisions are built on assumptions. These assumptions may not be valid. What is needed then is a way of testing the assumptions of the alternatives to see how well they stand up to criticism. The polarised views, of which there will be two or more, are assessed in terms of their strengths and weaknesses, are then compared and from this analysis a synthesised plan for action is formulated. A trained facilitator is essential to the successful employment of the method described below.
    The method has four steps.

• Group formation.
• Assumption surfacing.
• Investigative debate.
• Synthesis.

Group formation. The aim of group formation is to organise people into groups in such a way that the best plan for action will be generated. There are two rules to follow.

• Group people together who share the same view. This means that each view will be strongly supported by its group of advocates.
• Maximise the difference in opinion between the groups. This

means that the view of each group will be strongly challenged during investigative debate.

Suggested criteria for group formation include the following.

- Advocates of identifiable alternatives.
- People with vested interests.
- Managers from different functional areas.
- Managers from different organisational levels.

Choice of criterion depends on circumstances. The facilitator must ensure that the right criterion is chosen in the circumstances. The facilitator then arranges for the groups to work in discrete areas free from interruption by other groups.

Each group initially formulates a clear and concise statement about their preferred alternative. Once this has been achieved the process moves on to assumption surfacing.

Assumption surfacing. Each group has a clear view on which alternative must be selected. What is not clear in most cases are the assumptions on which that view is based. Unseen weaknesses can often be found when assumptions about the viewpoints are surfaced. The next task, then, is to surface assumptions to be tested.

Assumption surfacing employs three quite simple but very effective techniques: stakeholder analysis, assumption specification and assumption rating. There is no time limit imposed on the process but 90 minutes is often sufficient time for groups to complete assumption surfacing.

Stakeholder analysis. Each group must identify key stakeholders on whom the success or failure of their preferred design or decision depends. Stakeholders include the following.

- People affected by the alternative.
- People who have an interest in it.
- People who can affect adoption, execution, or implementation of it.
- People who care about it.

Assumption specification. Each group constructs a list of assumptions that they have made about individual stakeholders in trusting that their preferred alternative will work. There is no limit to the number of assumptions that may be included in the inventory. Working initially with five key assumptions, however, gets things going and prevents the process from getting weighted down with a large volume of assumptions. More assumptions can be added at any time.

Assumption rating. Each group now plots the assumptions on a chart. This begins the process of testing how sound they are. It begins to test the alternative as a whole. The chart comprises the following two scales.

- The importance of the assumption in terms of its role in the success or failure of the alternative – from least important to most important.
- The degree of certainty that the assumption is justified – from least certain to most certain.

The scales are put together to form a chart (see Figure 9.22). Assumptions plotted on the right-hand side of the chart are evidently important. Those in the lower quartile of the right-hand side are risky. These are the assumptions the group is making

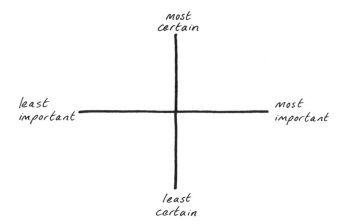

Figure 9.22 *Example of an assumption rating chart used in Testing Polarised Viewpoints (TPV)*

that are likely to be the root cause of any failure – hence this part of the chart is known as the problematic planning region.

Investigative debate between participating groups is the next step. The groups are brought together by the facilitator. Each group then makes a presentation. They explain their alternative and then talk through the results of their assumption surfacing. The groups present for about five minutes. No discussion is permitted at this stage but the facilitator should allow for points of clarification.

When each group has completed their initial presentation the facilitator starts a second round of deliberation, this time encouraging reasoned criticism about alternatives. Each group has to defend their alternative against the most penetrating reflections other groups can muster. The critics may begin by pointing out one or more of the following.

- There are stakeholders who are not taken into account.
- There are assumptions of stakeholders which have not been taken into account.
- There are assumptions shown on the rating chart that should have been plotted in the problematic planning region.
- Certain stakeholders have greater or lesser prominence than other groups and this needs explaining.
- Certain assumptions are rated differently from other groups and this also needs explaining.

After approximately 30 minutes of adversarial debate, the facilitator asks another group to defend their position. After all groups have been in the hot seat, the facilitator asks the groups to retire once more to reconsider their assumptions and alternatives. Assumption modification takes place. The modification process must not be curtailed too early, continuing within reason for as long as there is progress. Once modification is complete, the facilitator brings together the groups for further debate in the form of synthesis.

Synthesis. The aim of synthesis is to reach a compromise between groups on their alternatives and assumptions. This is a process of negotiation and further modification. A list of agreed assumptions is constructed. Using this list, efforts must be made to work out a compromise between the polarised groups. The ease with which this happens is determined by the substantive content of the agreed list.

There are four further issues to take into account during the process. Each one has a recommended method.

- Has the process sufficiently taken into account the issue of whose interests are being served and why? Use the method for Critically Evaluating Designs and Decisions (CEDD).
- Is there a genuine synthesis or are there still many points of disagreement? Use the method for Exploring and Choosing Decisions (ECD).
- Is the synthetic alternative about organisational design? Use the method Diagnosis for Effective Organisation (DEO).
- How can the alternative be implemented? Use the method for Implementing Designs and Decisions (IDD).

Example. (The name of the hospital featured in this example is not mentioned to maintain confidentiality as requested.) The following case is an application of TPV written by my colleague Robert Cross, director of the hospital where the intervention was carried out. I wish to thank him once again for the time taken to prepare this study for *Solving Problem Solving*. The case reports on a decision to be made concerning substantial capital expenditure on a swimming pool for the social club of a hospital in the Middle East.

The hospital is located in the capital city of a country in the lower Gulf in the Middle East. The location is a crucial factor that must not be forgotten. The hospital is managed under a renewable fixed-term management contract by Allied Health Company on behalf of the owner, which is the local government. The hospital employs approximately 750 people from a wide range of nationalities, cultures, ethnic groups and religious backgrounds. There are quite a large number of Western expatriate single female nurses and paramedical staff who are generally recruited through the company's recruitment offices in the UK and Eire.

The hospital moved into new buildings in 1984. Part of these new buildings included a purpose-built staff social club, located on the beach front adjacent to the hospital. The majority of the staff accommodation is located in blocks of flats situated throughout the city. The social club facilities have been considerably developed over the last few years, including extensive landscaping of the beach front area with grass and trees forming a large garden area.

Although the club is situated on the beach, many of the staff prefer not to swim in the sea because an extensive area of the beach comprises shingle and pebbles. Also, the amount of tar being washed up had greatly increased since the Gulf War. Tar becomes attached to swimmers' bodies and costumes and is very difficult to remove.

From time to time staff and members of the hospital management team raised and discussed the option of a purpose-built swimming pool in the social club grounds. It would alleviate the problems associated with sea swimming and might provide an extra attraction helping recruitment of the best-trained single female nurses and paramedical staff. Despite these immediate gains, digging a little deeper soon revealed as many disadvantages as advantages, accentuated by the increasingly polarised views of staff members. Two positions therefore emerged, those in support of the argument for a swimming pool and those against, but relations between the people were quite amicable. This is a classic situation where TPV can come into its own.

Group formation was relatively straightforward; one group in support of having a swimming pool and the other against. Selecting membership of the groups was, however, problematic. Certain assumptions to be explored might be interpreted as political, racist, sexist or criticising a religion (anyone sensitive to these issues will experience some discomfort later on in the study!). It was therefore decided to contain membership within the management team, where there was strong polarisation on the issue anyway, who would act on behalf of those requiring representation. Views of other stakeholders were sought informally and introduced into the exercise by representatives on the management team. This enabled problem solving to approximate the ideal of participation whilst at the same time avoid the problem of negative conflict. These are the realities of managing an organisation in the Gulf region, where there is multi-cultural diversity, having to balance societal, organisational and individuals' needs equitably without triggering off fruitless conflict and strife.

The groups were composed as follows.

- In support.
  - Matron.
  - Hospital director.
  - Hospital works officer.
- Against.
  - Hospital administrator.
  - Financial controller.
  - Support services manager.
  - Supplies manager.
  - Medical director.

Assumption surfacing. The preferred strategies for each group were crystallised in concise statements. Those in support wanted:

To utilise the existing financial funds of the hospital social club, supplemented by additional fundraising activities and ongoing financial subscriptions from members, to build and maintain a swimming pool in the social club grounds.

Those against wanted:

To continue to utilise the sea as a swimming facility, in view of the potential problems associated with additional responsibility for safety, cultural problems, planning restrictions and cost of building a swimming pool.

Stakeholder analysis. The group in support identified the following stakeholders.

- Western nurses.
- Developing countries' male staff.
- Arab families.
- Matron.
- Residential medical staff.
- Government liaison staff.
- Recruiters.
- Swimming pool manufacturers.

The group against identified these stakeholders.

- Financial controller.

- Hospital administrator.
- Support services manager.
- Western nurses.
- Hotels in the city.
- Religious fundamentalist groups.

Assumption specification. A list of key assumptions was drawn up by each of the two groups, being assumptions that they were making in believing their preferred strategy would be successful. The group in support of the swimming pool came up with the following key assumptions (there were many more).

- Western nurses
  - want a facility of their own
  - find hotel facilities expensive
  - find that hotel facilities expose them to preying male hotel guests
  - will use a facility of their own
  - want to learn to swim
  - prefer a cleaner option
  - prefer a pool because it could be kept cooler in the summer (when temperatures are stifling).
- Developing countries' male staff
  - enjoy viewing Western nurses
  - would have a facility that they could not otherwise afford
  - want to learn to swim.
- Arab families
  - would have a facility that they could not otherwise afford
  - want to learn to swim
  - would use the pool as a place to leave children enabling them to do other important things
  - would enable them to get out of their flats.
- Matron
  - would raise morale of nursing staff
  - would assist with recruitment
  - would add support to the social club.
- Residential medical staff
  - would raise morale
  - would help with recruitment
  - Want to learn to swim.

- Government liaison staff
  - would raise staff morale
  - would add to the recreational facilities which may be attractive to the government if they took over.
- Recruiters
  - would help with recruitment as a recreational facility and through image enhancement.
- Swimming pool manufacturers
  - will be keen to make a sale
  - can offer attractive variations.

The group against the swimming pool came up with the following key assumptions (there were many more).

- Financial controller.
  - additional costs will be unreasonable, e.g., heating/cooling, water, maintenance, pool attendant.
- Hospital administrator.
  - difficult to supervise even with pool attendants
  - problems with families leaving children unsupervised
  - policing unauthorised guests
  - tension with the male Arab and developing countries' staff ogling at Western staff, in particular the female staff
  - gaining planning permission for this type of facility would be excessively time consuming.
- Support services manager.
  - there would be onerous cleaning requirements to avoid fungal infections from leaves, litter and urine.
- Western nurses
  - will object to being ogled at and stay away
  - want to get away from the workplace for leisure activities.
- Hotels in city
  - will resist because they will lose indirect benefit from single Western females adorning their beaches
  - will resist because they will lose direct sales from nurses.
- Religious fundamentalist groups
  - will strongly resist because the scheme breaks with the cultural norms of the indigenous society.

Assumption rating. The two groups rated the assumptions

according to the criteria of importance and certainty. The groups recognised considerable overlap between some of the assumptions they had made and found it helpful to lump them. The group supporting the swimming pool consolidated their assumptions and numbered them for the rating chart as follows.

- (1) Would help with morale of staff.
- (2) Many staff want a facility of their own.
- (3) For some staff it would provide them with a facility that they otherwise would not be able to afford.
- (4) Staff find hotel facilities expensive.
- (5) Would assist generally with recruitment.
- (6) Provides a better alternative to the sea because it is cleaner.
- (7) Provides a better alternative to the sea because it can be kept cooler in summer.
- (8) Would enable some staff to get out of their flats.
- (9) Staff will use a facility of their own.
- (10) Hotel facilities expose Western nurses to preying male hotel guests.
- (11) Many staff want to learn to swim.
- (12) Some staff would be able to use it as a place to leave children whilst they did other important things.
- (13) It would help support the social club.
- (14) It would be an added recreational facility for the Government if they took over the running of the hospital.

The group against the swimming pool also consolidated their assumptions and numbered them for the rating chart as follows.

- (1) Certain male staff would ogle at female Western staff.
- (2) Difficulty in supervision even with an attendant.
- (3) Problems would arise if families left children unsupervised for hours on end.
- (4) It would require planning permission which would be a lengthy process.
- (5) The scheme breaks with the cultural norms of the indigenous population.
- (6) It would lead to onerous cleaning requirements to avoid fungal infection, e.g., from leaves, litter and urine.

- (7) Additional costs would be unreasonable.
- (8) It would lead to policing problems with unauthorised guests.
- (9) Staff want to get away from the workplace to enjoy their leisure.
- (10) Hotels want the indirect benefits arising from single Western girls adorning their beaches.
- (11) Hotels do not want to lose the direct sales of drinks, etc.

Assumption charts. The two groups plotted the consolidated assumptions on separate assumption rating charts as shown in Figures 9.23 and 9.24. The ratings among the group in support of the swimming pool raised only a couple of potential problem areas that might be of significance. The group was confident in their certainty about the vast majority of their assumptions. The key assumptions of the group against the swimming pool were more evenly spread across the four quadrants. Nevertheless, they remained confident.

It is interesting to note that up until this stage the two groups were still bullish about their strategies. This is despite the groups' undergoing self-analysis in the process of assumption rating and charting, which can lead groups to uncover weaknesses in their strategy. In fact, the two groups felt that they had identified some very important assumptions and were con-

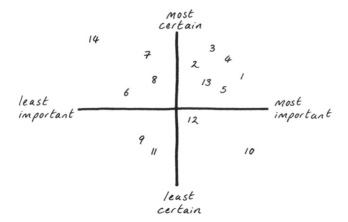

Figure 9.23 *Assumption rating chart of the group in support of the swimming pool used in the Testing Polarised Viewpoints (TPV) case*

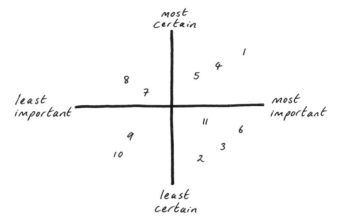

Figure 9.24   *Assumption rating chart of the group against the swimming pool used in the Testing Polarised Viewpoints (TPV) case*

vinced that they were correct. If nothing else this underlines the strong adversarial nature of the strategies of the two groups.

Investigative debate and synthesis. Debate was carried out in several open meetings over the course of five to six weeks. Periods of several days were left between meetings so that groups would have plenty of time to consider the content of debates. This also allowed time for representatives to hold informal discussions with interested parties. Managers put forward their own views and represented the views of other stakeholders who had a stake in the outcome of the debate but who were not included for reasons already explained.

Debate quickly uncovered new stakeholders that neither group had included. In particular a number of fundamentalist groups, who stood firm against the proposal for cultural reasons, had to be included. This added more weight to the position of the group against the swimming pool.

The group against the proposal also pointed out that some assumptions on the chart of the group for the proposal could well turn out to be more problematic than they had initially believed. For example, it was not so certain that the pool would assist that much with recruitment, that learning to swim was important to many people or that there really would be advantages overall in children being left at the poolside. Furthermore, the capital and running costs were very hard to justify and it would not be sensible for the hospital to step out of line with cultural norms of the indigenous population. The group for acknowledged these concerns and readjusted their chart and viewpoint radically. They eventually dropped completely the idea of a swimming pool.

The group against the proposal, however, saw some value in the ideas of the group for the swimming pool that they did not want to lose. For example, more recreational support would help with staff morale and possibly improve recruitment. They formulated a new proposal to harness the worth of those ideas. The proposal requested management to consider utilising financial resources to subsidise use of outside clubs and hotels, whilst concentrating on utilising hospital social club funds on other more modest ideas that would increase the club's attractiveness to staff. This synthesis ultimately became the foundations of a new strategy that was implemented.

9.2.3.8 Disimprisoning – Critically Evaluating Designs and Decisions

- Critically Evaluating Designs and Decisions (CEDD) helps managers to think about whose interests are being served in the following.
  - Design work: it is ideally used right at the start to formulate properties of the design, but can usefully be drawn in to criticise a design at any stage of development.
  - Decision making: it is ideally used at the start to identify the interested and disadvantaged parties who should be involved, but can be usefully drawn in to criticise the decision-making process at any stage.
- The immediate and given purpose in simplest terms is to ensure that even the most disadvantaged people have been explicitly accommodated.
- The output will be designs and decisions that have taken into account freedom of choice to design better organisations or make better management decisions; but what is happening when you problem solve with this method is explained in detail in Chapter 6.
- There are four main principles proposed in CEDD.

- *Purposefulness*. Designs and decisions have a meaning to involved and affected people and matter to them, which must be respected.
- *The systems idea*. Human knowledge is not comprehensive. The idea of whole systems thinking forces us to consider this matter.
- *The moral idea*. Assess what values are built into designs and decisions and therefore what moral imperfections exist.
- *The guarantor idea*. There is no absolute guarantee that designs and decisions will lead to improvement in human well-being, but planners and decision makers must reflect on this issue and incorporate procedures for consultation and agreement to guarantee improvement as far as possible.
- The method has two modes of evaluation.
  - Mode 1 – to critically evaluate extant designs or decisions, by comparing what is with what ought to be.
  - Mode 2 – to evaluate in advance what should be the main properties of designs, or to identify interested and disadvantaged parties to be included in the decision-making process.

  Results of evaluation are fed straight into the design or the decision-making process.

During the process of designing or decision making it is often the case that issues concerning whose interests are, or are not, being served get neglected. There may even be coercive processes at work. Such processes are employed unwittingly or wittingly.

- Processes can unwittingly affect the way designs and decisions are formulated, e.g., the influence of a senior member of staff, of someone's ability to articulate points well, of an expert's superior technical knowledge, or of biases in organisations and society such as race and gender.
- Processes can be used wittingly to affect the way designs and decisions are formulated, e.g., someone might use their power to bear on a design or decision using money, or their position in an organisation or society.

These matters are of great concern to TSI whose philosophy and principles argue for human freedom by managing conflict and coercion in a reflective and participatory manner, therefore upholding TSI's systemic principle. Without the systemic principle effective management is lost because there is no freedom of choice to design better organisation or to make better decisions about them; that is, better in the sense that all people involved and affected have had a reasonable opportunity to influence the design or decision thus preventing undesirable counter-intuitive consequences from occurring later on. This provides the conditions for more effective management.

CEDD strongly promotes the reflective principle of TSI. It critically reflects upon

- the purpose and means of designs
- how decisions are made and what the consequences of decisions are likely to be.

No design or decision is comprehensive, they are always partial. The normative content of designs and decisions therefore must be revealed and the consequences explored for all persons involved and affected by them. This can only be done by asking questions of the sort, 'What ought we do, why, whose interests are likely to be served and what will be the likely consequences of all of this?' The CEDD method described below operationalises these lines of inquiry.

Critical evaluation gets beneath intended or sales pitch consequences of designs or decisions, even though they may be applaudable, and explores what the actual consequences are likely to be. It does this through two forms of questioning. The two forms tease out the consequences of the design or decision by asking questions about

- things as they currently stand with the actual client (Form 1)
- things as they ought to be with disadvantaged parties as clients (Form 2).

There are two modes of CEDD which use the two forms of questioning.

- *Mode 1 – to critically evaluate extant designs or decisions.* If there is already in place a design or a decision, then Forms 1 and 2 are operated and compared.

- *Mode 2 – to choose the main properties of designs or to identify interested and disadvantaged parties to be included in the decision-making process.* If CEDD is being used to kick off implementation in TSI's Problem Solving Mode, then move straight on to Form 2, using it to generate the properties to be included in the design process, or to generate a set of interested and disadvantaged parties to be included in the decision-making process.

There are 12 questions that are addressed by each of the two forms of questioning in each mode. The 12 questions target four types of stakeholder. The four types of stakeholder are

- the client of the design or decision-making process
- the designer or decision taker
- experts involved in the design or decision-making process
- those people who are affected by the design or decision-making process but are not involved in it.

Form 1 asks the following 12 questions about things *as they currently stand* with the actual client.

The client.

- Who is the actual client? That is, whose interests are served by the design or decision?
- What is the actual purpose? That is, what are the actual consequences of the design or decision?
- What is the built-in measure of success? That is, what measures are used to judge whether the purpose of the design or decision is being met?

The decision taker.

- Who actually is the decision taker? That is, who can actually change the measure of success of the design or decision?
- What does the decision taker actually control? That is, what is the actual span of control of the design or decision?

- What does the decision taker not control? That is, what is outside of the span of control and is in effect environment for the design or the decision?

The expert.

- Who is actually involved as planner? That is, whose expertise is being drawn upon to formulate the design or decision?
- Who is actually involved as expert, with what kind of expertise, playing what role? That is, what expert knowledge is being used to shape the design or decision?
- What guarantee do the experts give that the design or decision will be successful? That is, is there technical competence, experience and intuition, a consensus among experts, political support from interest groups, etc.?

The affected but not involved.

- Who will actually be affected but not involved? That is, who will be affected by the design or decision but has no direct say in its construction?
- How are the interests of the affected dealt with? That is, do the experts decide what is right for those affected by the design or decision, or are the affected used as tools to serve the purposes of others?
- What world view actually underlies the design or decision? That is, is the world view of (some of) the involved or of (some of) the affected?

Form 2 asks the following 12 questions about things *as they ought to be* with interested and disadvantaged parties as clients.

The client.

- Who ought to be the actual client? That is, whose interests should be served by the design or decision?
- What ought to be the actual purpose? That is, what ought to be the actual consequences of the design or decision?
- What ought to be the built-in measure of success? That is,

what measures ought to be used to judge whether the purpose of the design or decision is being met?

The decision taker.

- Who ought to be the decision taker? That is, who ought to be able to change the measure of success of the design or decision?
- What ought the decision taker actually control? That is, what ought to be the actual span of control of the design or decision?
- What ought the decision taker not control? That is, what ought to be outside of the span of control and is in effect environment for the design or the decision?

The expert.

- Who ought to be involved as planner? That is, whose expertise ought to be drawn upon to formulate the design or decision?
- Who ought to be involved as expert, with what kind of expertise, playing what role? That is, what expert knowledge ought to be used to shape the design or decision?
- What guarantee ought the experts give that the design or decision will be successful? That is, ought there be technical competence, experience and intuition, a consensus among experts, political support from interest groups, etc.?

The affected but not involved.

- Who ought to be affected but not involved? That is, who ought to be affected by the design or decision but have no direct say in its construction?
- How ought the interests of the affected be dealt with? That is, how should the experts decide what is right for those affected by the design or decision, or are the affected used as tools to serve the purposes of others?
- What world view ought to underlie the design or decision? That is, ought the world view be of (some of) the involved or of (some of) the affected?

The results of the critical evaluation must be recorded and fed straight into the process of design or decision-making and taken account of. There are two obvious possible outputs of the CEDD method that will be fed into the design or decision-making process.

- Evidence that the most disadvantaged have been accommodated for.
- Evidence that the most disadvantaged have not been accommodated for.

Example. The following example reports a Mode 2 application by Claire Cohen and Gerald Midgley from the Centre for Systems Studies at the University of Hull in the UK. The intervention is known as *The North Humberside Diversion From Custody Project for Mentally Disordered Offenders* (see Further Reading). I am grateful to both problem solvers for allowing me to share a portion of their work with readers of *Solving Problem Solving*, not only the steps that they undertook, but also the valuable discussion they have contributed concerning problem solving when the main issue being tackled is whose interests are being served and what the likely consequences will be.

There are in the region of 80 Diversion From Custody schemes currently operating in the UK. The Centre for Systems Studies was asked to support the development of the North Humberside Diversion From Custody Project through process consultancy and evaluate it at the end of its first year. The focus of the part of the intervention reported herein was the design of an ideal diversion service. It involved looking at what clients and professionals in the field thought the system ought to be, using CEDD. This enabled the following things to be achieved.

- Making comparisons between client and staff views, revealing discrepancies, discussion of the discrepancies and from this making recommendations.
- Exploring the possibility of a shared ideal vision of the future direction of diversion activities.
- Evaluating current activities in terms of whether they are moving toward the ideal.
- Helping people with mental health problems caught up in the

criminal justice system to get involved in the evaluation of the diversion service in a constructive way.

Two one-day workshops were run. The first was for people with mental health problems who were, or had been, caught up in the criminal justice system. A trawl for participants was conducted by sending out letters to all clients and ex-clients of the Diversion From Custody Project. In addition, letters were sent to 30 users of North Humberside MIND. Twelve people chose to take part. Their experiences of custody ranged from being held overnight in a police cell following arrest to a six-year prison sentence. The second workshop was held with the staff team and management group.

Both workshops followed the same basic format. Firstly, participants were asked key questions in order to generate a list of desired properties of a diversion system. This entailed using the questions of CEDD in advance of idealised planning using Exploring and Choosing Designs (ECD). This part of the intervention is reported below. The second part of the intervention reported only briefly herein went on to design the skeleton of an ideal diversion system using ECD – a system that contained all the desired properties generated using CEDD up-front.

The desired properties of an ideal diversion system as visioned by professionals and by clients is detailed below in the form of questions and answers. The questions were used to elicit the desired properties. Occasionally text has been placed in brackets, being comments that the group wanted to record but were digressions from the main theme being discussed.

Who should benefit from the system?

- Staff/management response.
  - Mentally disordered offenders.
  - All agencies involved because: this saves cost, makes processing easier, leads to more desirable outcomes and enhances job satisfaction.
  - Public purse will benefit.
  - However, mentally disordered offenders should be the primary beneficiaries.
- Client's response.

- The main beneficiaries should be patients.
- Families should benefit.
- (Local general practitioners should be involved in visiting.)
- Children of clients should benefit.
- Police and judges, social workers, probation officers, community psychiatric nurses should benefit.
- However, people with mental health problems and families should benefit most.

What should the goals of the system be and what should it try to achieve?

- Staff/management response.
  - Divert at the earliest opportunity into more suitable service.
  - Get people out of the criminal justice system.
  - Early identification of problems by one agency.
  - Assessment of need.
  - Production of plan of care and treatment (if appropriate).
  - Need education of professionals involved in mental healthcare.
  - Need adequate quantity of alternatives, especially accommodation.
  - Avoiding oppressive systems – support rather than supervision.
  - Need improved access to existing services.
  - Faster response from medical staff: 'When it is asked for', 'Within 24 hours'.
  - Make agencies and individuals aware of diversion.
  - Training with the police service.
  - Co-operation, particularly with police.
  - Spread the service across Humberside, but not too thinly.
- Client's response.
  - Not enough training or understanding – police need more training in all medical needs.
  - To stop people going into custody.
  - People should be able to meet to discuss issues of custody and diversion.
  - Make more time for people; especially important that the police do this.
  - Not to be kept in custody longer than a mental health patient needs to be.

- Help with employment.
- Raise public awareness.
- Less drugs, more counselling. However, drugs may be the only answer for some people.
- Provision of advocates.
- To be treated as a human being.
- Make sure patients know their rights.
- No one should be in prison with mental health problems.
- More communication between police and general public about their activities.
- More than one policeman should be with a person if they are a danger to themselves.
- Social worker or an appropriate adult should be called when a person is taken into custody.
- Solicitors should not drag cases out. This may need monitoring. There may be a need for a ceiling on salaries that can be earned from dragging cases out.

What should be the measures of success?

- Staff/management response.
  - Numbers of people diverted.
  - Quality of diversion, meaning: incorporating users' views and getting them involved, having a quality process, reduction of reoffences, incorporating different agencies' views and reducing numbers of referrals from solicitors and others.
- Client's response.
  - (Need to evaluate the scale of the problem.)
  - Number of people diverted.
  - Number of people reoffending.
  - Need to know if people have effective follow-up.
  - (Need more family involvement.)
  - (Alternatives: hospital for some; special unit for assessments, but without bars, different units for people with different degrees of mental illness; assessment *with* patients, rather than *of* them.)

Who should be able to change the system? Who ought to be the decision taker?

- Staff/management response.
  - Managers of agencies involved, with project workers and users.
  - No decision making should be unilateral.
- Client's response.
  - Department of Health.
  - Council.
  - Through public involvement.
  - Police.
  - Health service.
  - Social workers.
  - Select committee from public, including people who have been through the system and people from agencies involved.

What resources and limitations should the decision taker have?

- Staff/management response.
  - Central budget from Home Office and Department of Health to be managed by the project. This could provide staff and support. There was some discussion over whether alternatives to custody could be purchased with such a budget.
  - Project could contract directly with purchasing agencies and providers.
  - One constraint is that the project should only deal with mentally disordered offenders, not other people.
- Client's response.
  - Training for patient representatives.
  - Should any agencies be able to say no to being involved? Once committed, they should be made to stay.

Who ought to design the system?

- Staff/management response.
  - All those who were involved at the beginning, plus users through consultative workshop and NACRO.
- Clients' response.
  - Same as staff/management.

Who should be considered an expert and what are their roles?

- Staff/management response.
  - Users.
  - Could say all agencies, but there is no overall expert.
- Client's response.
  - Former patients.
  - Patients themselves.
  - Ex-prisoners.
  - Families.
  - Some disagreement whether psychiatrists should be included. Only one person thought they should.
  - Same again about doctors and nurses, but more people thought they should be included.

Who ought to guarantee that a new system is designed and put in place?

- Staff/management response.
  - Home Office and Department of Health through funding and legislation.
  - Project workers, other individuals and management.
  - Other agencies.
  - Primary responsibility should lie with the Home Office and the Department of Health.
- Client's response.
  - Parliament, in particular the Health Minister.
  - Home Secretary.

Is there anyone who is going to be affected by the system being designed who has not yet been mentioned?

- Staff/management response.
  - Mainstream services will be affected; there may be indirect involvement via representatives of agencies involved.
  - Some families; not to be involved because they are too diverse for representation.
- Client's response.
  - No.

To what extent should people have their fate in their own hands?

- Staff/management response.
  - Whether involvement in diversion is a matter of personal choice depends on extent of mental disorder – a person might not be capable of making an informed decision.
  - Mentally disordered offenders could express a preference if they are properly informed and capable of making a decision.
- Client's response.
  - Patients say that they should have their fate in their own hands as long as they are not a danger to themselves or to the public.
  - However, courts should be able to enforce an alternative to custody whether or not a person wants it if there is an issue of public safety or punishment.

What is the moral basis upon which the system should be based?

- Staff/management response.
  - It is immoral to put someone in prison who is so mentally ill that they are not in control.
  - There is a need for treatment, not punishment or 'rehabilitation of criminal tendencies'.
  - People should not be disadvantaged because they are ill.
- Client's response.
  - People should not be sent to prison for doing a crime if they suffer mental illness.
  - It must help the patient and not make him or her feel worse.
  - An alternative to custody is needed for people with a history of mental illness who cannot help themselves.

Scanning the above analysis soon reveals that there are points of similarity and points of difference. The points of similarity between the client and the professionals are reviewed first. In the vast majority of cases professionals and clients gave the same basic answer. The following issues are worthy of note.

- Clients and professionals were unanimous in agreement that people with mental disorders should be diverted from custody and that no form of custody is ever appropriate for a person with a mental disorder.

- Clients and professionals agreed that there should be secure therapeutic provision as a replacement for custody when there is a need for the public to be protected from people who are a danger to others or themselves.
- Clients and professionals assumed that a diversion system had to be multi-agency.
- Clients and professionals identified the police as a key agency in the system, hence an ideal property of the system would be suitable training for police officers so that they become more aware of the needs of mentally disordered offenders and how to deal with them.
- Clients and professionals identified the Home Office and the Department of Health as key agencies which should ultimately be responsible for ensuring that an adequate system is put in place.

In this case there was broad agreement on some of the most fundamental issues surrounding diversion from custody. Everybody agreed it should happen, that it should be multi-agency, that ultimate responsibility should be governmental and believed that protecting the public does not have to be compromised by finding alternatives to custody. This is important because it suggests that, if these desired properties are actually used as guiding principles of a diversion service, there will not be a perception on the part of the clients that they are being oppressed. This would part way with the usual perception of clients in the mental health services.

Although the majority of the desired properties of a diversion system were the same for both clients and professionals, there were some points of difference to take into account. The main ones are listed below and then discussed.

- Clients explicitly emphasised the need for all parts of the system to treat mentally disordered offenders as human beings. This value was less evident in the list of desired properties produced by the professionals, often remaining implicit in other comments.
- The professionals discussed funding arrangements, looking at

the possibility of the Home Office and the Department of Health providing a budget that could be managed by the project to fund salaries and purchase alternatives to custody. The issue of funding was not discussed at all by clients.
- Clients were concerned about details of the procedures of some agencies, most noticeably the police. Comments made by professionals tended to be much more general.
- Professionals wanted the expertise of all the agencies to be recognised along with the particular expertise brought in by clients, but insisted that there was no overall expert. The clients, however, prioritised expertise.

Each of the above differences is explicable if it is recognised that clients and professionals have a different knowledge base, different experience of criminal justice and different experience of mental health systems.

Most obviously, funding was only discussed by the professionals because they have specialised knowledge about the various possibilities available. Similarly, clients have specialised knowledge about the day-to-day realities of custody, such as the kind of supervision provided when they are in police cells. Clearly it would be useful for both parties to learn from each other. In particular there was a need for clients' knowledge to be included in the ongoing design of the diversion system and to inform the practices of the individual agencies involved.

The fact that clients explicitly emphasised the need for a recognition of their humanity, whilst the professionals left this largely implicit, can also be explained by understanding the different experiences of the two groups. Professionals often have to think freely about how they can balance the need to gear services to individual requirements with the need to provide services for a large number of people. Serving large numbers within a restricted budget means inevitably that systems are created into which people are slotted. The fact that some form of balance has to be struck does not mean that professionals disregard people's humanity, but it does mean that what is or is not defined as dehumanising will often be seen in the context of the wider constraining system in which people work. In this way a practice that is far less than ideal may be considered acceptable in the circumstances.

In contrast, the context in which clients judge what is and what is not dehumanising is largely a function of their direct personal expectations. It is easy for service users to disregard the difficulties of providing a service with limited resources, but it is also easy for professionals to fail to notice just how much individual choice is removed from people when they are provided with services and the depth of outrage this can give rise to. Once again this indicates the need for communication between users and professionals, with users and staff becoming involved together in the planning process in a meaningful way.

Finally, there is the difference over the emphasis placed by the clients of their own expertise over the expertise of others. For the professionals, recognising everybody's expertise was not at all problematic. Indeed, it was necessary given the array of professions and agencies involved in diversion. This was not the case for clients, however. Historically their knowledge has never been regarded as expertise. What the client group did in the workshop was to invert the usual hierarchy of expertise in the mental health system so that psychiatrists (who are normally the principle authority) lost theirs and the service users gained it. They were, however, very clear that this was not a simple reactionary gesture. They said that the psychiatrists had least expertise because they spent least time with the person with the mental health problem. Expertise is said to increase the more time the professional spent in productive communication with the service user. Of course, by this logic the user must be the principle expert because they spend more time with themselves than anyone else. In fact, there was a categorical denial of the value of psychiatric knowledge by all but one of the clients: the pro-psychiatrist exclaimed to his friend, 'But your psychiatrist helped you', to which the response came back, 'I beg your pardon, I helped myself!'

This issue is important because it illustrates that multi-agency collaboration in planning and management, especially when it involves users, will raise serious problematic issues, that is, if there is a genuine attempt to develop the service rather than simply co-ordinate what already exists. Nevertheless, the purpose of bringing people together in multi-agency groups must surely be to tackle just such difficult issues. Without facing thorny problems head-on, and designing ways around them, the practice of multi-agency co-operation is merely notional.

From hereon the problem solving process moved into a phase of idealised design using the method for Exploring and Choosing Designs (ECD). This is fully written up in a report available from the Centre for Systems Studies (see Further Reading).

9.3 CRITICAL REFLECTION MODE

- The Critical Reflection Mode plays an important role in evaluating whether the method(s) chosen was/were most suitable and whether the output of the method(s) was appropriate in the circumstances.
- The aim is to evaluate critically the ongoing process of problem solving.
- The output will be assessment of the suitability of any method or its output in the circumstances; and increased knowledge of the utility of the method.
- There is one main principle of the Critical Reflection Mode – always accept that there may have been a better way of 'doing it'.
- The method raises a set of questions that targets from many positions the question of suitability of method and output of method in the circumstances.

The Critical Reflection Mode makes use of the three general questions, 'How?', 'What?' and 'Why?' These three questions are moulded to enable the problem solver to address two crucial reflective questions.

- Was the most suitable method used in the circumstances?
- Was the output of the method used appropriate in the circumstances?

Each question is moulded into a 'did', 'should', 'could' and 'would' form.

The 'How?' questions are presented first.

- How did the method achieve the output?
- How should the method achieve the output?
- How could the method achieve better output?
- How would another method achieve better output?

The 'What?' questions are as follows.

- What did the method do?
- What should the method do?
- What could the method have done?
- What would another method have done?

And the following are the 'Why?' questions.

- Why did the method achieve the output?
- Why should the method achieve the output?
- Why could the method achieve better output?
- Why would another method achieve better output?

The questions are put together in Table 9.1. This forms a matrix which can be used to review critically the output of the three phases in the Problem Solving Mode. The rows and columns of Table 9.1 address one of the two crucial questions, 'Was the

Table 9.1   *Summary of Critical Reflection Mode of TSI*

'How?' questions	'What?' questions	'Why?' questions	The 3 questions ask if the . . .
How did the method achieve the output?	What did the method do?	Why did the method achieve the output?	Output appropriate?
How should the method achieve the output?	What should the method do?	Why should the method achieve the output?	Output appropriate?
How could the method achieve better output?	What could the method have done?	Why could the method have achieved better results?	Output appropriate?
How would another method achieve better output?	What would another method have done?	Why would another method achieve better results?	Method most suitable?
'How?' questions ask if the output was most appropriate	'What?' questions ask if the method used was the most suitable one.	'Why?' questions ask if the method used was the most suitable one.	

most suitable method used in the circumstances?' or 'Was the output of the method used appropriate in the circumstances?' These results are carefully sifted through. Ultimately, the Critical Reflection Mode questions the adequacy of the output of the Problem Solving Mode and makes the problem solver think very carefully about the result of their efforts. The results of this analysis are passed on to the Creativity phase of TSI where the process of problem solving continues.

9.4 OTHER PROBLEM SOLVING METHODS

There are many more approaches to problem solving not covered in this book. You may currently be using an approach that is working well and will want to run it through the Critical Review Mode of TSI to incorporate it properly in your own system of methods for problem solving. Methods and techniques that I would like to draw your attention to that you may not be familiar with are listed below with a brief commentary. Most of these I use within my system of methods reported in this chapter, but unfortunately do not have space to detail them given that the overriding aim of the book is to develop an appreciation of problem solving as a whole (also see Further Reading).

- *Operational Research.* Operational Research comprises a range of optimisation techniques that are typical of a means-end approach. It emerged as a way of tackling the vast logistical problems that were encountered during World War II. Subsequently, a whole variety of formal quantitative techniques have been developed for use in manufacturing for technical matters such as manufacturing production. Examples of techniques include queuing theory, inventory and stock control, linear programming, etc.
- *The seven tools of quality management.* Ishikawa, a Japanese quality guru, developed an approach to quality management called company-wide quality. In this he wanted everyone to be involved in the process at all levels across all functions. To help them he came up with a set of simple tools that any person can be trained to use. The tools help people to identify

causes of variation and hence aid their eradication. These tools have become known as 'the seven tools' of quality management. The seven tools are given below.

- *Process Control Charts*. Graphs that plot samples of data over time looking for types of variation and assessing whether the process is within acceptable control limits. Useful to discover causes of variation and to grasp the control dynamics.
- *Fishbone diagram*. A fishbone-shaped diagram that uses the cause–effect principle to identify causes of problems. Useful to grasp the causal relationship between cause and effect and to stratify. The Quality Management (QM) example in this chapter uses a fishbone diagram.
- *Scatter diagram*. A graph that compares two sets of data looking for a congenial relationship. Useful to grasp the past and present situation and to ascertain any correlation that exists between the two data. The Quality Management (QM) example in this chapter uses the scatter diagram technique.
- *Pareto diagrams*. Using data to rank problems according to their size and importance. Useful to help grasp the problem, the past and present situation, to stratify and to confirm the improvement results.
- *Tally sheets*. A table or diagram used to analyse data and to surface important questions to be addressed. Useful to help grasp the past and present situation, to stratify, to monitor changes over time, to demonstrate results and confirm standards.
- *Histogram*. A columnar graph that plots data looking at frequency of occurrence. Useful to grasp the past and present situation, to stratify and to confirm improvement results.
- *Pie charts*. Recording information about control and improvement in a pie-shaped diagram that shows proportions. Useful when analysing causes and to make comparative assessment of data.

• *Just In Time (JIT)*. JIT emerged after World War II in Toyota's production system. In the 1970s JIT spread throughout Japanese manufacturing and in the 1980s began to influence Western practices. JIT is an integrated systems approach to optimising the use of company resources based on the goal of continual elimination of waste and consistent improvement in productivity.

- *Supplier Development Strategies.* Supplier Development Strategies, or 'comakership', is another approach linked in to Quality Management (QM). Supplier development means bringing together organisational members and their suppliers to pursue a common goal. It means establishing long-term business partnerships with selected suppliers. It is based on the principle that suppliers and clients can gain more benefit through co-operation rather than pursuing their own interests separately.
- *ISO 9000.* ISO 9000 is a general standard that applies to a broad range of businesses and organisations. It is in a sense a seal of approval that is given by an independent authority. It is not a product-specific standard, but a management system standard. The aim is to achieve consistency in processes. This necessarily involves all functions and departments. Documentation required for accreditation places emphasis on organisational structure and employee participation. Manuals have to be prepared that document the way the processes work and these are carefully audited against the actual operations before the award is given.
- *System Dynamics.* System Dynamics is a theory of information feedback and control as a means of evaluating business and other organisational and social contexts. It is argued that any situation can be considered as complex, but mainly in terms of elements and flows; flows being the relationship between elements. All influential elements must be included in a boundary. Connecting elements may form loops and hence feedback analysis is considered very important. Analysis using these ideas is along a closed sequence of causes and effects, a closed path of action and information.
- *Cognitive Mapping.* Cognitive Mapping is a method for problem structuring based on a theory of cognition that focuses on human beings as problem solvers. It is a theory relevant to model building for problem solving. It seeks to portray the way in which problem owners are making sense of their situation. It aims to set out their explanations for why the situation is as they construe it and why it matters to them. A cognitive map is designed to help depict the structure of a problem. It is a representation of the way in which a client believes a situation has come about and why it is problematic.
- *Project Planning.* Project Planning is a technique that helps to

organise large numbers of activities in an efficient way. It identifies which activities follow which other ones and in this process also finds out which ones can be run in parallel, thus saving time. A project flow diagram is produced. Its use can be extended to calculation of optimal resource use.

9.5 ENDNOTE

This chapter presents a system of methods that operationalise the three modes of TSI. Throughout the chapter cases have been given that illustrate individual methods. In the next chapter, the emphasis remains on practical utilisation, but the theme is all about how the process of TSI has been used by practitioners. There are nine cases employing TSI in the following chapter. Each one is written by either the managers or consultants who carried out the work. Let us now find out what they have to say about TSI.

10
Nine Cases Employing TSI, Written by Managers and Consultants – 'An International Perspective'

The previous chapters document the philosophy, principles and methods of the problem solving system TSI. What is happening when you problem solve with TSI and pitfalls to avoid have also been covered. Now it is time to hand the whole thing over to practitioners to give them a chance to tell us what use they have made of TSI in their working lives.

There are nine cases in this chapter written by managers and consultants. The cases are not step-by-step accounts of how methods were used. This type of account has been given in Chapter 9 alongside the presentation of the methods themselves. The aim of the cases in this chapter is different. The cases are discussions about the merit and scope for use of the problem solving system TSI focusing mainly on the process.

Each case has original content of value and worth that you will want to extract. You will find that they substantiate the ideas that I have been pressing home in this book, although honest reflections are included that point to difficulties the authors encountered. You will learn much more about the extent to which the problem solving system can help you. So, let me hand the book over to managers and consultants. You and I will meet up again at the end of this chapter when I consolidate the findings in an overview of the nine cases (although I do provide a brief background to each case).

Case 10.1
Normet Pty Ltd (Australia and Asia) (Finalist, Western Australian Best New Exporter Award, 1991)

PHIL HEARSE, MANAGING DIRECTOR
(Finalist, Western Australian Individual Export Achievement Award, 1991)

Focus: Strategic Management – planning the future.

Methods discussed: Metaphors, Exploring and Choosing Designs (ECD), Diagnosis for Effective Organisation (DEO), Implementing Designs and Decisions (IDD), Quality Management (QM).

BACKGROUND TO THE WRITER AND ORGANISATION

Phil Hearse is a metallurgist. He commenced his career in the mining industry at Broken Hill in Australia before moving on to the large Bougainville Island copper project in Papua New Guinea, where he worked for five years. He returned to Australia and worked in the nickel and alumina industries and then joined the Northern Territory Department of Mines and Energy.

In 1984 he launched the metallurgical services company Normet Pty Ltd to provide operations consultancy services to the mining industry. Phil has pushed Normet into Asia where the company has a laboratory base in Indonesia, Malaysia and Thailand. The company, of which Phil is the managing director, is now the largest metallurgical consultancy in Australia. Phil's key responsibilities are marketing and strategic management, but he still takes on some project management and consultancy roles.

The privately owned Australian company Normet Pty Ltd operates within the metallurgical services sector of the mining industry. Like so many companies, Normet grew from a one-person business providing a niche service, in this case the provision of on-site contract metallurgical services. From origins in 1984, the company expanded rapidly until by 1989 it had four metallurgical testing laboratories and consultancies within Australia and two overseas bases in Indonesia and Malaysia. The major services provided by Normet at that time were

- on-site metallurgical contract services
- metallurgical consultancy services
- project feasibility studies
- metallurgical process route testing services.

The company had a staffing of 50 people and was turning over US$4 million in consultancy fees. The family founders retained majority equity, with growth being financed through a combination of debt and equity funding.

In 1990, after a boom period particularly within the gold industry, the Australian economy began a rapid and hugely damaging economic decline. At the same time one of Normet's major off-shore projects wound up. Normet found itself in a threatening position of excessive debt funding in a declining market. The company was ill-prepared for this totally new business context, one which its members had not previously experienced. The case study begins from here, but an indication that there was successful management of this crisis is marked in Phil's personal achievement, being finalist, Western Australian Individual Export Achievement Award (1991); and Normet being finalist, Western Australian Best New Exporter Award (1991).

INTRODUCTION

There are many vital factors essential to effective management of companies. Some are aimed at maintaining and enhancing short-term viability, whilst others concentrate on long-term viability. The essence of strategic management in my book is to have the ability to recognise and anticipate changes occurring within our industries and to have the ability to respond to them. There are three possible forms of response.

- To react to unforeseen changes.
- To predict changes and prepare for them.
- To induce change in Normet and the industry – to plan their future and set the ground rules.

The last is by far the most desirable of the forms of response. So, how can we prepare strategies that plan the future?

There are many books and courses written on strategic management as well as numerous consultants always keen to help practitioners plan strategies, at a cost. However, what many of these aids fail to address is the individuality of our organisations and industries, and how different corporate cultures need their own relevant ways of getting to grips with problems encountered in planning the future. The aids are not sufficiently diverse to deal with the complexities that practitioners face. I have found that the problem solving system TSI presented in this book stands out from others in the way it directs practitioners to deal with the complexities faced and further encourages thinking about dimensions of organisation that are often neglected but ultimately must be managed.

I have written this case from the perspective of an owner/operator of a technologically based service organisation in the mining industry. The case study shows how TSI has been applied to conceptualise Normet in terms of systems thinking and how this individualises the organisation, setting the stage for the application of highly relevant problem solving methods to assist with strategic planning. The outcome of Normet's use of TSI is broadly reviewed in terms of the theme of Chapter 6 'What is Happening When You Problem Solve'. The effectiveness of the chosen methods is also reflected upon.

THE STUDY

As seen in Normet's history sketched out above, in 1990 we faced a massive uphill struggle to put the company back on a firm footing and stake ownership as the leading company in our field in Australia. Our strategies had to change to corporate survival initially. We applied strategies aimed at cost containment and debt reduction. Normet is now debt free. Over the next year or so Normet pulled through the short-term problems of financial viability and increasingly concentrated on strategies aimed at controlled corporate growth. The adoption of Quality Management (QM) principles at this time profoundly affected the way the company managed itself and its clients. QM remains an integral part of Normet's *modus operandi* today and has more recently taken the form of QM as described by Professor Flood in Chapter 9. TSI has been used extensively in the strategic planning process as discussed later.

Significant developments that have taken place over the last few years include the introduction of additional equity holders into the laboratory side of Normet. This has significantly boosted our technical expertise. Also, a strategic alliance has been established, forming a tripartite Australian/French/USA link for the application and marketing of internationally developed metallurgical software to the Australian and Asian mining industries. Normet now employs 33 people, including 18 metallurgists, and turns over US$3.5 million per annum.

So, as you see, Normet has suffered from the sort of problems that many small growing companies face. I feel sure that many readers of this book will identify with this history and will have experienced similar problems. Many will have been forced to make dramatic changes like Normet.

The main point of this case study, though, is to demonstrate how a business person can use TSI, a systems approach, to understand its problems well and to overcome them by choosing relevant methods to tackle them. The case concentrates on Normet's strategic planning efforts in 1994 where TSI was used extensively. The aim was to determine a strategic direction for the next two to five years. The efforts began using TSI's Creativity phase.

A systemic description of Normet was developed as follows. Normet employs mainly professional personnel who are expected to work autonomously. Control is spread throughout the organisation. Decisions are made by the people most familiar with the kinds of problem faced, which normally means by the people as they encounter them. Normet is open to its operational environment, but we are particularly keen that, through innovative management, it can influence and on occasions control this environment.

The organisation is therefore organic in nature. The high level of uncertainty in its environment means that internal organisation must be intelligent and creative, able to foresee and even create the future. It is an intelligent system.

The culture is one of professionalism. On the whole people work well together forming a cohesive system pursuing shared goals. These goals include Normet's overall mission and so there is organisational integrity. Rarely do political dynamics surface as prevalent. As far as possible power is shared and does not surface as a main issue.

In some senses Normet operates with a family spirit. The mood and atmosphere is co-operative and very positive. For example, on Friday evening people start to congregate in the board room for beers and other end-of-week refreshments. Clients are encouraged to come along too. There is a happy feeling generated and a sense of achievement. Staff and clients talk openly about how they feel the company is progressing and concerns are heard and dealt with. The staff also socialise frequently out of work.

A metaphorical description that captures well the essence of Normet is, an intelligent organism with a strong culture of co-operation. This image can be further understood in terms of needs to be met in the strategic planning exercise undertaken in 1994. In one sense the following narration amounts to the most plausible explanation of the needs of the organisation, a slightly different tack to creative thinking with metaphors to surface problems than was recommended in the main text of this book.

The needs of Normet to be taken into account during the strategic planning exercise based on the above analysis were judged to be fourfold.

- The environment is extremely turbulent, therefore new goals and objectives need to be generated, and on a continuing basis.
- Human needs must be considered to ensure effective organisational development, particularly with the continuing implementation of QM which is an integral part of Normet's culture. All aspects of organisational development including strategic planning need to encourage participation to ensure successful implementation. A mechanistic, autocratic approach and management style would raise huge barriers across the organisation and severely constrain organisational development.
- The organisational-enterprise is a consultancy company that needs to have capabilities for rapid learning which further stresses the need for a locally autonomous structure.
- The company is relatively small in terms of number of employees at the offices in Perth, Australia, and has an informal atmosphere that needs to be maintained.

In short, Normet must be intelligent and capable of rapid learning, which can only be achieved through participation and local autonomy, in an informal environment. The problem was to connect these characteristics together. The features were loosely there, but we wanted to take a systemic approach and build them all into one carefully thought through coherent strategy. We needed to choose an approach to strategic planning that was relevant to these needs.

The process of choice of method was guided by TSI. We saw the main purposes of our problem solving being twofold.

- *How* to come up with an effective organisational design for strategic management.
- To debate the issues associated with strategic planning and choose *what* to do.

Three methods in TSI's system of methods as reported in this book seemed relevant. An effective organisational design could be pursued using Diagnosis for Effective Organisation (DEO). Exploring and Choosing Designs (ECD) would enable people to participate in the process and Implementing Designs and Decisions (IDD) would enable us to implement the new strategy.

The close relationship between ECD and DEO in the context of Normet's problem solving exercise led us to derive an integrated version of the methods for strategic planning and management. The approach that we adopted is shown in Figure 10.1.1. Practitioners of strategic management can see that in some respects it resembles conventional strategic management methods (indeed we took these into account during the strategic review, e.g., Porter's analysis and business cycles – see Further Reading), but the process is dominated by the main stages of DEO, ECD and IDD. Key differences include idealised design to conceive of the organisation and its strategy, the Viable System Model to design an organisation that can achieve the strategy and IDD to implement the organisation and its strategy. I shall concentrate discussion on the value and process of ECD and DEO in the remainder of this case. Details of the methods and their use can be found in Chapter 9.

The questions that Normet needed to answer were 'What?' strategies we should implement and 'How?' we should go about that implementation. The question of 'Why?' we should go about strategic planning and the concern over whose interests will be served were not judged to be the most relevant questions by Normet's staff (except for wider issues such as environmental concerns that are always on our agenda). Sure, differences of opinion surfaced between participants involved, but this occurred within a spirit of co-operation and pulling together. ECD therefore was able to nourish creative thinking through open and meaningful debate about 'What?' we should do.

ECD helped people to disregard constraints, mainly about feasibility, that might otherwise have prevented creative thinking. It encouraged reflection that challenged core management beliefs. It also helped produce a 'big picture' of Normet. All in all it lead to systemic thinking.

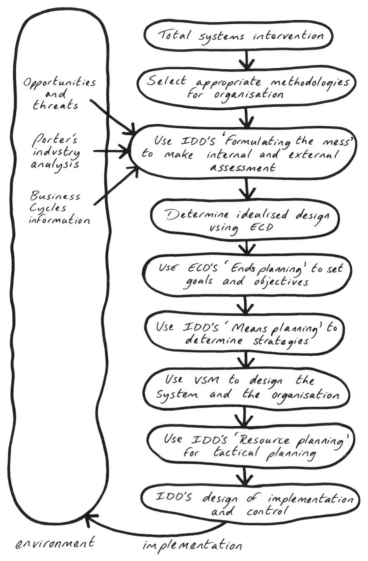

Total systems intervention

Select appropriate methodologies for organisation

Use IDD's 'Formulating the mess' to make internal and external assessment

Determine idealised design using ECD

Use ECD's 'Ends planning' to set goals and objectives

Use IDD's 'Means planning' to determine strategies

Use VSM to design the system and the organisation

Use IDD's 'Resource planning' for tactical planning

IDD's design of implementation and control

Opportunities and threats

Porter's industry analysis

Business Cycles information

environment   implementation

Figure 10.1.1   *Normet's systems model for strategic planning*

A number of important strategies consequently surfaced. We decided that Normet needed to adopt strategies that developed specialist skills which are valuable to our clients. We decided to be different from our competitors as a matter of policy – our integrated approach with the laboratory group, our commitment to quality principles and our commitment to international marketing already differentiate us, but we wanted to go further. The following new strategies were chosen.

- Implementation of control modelling software.
- Further development of iron ore support services.
- Working towards strategic alliances thus growing our number of specialist services.
- Running training courses and generally moving into the educational arena.
- Offering project management for small-scale activities.
- Seeking site operations contracts.
- Providing environmental services to Asia.

Thus a suite of strategies was surfaced for Normet to implement. A resource allocation and responsibility/accountability plan was prepared to ensure that implementation would proceed. Implementation of the strategies commenced immediately after the planning work was complete. Within three months most of the strategies had been refined, expanded, elaborated and a few were chopped.

The debating part of the process of ECD that led to these outputs mainly encouraged learning about the company. ECD also helped to develop ownership over strategies since people participated in the process. The strategies were to a large extent their own. People saw the need for new directions, such as projecting a more technological image. The process of planning was probably of greater value to the participants than the strategies themselves.

Following on from debate, the emphasis shifted to the question of 'How?' the strategies could be implemented and 'How?' the organisation could be (re)designed to accommodate for these changes. The process of design was led by DEO incorporating the Viable System Model. DEO proved very effective in deriving a design and allowing participants to gain an understanding of the essential requirements for effective organisation. You may remember that the model organises five key management functions: implementation, co-ordination, control, intelligence and policy.

Implementation is what the organisation is actually doing. For Normet the main divisions relate to types of project work. There is extensive interaction here with our clients. The divisions are where all of our income is generated and so must be well served by the other management functions. *Co-ordination* is vital so that our resources are effectively deployed, people know what is going on and conflict is kept to a minimum. Co-ordination of on-site projects is a most crucial part of our activities although we found through DEO analysis that it was badly neglected.

Control and audit for us ensure that the activities of implementation do not diverge from the overall mission and identity of Normet. This is largely achieved through informal group discussions. A formal system has also been put in place in the form of a weekly meeting. Information used to assist in this control and audit function is provided in the form of monthly profit and loss figures and monitoring and comparison of budgets, with divisions being cost centres. Now, through quality audit, information on quality performance is reviewed and controlled. Information from intelligence gathering also comes to the weekly management meeting, which means that this meeting considers policy as well as control. Such an eventuality is quite proper and likely to occur in small organisations.

Intelligence gathering is fulfilled by all personnel. Everyone gains knowledge about events and activities, internal or external, that may affect Normet. Everyone therefore is tasked to pass on this information. This happens informally and at the weekly management meeting.

Policy is driven by the executive directors and, as made clear in this case study, strongly supplemented from all personnel. As strategy tends in practice to happen incrementally as well as through planning exercises, it is particularly important to ensure everyone is thinking about strategy. This is strongly encouraged. The Friday night sessions are one way people can pass on their thoughts.

A number of systems were also established that put in place procedures to complement those already existing, in line with our quality philosophy, to operate the design.

- An overall organisational system.
- A marketing system.
- A personnel and staff development system.
- A financial targets system.

Together with organisational design, these systems completed the overall design needs of Normet. The output had produced an effective organisational design ideal for the future. The process increased participants' awareness of the need for this ideal design and their involvement developed ownership of the management systems that were introduced.

REFLECTIONS

Taking on a corporate strategic planning exercise is a major and time-consuming project at the best of times. Introducing methods like ECD significantly increased the time involved. To have followed the method closely including IDD requires a huge time commitment which is testing for a smaller company with limited resources. It was therefore necessary to modify the methods used so that the resources of the company were never stretched too far. However, I believe that this is consistent with the idea of TSI that wants users to work out a system of methods most suitable to them and their organisational context. This respects individuality of organisations.

We believe the time spent in the strategic planning exercise was a great investment. First of all the planning resulted in the recommendation of clear strategies to be pursued. These will enhance the group's distinctive competencies and encourage further innovative thinking laying a platform for future change. The work also resulted in the design of an organisational structure that facilitates the group's ability to increase performance; a number of new organisational systems and processes were designed within the QM approach Normet implemented some time ago.

Furthermore, the planning process was enlightening for the participants. It has formed an excellent basis for the next stages of detailed planning, resource allocation and implementation of the selected strategies. Although the process was more time consuming than a conventional strategic planning process, it delivered far more – in terms of depth of information, exposition of core weaknesses and fundamental understanding of the organisation.

One difficulty that we encountered was achieving TSI's principle of participation. The participative principle is important but can be difficult to incorporate in all aspects of the planning process. The practical realities are that work commitments of certain employees, perhaps peaking at the time of the planning exercise, may force them to have a limited involvement. In this case their ideas need to be gathered informally and represented at strategy meetings. Indeed, all types of stakeholder must be at least represented in this way.

There are particular features of the methods used that I want to comment on.

- Systems analysis in IDD helped people to think about the organisation in a manner conventional strategic planning methodologies do not. It produced a big picture.
- Obstructions analysis in IDD helped to determine weaknesses in the organisation that would not have been raised by a traditional strengths and weaknesses analysis – in particular, when the discussion raised differences between what the organisation believed was happening and what was actually happening. This brought out weaknesses in both our marketing and our commitment to QM. It is doubtful that these more sensitive issues, which reflect core management beliefs in itself, would have surfaced if we had directly asked what are the weaknesses.
- Idealised design in ECD proved wonderful to work with. The process shed at least some of the participants' prejudices about their views of the world and in this injected creativity into the planning process. In addition, the concept of a strategic plan filling the gap between the future as it currently exists and the idealised future cemented the purpose of strategic planning into participants' minds.
- The Viable System Model in DEO proved particularly powerful at revealing the key systems required for effective organisation and facilitated the process whereby personnel recognised the importance of those requirements. It is a great tool for explaining organisation and can readily be understood and used by managers.
- The Viable System Model in DEO introduces and explains systems that are lacking in many organisations. Its application to Normet's consulting group has confirmed the need for the

five main management functions integral to the DEO method. It made participants in the planning exercise aware of these key needs for effective organisation and has strengthened the management principles of autonomy and control spread throughout the organisation.

- The Viable System Model in DEO has glaringly shown up shortcomings in co-ordination between Normet's consulting and laboratory groups. This came through when looking at the operations at different levels as the method for DEO recommends. This vertical understanding of the organisation turned out to be crucial in the successful implementation of our suite of strategies.
- The principles of DEO also proved particularly useful in specifying the desired properties of the consulting group within the ECD part of the planning exercise. Most of the desired properties for the organisation itself emanated from DEO's principles.

In conclusion, what overall recommendations can I pass on to practitioners wanting to use TSI in strategic planning? There are perhaps four main ones.

- Give yourself a generous time allowance if you are going for a major strategic planning exercise using TSI. If you are topping up your plans then an abridged version will take much less time, but still can be rewarding. In any case, be sure to plan your planning and take a project management approach as a first stage of preparing for the strategic planning exercise (see Further Reading).
- Whenever practicable, I would encourage managers to learn about the methods and actually use them, with minimal use of consultants. This will enhance knowledge about the technical side of the organisation and the industry and the culture of the people, which will prove advantageous in managing a planning exercise.
- In line with systems thinking, take all aspects of organisation into account when undertaking a strategic planning exercise. Get out among your clients, both before and after the main strategic work, to see what their needs are. You will learn a lot from them that will help in the preparation of your own

strategic plans, for example making sure that you will be proceeding in the same technological directions. Research current trends in your industry as part of the work.

- And finally, do not set your plans in concrete. Be prepared to flex around them as you learn more after implementation of the plans.

Perhaps my overall message of the need for rigorous strategic planning is reflected in a comment made to me by a colleague, Mark Miller, a mining man of many years, when after several beers in a bar in Jakarta he confessed, 'Phil, the longer I'm in this business the more confused I get by it.'

Case 10.2
Sintech Construction Pty Ltd and Nakamaya Corporation (Singapore and Japan)

CHOW KOK FONG, DIRECTOR OF PROJECTS

Focus: Human dimension of establishing an international joint venture.

Methods discussed: Metaphors, Diagnosis for Effective Organisation (DEO), Exploring and Choosing Designs (ECD), Exploring and Making Decisions (EMD), Operational Research (OR).

BACKGROUND TO THE WRITER AND THE PARTNERS

Chow Kok Fong is the Director of Projects with City Developments Ltd in Singapore, responsible for a real estate project portfolio of more than US$3 billion. He is concurrently Vice Chairman of Acropol Johnson Controls, a leading facilities management contractor in Singapore. Prior to this he established the Construction Industry Development Board where he subsequently served as chief executive. At the CIDB he was credited with launching several initiatives to raise the level of cost competitiveness and quality in the construction industry. He has served as an arbitrator on international construction disputes and is a fellow of the Chartered Institute of Arbitrators. He is consulted by the World Bank as a construction industry specialist. Kok Fong is an Associate Professor with the Centre for Advanced Construction Studies at Nanyang Technological University. He is author of four books including *Construction Joint Ventures,* and *Construction Contract Claims* which is now in its second edition.

(A pseudonym is used for the partners in this case study to maintain confidentiality as requested.) Sintech Construction Pty Ltd was founded in 1947 in Singapore by Richard Cheng's father as a small jobbing contractor. It grew steadily and went into housing construction in 1955. A significant turning point for the firm was the launch of a major public housing initiative by the Housing Development Board (HDB) during the late 1960s and 1970s. These programmes enabled the firm's turnover to grow dramatically from Sing$600,000 in 1969 to Sing$19 million in 1977.

Richard Cheng worked for several years with an engineering design firm before joining the family business in 1979. In 1983, Richard assumed the mantle as managing director and changed the name of the company to Sintech Construction Pty Ltd. In that year, the company secured more than Sing$80 million of HDB work and another Sing$30 million of orders from other government departments and the private sector. Private sector work was to become an increasingly important source of revenue as the volume of HDB construction tapered off during the latter part of the 1980s. By the end of 1992, the company had an order book of Sing$260 million, consisting of an assortment of HDB, government and private sector work.

The bulk of Sintech's work is secured through direct contracting. Between 30% and 40% of the work is subcontracted from established names. Sintech normally pays a 'finder's commission' for such work, amounting to between 1% and 2% of the price. On the whole, the margins made on work secured through direct contracting average between 5% and 7%. In the case of work sourced from other general contractors, what remains after deducting the finder's commission is commonly between 3% and 4%. While the latter represents a barely adequate cover for the risks inherent in construction projects,

Richard felt that strategically he had to generate a sufficient volume of work to enable him to retain a basic technical support infrastructure and develop sufficient bargaining clout with his suppliers and subcontractors.

Nakamaya Corporation was founded in 1865 in Osaka. In 1992, it had a turnover of US$1.45 billion. Overseas work typically accounted for 9% of turnover. The company's reputation had been largely built on its civil engineering construction work, particularly in long span bridges, deep foundations and petroleum facilities. Consequently, Nakamaya's overseas work has been mainly confined to projects of large Japanese corporations and those funded by the Japanese government and bodies such as the World Bank and the Asian Development Bank (ADB).

INTRODUCTION

In September 1992, a scandal involving two of Nakamaya's top officials, coupled with a depressed domestic economy, threatened to reduce their volume of infrastructure work at home. Abroad, increasing competition from Korean, Taiwanese, European and US contractors has made it more difficult to secure work through competitive bidding. At the same time, project spending by the major oil concerns had been cut back considerably following the global slowdown in oil consumption growth. Simultaneously agencies such as the World Bank and the ADB reduced the financing of large infrastructure projects. As a consequence, Nakamaya's turnover from these operations shrunk by more than 45% between the 1988 and 1993.

Recently, the company decided, as a corporate strategy, to diversify into building construction overseas and that this would be best undertaken through strategic alliances in key overseas markets. An opportunity for developing a toe-hold in Singapore emerged when Kurosawa Fudosan decided to take a 40% interest in the development of the 660-room Reichman Hotel. Kurosawa Gumi is a large conglomerate with extensive investment and trading activities around the world. Nakamaya had a strong business relationship with Kurosawa Fudosan going back more than 40 years.

In January 1993, Toshiyo Suzuki, the Vice-President for International Operations, visited Singapore with a team of officials and reported favourably on the business environment in Singapore. The team was confident that Nakamaya could tap Kurosawa's goodwill to swing the project their way so long as Nakamaya's bid was not unduly excessive. They were further encouraged by the fact that of the seven banks lined up to finance the development of the project, five were Japanese banks which are likely to prefer the participation of a Japanese contractor such as Nakamaya. However, the team noted the tight labour market in Singapore and the fact that a considerable proportion of the work had to be carried out by local subcontractors. A Singapore partner was thus considered highly desirable.

After studying seven potential joint venture candidates, Suzuki's team closed in on Sintech Construction. They were introduced to Richard Cheng by Mr Akiro Sasaki, Singapore General Manager of the Japanese Credit Bank, and Mr Fumio Hasewaga, the Japanese Ambassador in Singapore. Mr Sasaki had known the Cheng family well through the business which the Japan Credit Bank had done with Sintech in the past.

In the weeks that followed the proposal was discussed, debated and refined before a formal commitment was made by both parties to the joint venture. Whilst the joint venture negotiators on both sides applied the usual array of financial management tools in evaluating prospects, Richard Cheng felt that these could not deal adequately with the strategic and organisational implications of the proposal. I have known Richard Cheng for 14 years, initially as a colleague and subsequently as a confidant. Richard invited me to facilitate an evaluation exercise, mainly because of the array of human perspectives which had to be considered. This case study describes how the process and methods of TSI were invoked to enrich the assessment of these perspectives and the formulation of the organisational response.

THE STUDY

Joint ventures are essentially corporate marriages. Each party to a joint venture has to ensure that the financial and operational attributes of the participating partners are compatible with its corporate attributes and agenda. It is necessary, in particular, to consider organisational fit and the strategic dimensions of the proposed joint venture from a myriad of behavioural and cultural perspectives. Whilst much of conventional management literature deals with management accounting and other financial analytical tools to assess the risk and return of such a venture, the human perspectives are seldom addressed. Yet these issues are crucial to the operational efficiency if not the very viability of most joint ventures – especially when there is an international dimension. Parties from such diverse backgrounds can be easily instigated into mistrust and suspicion because cultural expectations, mutual respect and consequently effective communications are not addressed properly. Human issues deserve to be identified and evaluated thoroughly.

Thus, the concepts of TSI were applied firstly to assess the organisational traits which each of the parties is likely to bring to the joint venture and hence fashion their expectations. This stage may be appropriately described as image generation in TSI terminology. The second major aspect where TSI methods were applied is in the conception of what the resulting organisation should be like if the joint venture were to proceed and if it were to attain the qualities of viability and integrity. A wide range of plausible solutions was generated and the means (resources) to proceed were fashioned.

A total of 14 sessions was held between the writer and seven of the senior managers of Sintech. During these sessions, the writer provided an overview of TSI, introduced some of the concepts and facilitated the working sessions which applied these concepts to the subject case study. Some of the ideas generated through these deliberations were raised with Suzuki. A number of them were factored into the final proposal submitted eventually for Richard Cheng's formal response.

The process began with creative thinking using image generation. Metaphors were used to provide a snapshot of characteristics of the organisations. The use of metaphors facilitated recognition of those cultural and behavioural differences between organisations which may affect their compatibility as partners in a joint venture situation. This was vital. The process employed to identify the appropriate systemic metaphors to

describe each organisation is summarised in Figure 10.2.1. Basi-
cally, it involved a study of each company's organisational
traits. Each metaphor was used to guide thought until the dominant metaphor or a group of metaphors describing adequately
the subject organisation was identified. The results of this process are recorded in the table starting with Sintech.

Despite the volume of its business, Sintech Construction was
still very much an *evolving organisation* at the time of this study.
The company was in the process of formulating new organisational norms and procedures, brought about by Richard
Cheng's installation as the chief executive officer. Richard felt
the need to modernise and place the company on an efficient
footing. However, he was patient and wanted to learn and
understand the operations set up by his father. Both the general
manager and the financial controller had helped the transfer of
authority within the company to Richard from his father.

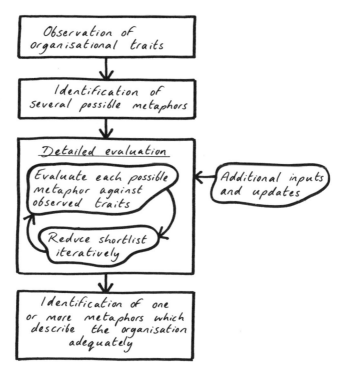

Figure 10.2.1   *Routine used by Sintech for the identification of systemic
metaphors for the Creativity phase of TSI*

Together they provided the continuity in the company's dealings with employees and various external parties. This is important in a setting like Singapore where the extent of credit and financial facilities depended significantly on the length of personal acquaintance and reputation. Indeed, the company's traditional source of strength stemmed substantially from its relationships with the company's subcontractors and suppliers as well as the major Japanese construction firms which periodically passed surplus work to Sintech.

Accordingly, despite the focus of decision-making authority in a small handful of individuals, the organisation of Sintech was not *a mechanistic or closed system*. It was useful to see Sintech's organisation as *a viable system with a strong cultural bias*, in the sense that it was not conditioned by rigid institutionalisation of procedures and processes. Each one of the three key players in the company – Richard, the general manager and the financial controller – was responsible for several areas. They were not organisational personalities operating only within narrow functional specialisations. All three might be expected to be versatile and know the market terrain well. They were clearly motivated by the fact that they had grown up with the firm and hence formed a strong sense of identification with it. The same *cultural flavour* extended to relationships between Sintech and its various subcontractors and suppliers. These long-standing relationships operated on trust, a spirit of 'give and take' and a history of mutual support, the essence of which may not be readily captured through formal obligations set out in written contracts. Indeed, Sintech's *culture* was probably a critical factor in leading Nakamaya to view it as a prospective joint venture partner. Consequently, an important task was to ensure that any proposed organisational change did not undermine these relationships.

Nakamaya was different. Given its 130-year history, the management style and corporate institutions of the Nakamaya Corporation were well-matured systems. The corporate headquarters in Osaka directed all strategic moves and approved key decisions. The organisation was characterised by a structure set up with well-defined tasks associated with each corporate appointment. Its management ranks consisted principally of long-serving career corporate officers, punctuated by a few highfliers such as Toshiyo Suzuki. The overall culture, like most of the large Japanese corporations, was thus not different from that of government institutions, being *mechanistic and strictly controlled*.

Suzuki had to establish his mantle in his current appointment without appearing to threaten his immediate superior, or any of the other senior executives overseeing the politically more important domestic markets. Although there was some consensus among the management ranks of the importance of the international operations, it is equally clear that the heads of the large domestic divisions overseeing Tokyo and Osaka respectively are positioned higher up in the company's hierarchy. As a career salary man Suzuki had to be also conscious of the unmistakable overlay of exacting *cultural norms* requiring him not to appear to accumulate all the credit for any successful venture for himself. He had to build up a support base within the organisation and this could only be done by drawing people into what were perceived to be successful projects. Officials further down the line would have similar concerns and, indeed, their actions would be influenced by similar *political considerations* at their respective levels in the overall corporate hierarchy. Hence, the dominant characterisation of the Nakamaya Corporation to be taken into account in the joint venture was that of a well-established *political system*.

The practical implications from Sintech's vantage were these.

- The priorities of Suzuki and his subordinates would focus initially on decisions which could generate an immediate impact on their corporate score card in Osaka. They would be expected therefore to push for the Reichman contract even if the margins were very thin in order to enable a large order to be registered quickly at home. The peer pressures to secure orders would be so great, therefore, that profitability might be sacrificed in bids for particularly prestigious projects.
- In common with most political systems, no component would be permitted to shine too visibly *vis-à-vis* the remaining components. Hence, if the international operations department became too successful too quickly, it might be expected to spawn internal dissension and jealousies.
- Sintech had to respect the system of checks and balances

which a large, institutionalised organisation would bring to bear on their operations. Sintech had to cultivate more than just Suzuki's team within the Nakamaya Corporation. It was important, for example, to appreciate the workings of the domestic operational departments including financial procedures because these might be called upon to support the project at board level and possibly to provide crucial technical services at some stage of the project.

Based on the assessment of the Creativity phase, the choice of the methodology for formulating the joint venture organisation was made. At the outset it was accepted that two very different sets of organisational values would be drawn together in the proposed joint venture: the controlled family culture flavour of Sintech with the political characteristics of the organisational institutions in Nakamaya. Whilst each would seek to dominate over the other, the broader interests of the joint venture suggest that this would be both unnecessary and undesirable. At the same time, it was felt that the resulting joint venture entity should not be determined merely by technical considerations and methods. Instead, given the strong flavour of culture and political metaphor in the description of the subject organisations, it was considered by Sintech's management team that an appropriate approach would be a planning process which is sufficiently rigorous to address the marriage of human elements and the technical process.

The search for a method was undertaken through a series of brainstorming exercises in the working sessions. By the fourth session of the 14 working sessions, it was decided that Exploring and Choosing Designs (ECD) should be applied as the principal chain of thought. It was by no means a clear-cut choice, but there was unanimity in pursuing the idea that this should be used as a debating construct on which other ideas were to be posited.

The possible contributions from other systems methods were not ignored. For instance, as discussed later on, the team efforts to build up understanding between the parties through forums for meaningful debate and other measures are ideas which were extensively borrowed from Exploring and Making Decisions (EMD). Similarly, it was considered that whilst the concerns for organisational integrity and viability are valid, they should never obscure the panoply of cultural, team-building and behavioural considerations underlying the organisational characteristics of the two joint venture parties. Nevertheless, the dimensions of command and control and the need for real time information through audit are contributions from the Viable System Model (VSM) employed through Diagnosis for Effective Organisation (DEO) which were considered important by the taskforce.

In addition, it was felt that the recursive character of the entire approach should be fully exploited. The Sintech management recognised that the matter was never going to be settled by an optimal technical solution. Instead, it was envisaged that the basic ideas and proposals had to evolve progressively through review, refinement and debate. New ideas and lessons learnt during the practice of working with the organisational arrangements would be expected to contribute to this review and refinement process just as the TSI process suggests.   The idea was that ECD would be used as a starting point. This would focus on an idealised design of the joint venture. After signing a memorandum of understanding, a group of senior corporate officers from Sintech went through the elements of an idealised design and explored these ideas with their Nakamaya counterparts through a series of informal meetings. The results were translated into a draft mission statement and placed before a meeting attended by both Cheng and Suzuki. After further deliberations and refinement a mission statement of the joint venture was adopted

> To provide a basis through which Sintech Construction Pty Ltd and Nakamaya Corporation could pool their expertise and resources to develop an organisation capable of undertaking an extensive range of building projects and establishing a major presence in the Singapore construction industry.

The primary stakeholders in this mission were taken to be the parties themselves for whom the joint venture would help to defray the entry costs for penetrating a new market segment, i.e., Sintech and Nakamaya. Other stakeholders would be the Japanese developer, Kurosawa Fudosan, as well as its Singapore partner in the Reichman project. These parties had more than a cursory interest in the joint venture since any disruption in the relationship of the joint venture partners would adversely affect the progress of the eventual construction work.

Following the specification of the desired properties of the joint venture organisation a number of important ideas emerged. At the outset, it was accepted that the joint venture should not be construed as a permanent form of collaboration at this stage. It was felt that the joint venture had to prove that it could enable both parties to realise their individual corporate agenda which neither could have attained alone. Nevertheless, some of the more distant objectives, i.e., commercial objectives beyond the Reichman project such as sourcing additional project work together, were acknowledged by both parties. Accordingly, it was felt necessary to include in the joint venture set-up some mechanisms which would pave the way for a longer-term business relationship. However, the initial priority remained the parties' commitment to get the joint venture started by securing the Reichman contract.

The approach chosen by the parties was to structure the joint venture in a non-integrated manner. The various parts of the contract were apportioned to each of the parties according to their respective strengths and know-how. For example, Nakamaya was assigned the responsibility for the foundation and structural work. Sintech was assigned responsibility for the procurement of labour and for the undertaking of the finishing work. In addition to the joint venture management board, each of the parties formed a separate steering committee to look after its package of construction work. The set-up contrasted, therefore, with an integrated joint venture in which one dedicated organisation is set up for the joint venture which then undertakes the contract as a truly separate organisation.

A number of risks are attached to a non-integrated joint venture. The chief of these are problems of communication and the propensity for the operational team looking after each part of the project to overlook the need for a co-ordinated effort in dealings with the clients, consultants, subcontractors and suppliers. For instance, if the procurement of general resources such as ready-mixed concrete, reinforcement bars and general labour are not properly co-ordinated, the joint venture may lose out in terms of bulk discounts and economies of scale and in so doing undermine the project's operational budget.

Other anxieties could be readily identified on both sides. Sintech was concerned that Nakamaya's size might eventually operate to take complete control over the entire joint venture. For example, if a contract dispute arises, it would be more likely for Nakamaya to ride out the cost of protracted and costly litigation comfortably whilst a legal bill of Sing$500,000 would have immediately rocked Sintech's bottom line for the year. Similarly, if calls for capital contributions were to be made which went beyond what had been initially agreed, Sintech was concerned that it might not be able to match Nakamaya's contributions with the same dispatch. Furthermore, given Nakamaya's extensive international reach, it was not inconceivable that it may practise some form of transfer-pricing which may operate to extract an excessive portion of the joint venture earnings to Japan. At the same time, because Sintech continued to source some of its work on a complete assignment basis from other Japanese main contractors, a very important consideration would be whether the joint venture may operate to extinguish this source of work.

On the other hand, from Nakamaya's vantage, there were anxieties that the Singapore company may not fully appreciate the strategic value of getting the job done right the first time, particularly in projects involving influential Japanese clients such as Kurosawa. Nakamaya was concerned here that their corporate image and reputation may be exposed to the risk that Sintech may not be able to deliver the level of quality or service which is normally expected of them by Japanese clients, and that in such an event a backlash may prove detrimental to its long-term interests at home. Questions were also raised as to whether Sintech was in the joint venture mainly to acquire Japanese construction management expertise and to exploit its financial clout. The consideration is whether Sintech can remain a long-term partner after its immediate corporate agenda of securing and completing the Reichman contract had been achieved. Clearly, if the joint venture was going to be a short-term affair, then it would not be possible for Nakamaya to share with Sintech the range of technical and management know-how necessary to establish a firm presence in the Singapore market. Equally important, Nakamaya considered at length whether Sintech would continue to source work from other main contractors (including their Japanese rivals) and, if so, the possibility that this might dilute Sintech's commitment to the joint venture. The parties decided that these and other related anxieties had to be addressed through the construction of 'trust building' mechanisms. These are discussed below.

The essence of the joint venture in idealised form was thus viability. It might be characterised in TSI terminology as organic but intelligent. However, as indicated earlier, there was a significant political flavour in the characterisation of the joint venture organisation. This recognises that the parties must co-operate and yet be fully aware of the other's interests and organisational territory. Any unsolicited encroachment or breach was considered likely to result in disruption or suspicion which might in turn operate to impede the progress of the project.

Consequently, a number of 'trust building' mechanisms were built into the joint venture idealised design. In formulating these mechanisms, the team applied some of the insights afforded by the VSM from DEO. The mechanisms were designed to allow the following.

- As much autonomy as possible for each area of critical project activity and accountability.
- Each part of the joint venture to communicate with each other as freely as possible.
- Performance standards and audit of the efficiency and integrity of key operations to be set.
- The business of pre-qualifying and securing the Reichman contract to proceed efficiently.
- Environmental changes to be accommodated efficiently and disagreements and differences to be settled expeditiously and without fuss.

The requirements for operational autonomy of each part were determined by adhering to the three-level analysis as propounded by the VSM (see Figure 10.2.2). Level 1 was assigned to the organisations of the joint venture partners with their diverse commercial interests. The joint venture is designated level 2. Implementation of the joint venture thus consisted of three divisions, in line with the non-integrated nature of the subject joint venture.

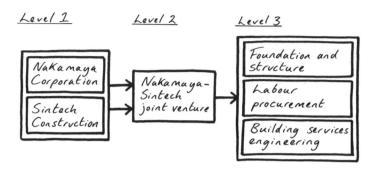

Figure 10.2.2 *Three-level representation of Sintech's joint venture with Nakamaya*

Division 1 is Nakamaya's portion relating to foundation and structural work. Division 2 is Sintech's portion of labour procurement and the finishing work. Division 3 is work such as engineering services which is to be undertaken by a principal subcontractor under the supervision of the joint venture. Procedures and reporting routines were agreed which determine the hierarchy of authority levels and the extent of direct costs and overheads for which each party would be responsible, thereby strengthening the vertical command axis.

Communication was enhanced by setting up an efficient reporting and communication channel between the various parts of the joint venture. The non-integrated nature of the joint venture made this a particularly crucial exercise. The design of the management information system for the joint venture, for example, required a careful study of the hitherto unchallenged information requirements of both companies. Executives from both sides had to be diplomatically persuaded to concede issues such as cutting back on the excess of management reports which may impede organisational responsiveness. Provisions were thus made for frequent executive meetings both formal and informal. The formal meetings would be through joint venture board meetings and major project meetings where Richard and his counterpart would normally be present. In addition, Richard spared no effort to receive senior Nakamaya officials in Singapore and help them to call on their clients. At the same time, Richard and his senior executives frequently stopped over in Osaka on business trips to Japan and the USA. The overall aim was to prevent 'them and us' type of confrontations at the operational level. All these management activities are consistent with co-ordination and management of conflict that derives from the VSM.

Targets for estimating margins, delivery schedules, quality attainment and profitability were also established. Some of these were developed from certain industry-wide benchmarks which enabled the parties to monitor the efficiencies of various joint venture operations continually. The whole process was fairly time consuming because the partners have slightly different profit expectations, with Nakamaya's executives being prepared to take a thinner margin because of the overriding goal of establishing a foothold in Singapore. Another area of initial difficulty was deciding how these standards were to be enforced and the incentives to be granted to operational personnel for the achievement of these targets. It was considered appropriate for auditors to be jointly appointed and for operational systems which concern both parties to be designed in consultation with one another. The parties would also consult each other closely on their dealings with other external parties such as subcontractors, suppliers, consultants and clients. These management ideas are consistent with control in the VSM.

It was also decided to designate a business development team for the joint venture, comprising representatives from both parties. This team dealt with Intelligence. It was charged with the task of calling on the Kurosawa project development team regularly and marketing the joint venture's strengths to them and their consultants. The team thus kept an eye on the preparation of pre-qualification submissions, client and consultant liaison and sourcing key suppliers and specialist subcontractors. The team's task also included establishing the pricing and negotiation strategies for the joint venture's contracts, including the sourcing of working capital. The team also identified opportunities where the joint venture could utilise the partners' combined resources and negotiation clout to improve their tendering competitiveness and positioning.

Finally, it was agreed that all decisions and differences would be calmly discussed and settled through consultations between the parties. Both parties realised that they would have to give a bit, but trust allowed this. Cheng and Suzuki would act as policy in the viable system. The overall VSM of the joint venture design is shown in Figure 10.2.3.

Attention then switched to implementation of the design. An implementation taskforce was formed. The team reported to a formal committee made up of Cheng and Suzuki. Their task was to translate the various ideas and concepts formulated for the joint venture entity into a plausible management proposal, review the demands of the joint venture in terms of manpower resources, materials, equipment and finance and to complete the formal establishments of the joint venture. A draft of the joint venture agreement was also simultaneously prepared, drawing on the ideas which emerged from the deliberations of the implementation team.

From hereon the activities took on a more conventional mould and included operational scheduling, information rout-

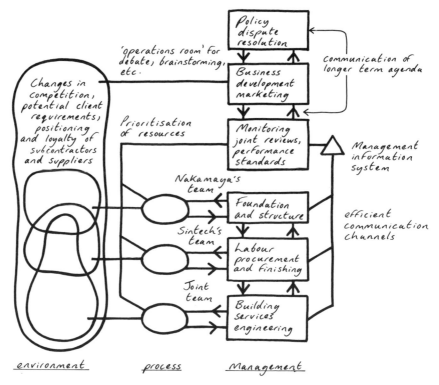

Figure 10.2.3 *Viable System Model (VSM) representation of Sintech's joint venture with Nakamaya*

ing, accounting and auditing systems, tax planning and other general administration matters. Also considered were alternative sources of finance (as compared to shareholders' equity) as well as procurement techniques which combined the strengths of both parties and the economies of their combined workload in the region. The team tasked with the establishment of the joint venture also arranged for business registration formalities. A separate technical group was established among members of the team, headed by a project manager designate, to determine the strategies for securing pre-qualification and preparing the tender submission for the Reichman contract.

The joint venture was duly established in August 1993 as a Singapore company with a paid-up capital of Sing$8 million. They were immediately pre-qualified for the Reichman project. In December 1993, the joint venture submitted what turned out to be the third lowest tender for the project. Nevertheless, the joint venture was invited to several rounds of discussions and negotiations with the client and consultants. Eventually the list was shortened to just the bid submitted by Sintech-Nakamaya joint venture and that submitted by another Japanese contractor, Hasegawa Gumi. Unfortunately for the joint venture, Hasegawa Gumi has an eight-year presence in Singapore, an established hotel construction record and offered to undertake the work at a price which was US$3.2 million lower than the joint venture's price of US$207 million. It turned out that because Hasegawa had just completed a large office building, it was able to bring to the Reichman contract scaffolding and plant items which had been essentially written off. Furthermore, the joint venture did not have sufficient time to source subcontractors for the extremely complicated mechanical and electrical engineering work on a sufficiently competitive basis. Following an exhaustive review of the pricing situation, both joint venture partners reluctantly concluded that they had to decline Kurosawa's offer to take the contract at Hasegawa's final price.

Nevertheless, both joint venture parties felt that the arrangements which they had formulated and put in place remained valid in so far as their respective longer-term interests are concerned. The four months spent on assembling the bid for the Reichman project, and the further ten weeks spent on negotiating the contract with the clients, enabled the parties to put many aspects of communication channels, in effect the 'trust building system', to work. As a result, when the Reichman project appeared to be slipping away sometime in January 1994, the joint venture decided to source other work. In April 1994, they managed to secure a Sing$46 million highway contract from the public sector which had been priced to provide a satisfactory profit margin of around 4.5%. Although from Nakamaya's vantage, this meant delaying the diversification to building construction, they managed to secure a useful foothold in the Singapore construction industry. In the meantime, the joint venture was pre-qualified for two other building projects, one of which was estimated at Sing$178 million. At the time of writing, they had just submitted their bids for both projects.

REFLECTIONS

Although my experience with TSI is still limited, the results from the application of its concepts to the present management situation are highly revealing. TSI's emphasis on creativity in the definition of the factors at work in the case, particularly the organic characteristics of the people and organisations concerned, permitted a comprehensive overview of the management issues confronting the parties to the joint venture. Metaphors were used as heuristic devices to transfer, in the words of one critic, 'knowledge from the (familiar) source domain to the (unfamiliar) target domain, thereby reducing a diverse variety of experience that otherwise may be difficult to conceptualise adequately because of the unavailability of literal terms'. Thus throughout the course of the exercise, they serve to underscore the task of marrying the perspective of the situation as seen from the closely knit family culture of Sintech with that as seen from a long-established, well-structured political system which epitomises a Japanese construction firm like Nakamaya.

The Choice phase enhanced the quality of deliberations in both the choice of the method and its implementation. Whilst the present paper reports principally the human aspects of the management situation, the subject case study demonstrated the complementarity between methods that deal with human problems and conventional technical diagnostic methods. Thus, recognition of the potential difficulties in the joint venture, given the respective backgrounds of both Sintech and Nakamaya and the different power and motivational elements of each of the protagonists in both companies, injected a concern for realism in the choice of organisational approach. This may serve as a helpful way of viewing the complementarity between human and technical dimensions of organisations within the broader TSI paradigm.

One other aspect of TSI deserves to be highlighted in the context of this case study. TSI does not adopt the 'pigeon-holing' approach of conventional management thought, where in order to cater to the limitations of particular management approaches, such as traditional Operational Research (OR), certain facts have to be held constant or assumed not to exist. TSI allows reality to be imported in full – warts and all. The TSI approach does not accept that there has to be one solution or one school of thought. The dominant relevance of ECD does not, for instance, exclude the application of DEO and its VSM to selected aspects of the case. Again the use of metaphors and the recursive nature the process used in conceptualising the situational context and in conceiving the idealised design of the joint venture suggest a wide latitude for incorporating 'untidy' factors in the overall problem solving approach. Admittedly, the participants of the process frequently complained that the approach appeared somewhat unwieldy at first, but, eventually, the rich exchange and juxtaposition of ideas, concepts and solutions persuaded them that the additional effort demanded was both highly necessary and worthwhile.

Case 10.3
Helderberg Boeing 747 Disaster (South Africa and International)

JOHAN STRÜMPFER, PRINCIPAL RESEARCHER

Focus: Problem solving in deep ocean search planning.

Methods discussed: Operational Research (OR), Testing Polarised Viewpoints (TPV), Exploring and Choosing Designs (ECD).

BACKGROUND TO THE WRITER AND SITUATION

Johan Strümpfer is currently Principal Researcher at the University of Cape Town. He is charged with managing the Programme for Systems Management, which is very closely linked with the University of Hull's Centre for Systems Studies in the UK. Previous employment includes Senior Researcher at the Institute for Futures Research and Senior Project Scientist at the Institute for Maritime Technology, during which time the events of this case study took place. Johan has been involved in technical and organisational problem solving for 15 years. He has been engaged in many projects ranging from basic engineering design to work with political organisations. He has a background in Operational Research and Systems Thinking.

In late 1987 the Helderberg Boeing 747 of South African Airways crashed into the Indian Ocean after an onboard fire. The crash location was 250 kilometres north-west of Mauritius, an island east of Madagascar. Despite modern technology the location of the wreckage at the time of the accident was as uncertain as the location of the Titanic when that famous ship sunk. A massive search and recovery exercise began immediately. Johan was responsible for deep ocean search planning. He applied Operational Research (OR) techniques and several systems problem solving approaches. At the time the search process was not guided by TSI, but Johan has written up the case showing how he used principles that indeed form an integral part of TSI. He also reflects upon the case through TSI's philosophy arguing that explicit use of this at the time would have enhanced the search process.

INTRODUCTION

The Helderberg crashed at night in the sea very far from land. It crashed approximately 20 minutes after an onboard fire was detected, which occupied the crew with fire-fighting attempts. Although requested by the Mauritian air traffic control, the crew were unable to give the location of the plane because of the fire-fighting activity. When the crew did manage to call in the location they used a wrong reference point that caused the initial search to be concentrated much too close to Mauritius.

It was 12 hours after the accident that the first surface debris was located. By this time it had drifted significantly from the geographic impact position. Other factors discussed later aggravated the uncertainty of the location. The wreckage was initially estimated to be anywhere within an area of 80 to 250 square nautical miles.

THE STUDY

The search process had three distinct phases.

- Sea surface search.
- Underwater search – pinger search.

● Underwater search – sonar search.

Each phase had its own particular challenges and problems. The information brought forward for search planning by each phase differed.

The sea surface search started with the emergency search hours after the accident and continued for approximately two weeks. The initial purpose was to locate and rescue possible survivors. None were found and so the search became one for drifting wreckage.

Wreckage was found 12 hours after the accident. Much more debris was found in the area around the last debris position and down current from that position. People began to believe that the best estimate of the wreckage position would be the location of the first debris sighting. The logic of this argument was that continued discovery of debris indicated surfacing wreckage from the ocean bottom. Much more information was to be gathered that suggested different estimates.

A standard technique for locating an object lost at sea is to 'back-drift' to the time of the incident. Using drift vector calculations used in search and rescue planning it is possible to estimate the initial impact area from the drift of surface debris. There are, however, uncertainties in back-drift calculation such as knowing the weather conditions for the interim period, the effect of wind and variations in the current. Nevertheless, a solution space for possible point of impact was calculated.

Early in the sea surface search a purse with three watches was recovered. One was still running whilst the other two had stopped due to impact damage. They both showed seven minutes past the hour, the time of the impact. This indicated that the aircraft had impacted some four minutes after the time of the last reported position. Speed was the only unknown variable. A solution space was therefore calculated for where the aircraft may have impacted according to this information source.

Underwater pinger search seeks to locate sound beacons on the flight recorders which emit a pinging sound when submerged. This is a recovery aid. The beacons have a 30-day workspan and a detection range of four kilometres. This meant that highly specialised equipment able to detect pinger sound had to be deployed rapidly. Great logistical problems and time deadlines dominated this phase of the search.

The underwater pinger did not conclusively locate the Helderberg wreckage, although 32 more possible positions were recorded that had to be considered. The search continued using side scan sonar, a system of using sound reflections to record the presence of objects on the sea bottom. The equipment again is highly specialised and suffered from its own logistical problems. Yet further location possibilities were forwarded.

Both the underwater pinger and sonar phases were searches involving ships towing equipment on long cables. This involved enormous effort and expenditure, requiring accurate navigation systems and satellites to support the search. At that time there was insufficient satellite coverage to accurately guide an underwater search of this nature.

On the night of the crash a mathematics teacher with a celestial knowledge observed from an island north of Mauritius a phenomenon described as falling balls of fire. Accurate bearings were taken. Through careful debriefing, and surveying of his position and observations, a cone-shaped space of the location of the phenomenon was derived. This was added to the mounting possibilities.

The overall search planning information calculated using the above means is summarised in Figure 10.3.1. The figure shows

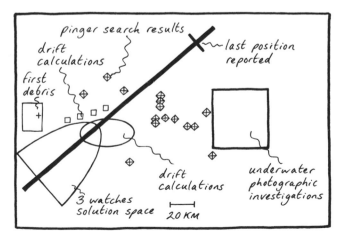

Figure 10.3.1 *Overall search planning information calculated in the search for the Helderberg*

both overlap and dissonance between the different information sources discussed above. The great amount of dissonance over-all led to much conflict. The search led to the mobilisation of resources and personnel from more than a dozen nationalities all holding different views about the validity of the six sources of information just discussed. Some of the groups favoured more than one of the information sources. The overall result was widely dispersed opinions on where the search should be conducted. The stakes were raised by the perception that those groups whose information sources were most accurate would be more likely to win the lucrative search and recovery contract.

The problem appeared to be a technical one, although exceed-ingly complex. Just how complex struck me at the moment the overall supervisor of the project slapped me on the back and said, 'Johan, you are my technical expert; sort it out.' So, it was down to me.

The classical Operational Research (OR) approach to search planning problems of this nature is to develop a probability distribution of the location of the object and to allocate search effort on this basis. Search results are then used to update the probability distribution. Search planning is a mathematical optimisation problem with enough technical intricacies to test the patience of the most experienced operational researcher.

The problem in practice is to come up with the search object probability distribution. For this a Monte Carlo simulation is commonly used. It has become the preferred method in cases where there are different and conflicting information sources such as the one under review. The approach works essentially by defining a simulation model for each information source or scenario and running the simulation to estimate positions given probability distributions on the uncertainties in each infor-mation source. The different information sources are simulated in turn. The resultant series of probability densities are com-bined in proportion to the relative credibility assigned to each information source.

This approach is technically quite sophisticated. With my background it is no surprise that I chose this route to resolve the search planning problem. Despite using systems methods, I did not consciously reflect as TSI demands, to think of alterna-tive systems approaches and then choose the best one in the circumstances. I resorted to what was the accepted specialist's way of dealing with an apparently clearly defined technical problem.

There were other dangers too although I did not know it at the time. The mathematical, statistical and computer wizardry involved in Monte Carlo simulation brings with it a kind of unquestioned credibility. Monte Carlo simulation almost certainly would have generated a seventh competing information source. Instead of reducing conflict around search areas it would have added to the overall confusion. At best it would have reduced the search areas only marginally.

During the planning process I viewed my assigned role of search planner narrowly. I carefully gathered information and worked with OR methods. Progress was problematic and the situation the so-called search committee faced was complex. This committee comprised between three to nine people who essentially were in control of the operation. We met at least once a day throughout the duration of the search. This meant that all conflicts and issues ended there.

Whilst reflecting on this situation a thought struck me, 'What we are busy with here is building an organisation.' I mentally renamed the operation the search organisation. The significance of this insight might not be immediately apparent, but what it did was to shift me mentally out of the mind trap that I was in. It opened the door to a whole new set of tools for inquiry. The trap had been to see my role in technical analytical terms, to determine the optimal search area using quantitative tools. Saying to myself that the purpose of the activity was organisation building led me to see the situation as a human system. This pointed to a whole different set of methods. The shock was that I had not questioned the relevance of the OR problem solving methods to the problems being tackled.

So I thought long and hard about the question, 'What does social systems thinking have to say about this situation?' From this came a second crucial insight for me. Search planning was actually a long-term strategic planning process for the search organisation. This perspective immediately got me thinking about two methods reported in this book, Exploring and Choosing Designs (ECD) and Testing Polarised Viewpoints (TPV). I started to look at the process of planning and the deliverables from such a process in a conscious manner.

Thinking about the situation in social system and strategic

planning terms generated ideas such as the need to create alignment and shared understanding among those involved. I
started to see my role as that of creating this alignment as
opposed to saying where the search should be conducted. This
was not to say that hard numbers were unimportant or that
search planning should not be conducted. It means that I
appreciated that the technical part of the problem solving
would need to be based on shared understanding of all participants, agreement and consensus about the meaning and implications of the underlying information. Alignment had to be created that agreed *why* and *where* the search had to be conducted.
This alignment would then be the guiding vision of every actor
in the situation.

This meant dealing with multiple perspectives, another
insight which hit me in this respect. The information portrayed
on Figure 10.3.1 surely was all 'true' at the same time. Of course,
the wreckage could not have been at all those locations at the
same time, but each information source did represent a viewpoint, each 'true' in its own right. The clamouring for the lucrative search contract had turned these into polarised viewpoints
instead of shared inquiry for an inclusive truth. Each viewpoint
was true in the sense that it was a reasonable view of reality
but was not the absolute truth. Each had to be considered valid
in its own right. None had indicated the exact location of the
wreckage. The fundamental question in this case was what
assumptions had each viewpoint made about reality for it to
have come to a conclusion about where the aircraft impacted
on the sea. What assumptions are critical in the sense that if
they were invalid that particular viewpoint would in itself be
substantially weakened? These are all questions that readers of
this book will recognise from the method TPV.

To proceed I had to change my role. Sticking to my official
role as search planner would have led to additional confusion.
I changed role to become a group learning facilitator for a TPV
process. I facilitated a process of group learning. Later I was to
use ECD to facilitate a process of planning.

Actively shifting to a facilitation role helped move the process
along. I did not view the process of information gathering as
merely clinical, but as a process of involving people and sharing
information. In this role I became accepted, not as a proponent

of one of the information sources, but as one knowledgeable
about the facts and able and willing to help in their sharing
and discussion. Each proponent therefore understood that their
viewpoint was being considered but that there were also other
viewpoints which, at this time, held equal weight.

Instead of trying to limit conflict by bounding the range of
people participating in the search committee, I consciously pro-
moted enlargement of the number of people and viewpoints
entering the learning process. For example, I invited people
responsible for set-up and operation of the navigation systems.
Their participation makes no sense from an optimisation point
of view, but makes sense when regarding the process as one of
building alignment.

The idea of critical assumptions underlying each of the different information sources gave rise to a very critical review of
each viewpoint and its supporting evidence. This meant careful
investigation that proceeded over some six weeks. Basic facts
were established through critical analysis, not accepting anything at face value but digging deeper to verify, verify, verify.

The process centred around identification of critical assumptions for each information source. Each source was examined
using the question, 'What assumptions are we making in believing that this information should be used to calculate a search
area?' Once a critical assumption had been highlighted, all supporting or contradictory evidence for the assumption was purposefully searched out.

A rich understanding of the overall picture was built up. It
was far richer than any one of the information sources on their
own. Furthermore, as the process continued, there was a grad-
ual de-politicising of the respective information sources. Individuals came to accept to varying degrees the value of the
whole set of information and let go of singular and much nar-
rower views.

Three search areas were decided upon at the end of January
1988. They are shown in Figure 10.3.2. What is not indicated
graphically is the high belief in Area 1. In fact, there was reasoned opinion that the aircraft would be located in the middle
of the eastern half of this area. The aircraft wreckage was found
using sonar search. It was located two days after the start of
this new search phase, within the primary area determined

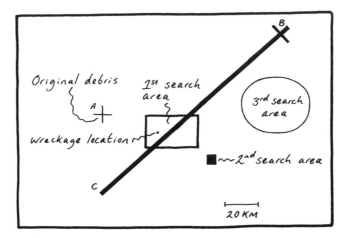

Figure 10.3.2 *Helderberg original debris and wreckage locations, also showing three search areas finally chosen*

through a process of group learning supported by conscious use of systemic principles. The wreckage location is indicated by a dot in the figure – if you have a problem seeing it then imagine the problem we had finding it on the ocean bed!

REFLECTIONS

In my view what is more remarkable than the success of locating the Helderberg and the dramatic reduction in search area, was the unusually high levels of consensus achieved in the latter stages of the process. The search areas were consensus decisions, based not on compromise, but on agreement as to the meaning of the underlying information sources.

With the advantage of hindsight it is clear that the reductionist and analytic thinking that characterised my initial way of thinking about the problem was a conceptual trap. By the same token I am under no illusion that the quantitative OR methods fulfilled a key supporting role. Without recourse to that, no amount of debating using systems methods like TPV would have succeeded. Yet blind adherence to OR would not have resolved the problem with the same effectiveness. The biggest trap of all then would have been the unquestioning acceptance of a particular method for problem solving without critically reflecting on which method is right in the circumstances. The Helderberg case study therefore provides a classic account of why TSI's problem solving process, including critically choosing methods, is essential for any problem solver in any situation all of the time. The argument of this book makes choice an integral part of problem solving and does not leave choice to default to conventional wisdom or individual bias. This case shows that this is true even in situations that are apparently very technical with well-proven analytical tools available.

The above example richly illustrates the advantages of explicitly following a TSI framework for problem solving. Where the example illustrates good principles for problem solving, TSI prescribes them. Where the example illustrates bad principles for problem solving, TSI guards against them. TSI's principles are constructed on a philosophy with essentially six main points as seen in Chapter 3. I round off with a brief analysis of this case study against the philosophy of this book, which again demonstrates the validity and value of the problem solving system TSI.

- *An organisation comprises technical and human activities.* In the Helderberg search planning the technical activities dominated massively in the earlier stages. When the human side of the activity was recognised too in the form of a social systems perspective a whole new set of possibilities arose that ultimately led to enormous changes in problem solving practice.
- *Organisational activities must be efficiently and effectively controlled whilst maintaining organisational viability in line with TSI's principles.* The daunting technical demands made for a situation dominated by specialised individuals. The actual management of the activities became highly problematic and received only secondary reactive attention. Up-front management reflecting on the TSI philosophy would have drawn direct attention to this.
- *Organisational activities must be directed to achieve some purpose.* The actual objective of the group involved remained contentious despite apparent clarity. The purpose seemed to vary between finding the aircraft, finding the flight recorders, find-

ing the cause of the accident, and apportioning blame. The importance of achieving accepted objectives and the need to manage alignment around purposes were unfortunately reactively addressed. The TSI philosophy would have placed much more attention on this.

- *People in organisations appreciate things in different ways.* The issue of attaching meaning to situations and the consequent need to manage the different perspectives is often improperly understood. Explicit use of TSI would have been more likely to place this issue under the spotlight. In the Helderberg case, it was the explicit management of multiple perspectives on reality that made a major contribution to the resolution of the search planning problem.
- *The last two stages must be harmonised through organisational design and management style.* The case study highlights the problem that would have resulted if a solely quantitative OR approach had been adopted. I mentally redesigned my little committee into an organisation and changed management style to be open and participatory.
- *Managers and problem solvers must accept the responsibility for the impact of decisions and policies on the physical, biological and social environment.* The ethical and moral issues of problem solving must remain part of the overall problem solving process if problem solving itself is to become less problematical. A reminder of these wider implications involved in any project is given in the following dedication.

This article is dedicated to the 159 people who died in the Helderberg in 1987, including the father of my friend Karin Osler. The deep pain and tragedy of so many people involved in the disaster should not be lost in the rational discussion of the problem solving exercise discussed above.

Case 10.4
North Yorkshire Police (United Kingdom)

STEVE GREEN, COMMANDER OF YORK DIVISION

Focus: Managing and developing a police division in a large bureaucracy.

Methods discussed: Metaphors, Quality Management (QM), Diagnosis for Effective Organisation (DEO).

BACKGROUND TO THE WRITER AND ORGANISATION

Steve Green is currently a superintendent in North Yorkshire Police commanding the York Division. His career began in the military. He attended the Royal Military Academy at Sandhurst and was commissioned into the Royal Corps of Signals. He served mainly in the British Army of the Rhine specialising in radio and line communications and the administration of field headquarters.

He joined North Yorkshire Police 'by accident' and served as a constable in Harrogate. Steve then attended the accelerated promotion course at the Police Staff College at Bramshill, served in various stations in the North Yorkshire area, rising to the rank of chief inspector and now superintendent.

North Yorkshire Police is a typical county police force covering a predominantly rural county, serving a population of 750,000. It covers an area of two million acres that contains 6,000 road miles. It has a gross budget of nearly £70 million a year.

Steve's recent tasks have been centred on restructuring North Yorkshire Police, aiming to remove unnecessary tiers of management and to devolve decision making across the organisation. He is heavily committed to removing bureaucracy from the police service and reforming its traditional militaristic model towards a community-based organic structure. He is currently involved in strengthening community links between the police and citizens of York by ensuring that police decision making is accountable to the communities that they serve.

INTRODUCTION

The purpose of this study is to portray one of several applications of TSI in North Yorkshire Police. The majority of case studies reported by exponents of TSI prior to this book have focused upon specific projects by internal or external consultants. In these cases, consultants manage the intervention and facilitate the events. This case study aims to show that TSI is of equal value as a method for managers to manage the organisation.

The case is based on my personal experience of taking charge over and managing a Territorial Policing Unit at York Headquarters at a time of proliferating workload and turbulent organisational change. It illustrates how a TSI-based analysis of the problems faced by the unit enabled my team to establish an agenda for managing the unit. Then a systems-based approach was used to develop the unit in response to that agenda.

The case study illustrates the benefits accrued by adopting a TSI-based approach to manage and develop the organisation. A special feature of the case is reflection upon the dilemmas encountered when the main holder of power in an organisation attempts to manage effectively whilst upholding TSI's core principle of human freedom.

THE STUDY

Policing in the UK follows a doctrine of policing by consent. This means in practice an unarmed police force working as members of the community, deriving their powers largely from the democratic consent that they are given by the population. Policing by consent works against the possibility of the development of an oppressive police force. It also makes the police force extremely sensitive to the matter of public confidence and support.

Despite, or even because of, these principles, the police force in the UK has recently been through a turbulent period. The first manifestations of this surfaced when a number of alleged miscarriages of justice received national prominence. Everyone in the UK knows of the releases, among others, of the convicted 'Birmingham 6', 'Guildford 4' and 'Tottenham 3'. At the same time opinion polls showed that public confidence in the police was declining. In addition, financial pressure built with central government's commitment to cut the level of public expenditure as a proportion of Gross Domestic Product; meaning that, among other things, resources made available to the police were closely scrutinised.

These events occurred against a backdrop of increasing crime. Recorded crime has risen from a half million post-World War II, to three and a half million ten years ago, to five and a half million now. Using crime as a broad indicator of all police activity gives some idea of the scale of the extra workload police have to manage today.

The picture I am trying to create has at the centre a police force operating according to a doctrine of policing by consent which is under pressure through proliferating workload, has had its confidence shaken by high profile adverse publicity and is under threat of growing financial scrutiny by a government committed to cutting public sector expenditure. In short, the police force has been stretched by a massive increase in the level of service required in the face of growing social upheaval.

The government have introduced a number of other significant initiatives. The Audit Commission scrutinised many aspects of police work including the way paperwork is dealt with, control rooms are operated, crime is investigated and details of management structure and financial systems. The overall goal was to improve value for money and increase operational effectiveness. Police forces across the country are under great pressure to respond to these reports and are also included in the requirements of the government's Citizens Charter. Yet more reform is obligatory following the Police and Magistrates' Court Act, which is all about accountability of the police for the results that they achieve and making them more responsive to local needs.

In 1990 the police service conducted a major review called Operational Policing Review. It found that the service had lost direction. Police wanted to operate with flashing blue lights, arresting criminals, etc., which represents a hard edge to policing. This was at variance with what the public actually wanted. The public were motivated toward police officers working in the community and generally being better oriented to local needs. The police were clearly 'out of sync' with the public that they served.

North Yorkshire Police began to respond to these pressures in 1989. They reviewed the management of the force and removed a tier of management. Power was devolved to local commanders whilst headquarters concentrated on a strategic overview of the force. The central challenge of that review was genuinely to destroy an old-fashioned bureaucratic model without simply creating a new one. Other forces which had already started the process of change simply created a more fashionable bureaucracy.

The first exposure that North Yorkshire Police had to systems thinking came in 1990 through staff at the University of Hull, now grouped in the university's Centre for Systems Studies. A Viable System Model developed (VSM) based organisation was using Diagnosis for Effective Organisation (DEO). This form of organisation is not overtly articulated, but it is paramount in underpinning the way that North Yorkshire Police is organised.

The second exposure to systems ideas came in the field of Quality Management (QM) through the Centre for Systems Studies. David Devlin and Professor Flood undertook a further review. The review recommended that local commanders be given the maximum amount of power and the maximum control over resources that would enable them to manage independently the services that they provided, geared up to the needs of the communities that they served. The force should be held together by an overarching strategic framework offered from the centre. In effect the recommendations proposed QM through the VSM, all guided by the process of TSI. The results of the review were implemented in January 1992. This was seen as Phase 1 of a larger process aimed at providing the public with the service that they wanted through a ministration that is not wasteful of resources.

The focus of the remainder of this article is to recount the management and development of one territorial division known as York Police Division using TSI. York Police Division is the busiest division in North Yorkshire Police. In 1993 it dealt with one-third of the force workload, involving 58,000 incidents of which 17,500 were crimes, and it made 7,000 arrests. Because of its size and the high profile that the City of York has in the region, York Division is seen as the flagship of the force.

I took charge of York Division in January 1993 and found that whilst implementation of the review was some 12 months on, the Division had not moved forward as far as it could have done, particularly in orienting its services to meet the public need. My problem, then, was how to analyse what those needs were and to determine how to satisfy them. The task turned out to be very tricky.

As a committed systems practitioner, indeed a TSI practitioner, I fought against becoming an autocrat and simply dictating needs and how to achieve them. A difficulty that I have faced, however, is being a systems practitioner whilst on paper being the main holder of power. That posed a whole set of dilemmas that I shall reflect upon later and which incidentally are not usually acknowledged by systems theorists.

What I needed to do to develop the division was to look at it as a whole, analyse all the issues, not just the obvious ones, and find out and tackle the causes of problems rather than their symptoms. I started my work with a TSI analysis of the division and built up my own shopping list of things to tackle as recounted below.

The TSI analysis drew upon three sources of information.

- The first source amounted to past experience, since the commander role is my third posting to the York Division. I knew

intimately the geographical region and the difficulties of policing in this large urban sprawl.

- Rural policing experience, my second source of information,
  provided a dramatic contrast to the resource hungry York.
  York is different. It is different from other divisions, must
  remain different and consequently must be managed differently, but it needs to aspire to the personal service and close
  community ties that characterise rural policing.
- The third source of information came through consultation. I
  entered into discussion with York's management team,
  inspectors, sergeants, operational staff, civilian support staff,
  public representatives including city councillors and the Community Liaison Panel, etc.

Of all these agencies, it may be surprising for you to find out
that it was the management team who posed me the trickiest
problems as a manager. Against the tide of change in leadership
style, my management team did not appear to want to share
power. They were adamant that current practices should be
kept. This in broad-sweep terms meant the team meeting
weekly to promulgate memos, backed up only by a meeting
with inspectors every two months at which they were informed
of the decision rather than invited to share in it.

The management style that I inherited, and was determined
to annihilate, predictably left people on the ground alienated.
They had no idea what the team was doing for them. A poign-
ant example from my first week in the post says it all. I met
with one of the four shifts as they prepared for the day's work.
Keen to find out their impression of the management style I
asked whether they were satisfied with the workings of the
management team. I was faced by 40 blank faces and perplexed
silence broken only when one wag said, 'and who are they Sir?'
The first task on my shopping list, then, was to break down the
power structure in place.

I wanted to see change. I wanted inspectors and sergeants to
take the initiative for the work that they did. In so far as it is
possible in any organisation I wanted all staff to tackle their
own problems as they faced them. In metaphorical terms, York
Division contained people with much talent in a kind of man-

agement prison that locked up talent; my second task was to unlock the talent.

The difficulties were accentuated by a long-standing corporate culture of which there were several lingering facets. The fountain of all power prior to implementation of the results of the review in 1992 was Divisional Command. This meant that practically anything of significance was sent up the hierarchy to a chief superintendent or higher. This one I knocked on the head immediately by sending the memos straight back to the manager directly in charge of the relevant operations and told them to deal with it. This procedural change focused attention on local operations; one small step forward.

The second cultural difficulty of note was the also long-standing rift that existed between police officers and civilian employees who help to administer affairs. The civilians were treated as second-class employees. It was perceived that they were not doing the real work that is of course policing. I strangled this problem early on too. In my judgement, and having taken on board other people's views; my intention was to increase involvement so now civilians are far more evident in direct policing matters such as working in the control room, on the crime desk, managing the public inquiry counter, and so on. I am also working on the management structure, getting rid of separate line management for civilians and police.

The third cultural difficulty to which I alluded earlier is the difference between York Division and other divisions. York Division polices a big city. It is an old city force with a tradition of independence. Since York is different, the management problem was maintaining this identity but keeping it on the corporate boat. This tension was added to the shopping list.

And then there were operational inefficiencies. Policing was reactive. York had a particular problem in the summer of 1993 that illustrates the point well. York is one of the UK's great tourist attractions with its intriguing history and valued architecture. Consequently, in the summer York is teeming with tourists. At night the tourists, here for only a day or two, prefer to take hand baggage only into their hotels, leaving the bulk of luggage in car boots. This creates a thieves' nirvana and sets off an explosion of car thefts. Panda cars and beat officers are run ragged dealing with one report after another. This is reactive policing.

What is needed is proactive policing on the part of the force. The force can only do this if it is intelligent. It needs to be an intelligent organism, but one that is adapted to its environment. Even within York there are many different areas each with their own type of policing demands. A simple example is the difference between middle-class communities and less affluent council estates.

Traditionally, policing has been undertaken on a shift basis. There are four eight-hour shifts which cover the whole of the York Divisional area. The shift structure encourages reactive management. Ownership is hard to install, grassroots policing is not possible and less competent officers are 'covered' by the next shift. Furthermore, anonymity exists between the police and public, at a time when surveys have shown that the public are calling for a return to community policing (I shall say more about the community a little later).

The shift system also sits uncomfortably alongside the small number of community beat officers who work in parallel with it. A tension has grown between shifts and community beat officers. The shifts see themselves as 'action men' hitting problems as they arise, but see the community beat officers as second-class citizens who only mop up after the action is finished. The community beat officers see the shifts as 'lockers up', or cavaliers, charging into battle and then charging off leaving a perplexed public. Their job, then, becomes placating the public. The public are therefore confused about the role of the police.

It has been my view for some time that proactive policing is needed. It was a great source of pleasure to me when geographic policing became national policy. This requires a geographic rather than a shift structure. Geographic policing aims to integrate the police with the communities, leading to better intelligence. It will give ownership to officers who get to know a patch, and its offenders, and who will be responsible 24 hours a day and be accountable for actions taken. Geographic policing also enables the police force to understand aspects of our work as reflecting wider social problems by being 'in contact' with people and their concerns. For example, the so-called 'criminal network' may actually be nothing more than a reflection of wider social problems; problems that we must be aware of if policing is to make a genuine contribution to the betterment of society. Indeed, the police force can and should make a contribution to these larger social debates.

The geographic model was bound to hit internal resistance and can be explained in the following way. Shifts have become like families. Shifts share a team spirit. There is camaraderie and an individual identity. They socialise. Each shift has its own subculture reflected by the style of management. The geographic model will tear these families apart. They will not all be working on the same patch. They may even see more of officers from other patches in the new scheme.

The dire need here was internal marketing. Attitudinal change was clearly the core problem. Officers had to have ownership over change, even though the strategy had to be taken as given.

Local Area Policing promises to help the force to move into the community. This meant that many things would improve, including intelligence. We carried out empirical research which demonstrated that the community beat officers, although only relatively small in numbers, accounted for the vast majority of intelligence that was fed into operations. Moving to Local Area Policing promises to increase dramatically the amount of intelligence flowing in and hence to provide the basis for proactive policing.

Furthermore, York Division was not organised in terms of being part of the social support system. There was no synergy between ourselves and other social agencies. We were not responsive. For example, the City Council set up cameras along the inner ring road for urban traffic control. They offered to extend this into the force's control room. Amazingly at the time this offer was turned down. There was a failure to see common interests with other agencies. Now we are working with the council to extend the system into the city centre with facilities for both organisations to receive transmissions. This is a symbol of partnership that we intend to build upon.

Another failing is that we have never educated the public about what we can do for them. We have never set out what it is that we do that they can ask us to account for. This is currently being dealt with through a public charter that will be distributed to all citizens, funded through sponsorship by local companies.

There are many other examples of the need to work together, but let me give just one more. The Department of the Environment have put up money under a scheme called 'Safer Cities'. The aim is to improve the quality of life in cities by making them safer places. Our response has been to set up a multi-agency steering committee. The committee represents all major stakeholders in the city.

The last problem we faced, which in some senses is reflected in the rigid organisation I took over, was that, frankly, there was no plan. There were received missions such as the move to Local Area Policing, but there had been no reworking of this mission in the context of policing in York. There was absolutely nothing put down on paper about what York Division would be doing a year on or further. Consequently, individuals followed their own agenda. Three decisions made in isolation illustrate the point.

- The operations manager decided he would reduce our presence at set-piece event policing such as football and rugby matches.
- The crime manager decided to change his bit of the operations to proactive policing.
- An inspector implemented people development for her own shift.

But none of this was linked together.

Now, up to this point, if it is not clear already, my thinking had been entirely of a systemic nature. I had wanted to appreciate, manage and develop the whole. To do this, drawing upon the three information sources set out earlier, I explored a series of management-based metaphors in the context of York Division. This grew strong images of York Division in terms of the four key dimensions of organisation recognised by TSI. I continued to develop my own agenda through diagnostic thinking, being guided by the VSM through my own form of Diagnosis for Effective Organisation (DEO). I knocked off a few difficulties on the way. The shopping list that remained had four main points of action.

- Break down the power structure with particular reference to the management team.
- Unlock the talent of all officers.
- Manage the tension between the corporate identity and the York individuality.
- Implement Local Area Policing to serve the communities in the knowledge of their views about wider social problems whilst managing corporate culture change.

The main problem was ultimately a political one. How could I bring everyone along? I wanted my desires to be wrapped up in force policy but there was no method to help do that. I had to review the instruments of power that would help me to get the outcomes I wanted. I had to take a tactical militaristic approach, but this only reflected the ancient traditions of the force, ironically the ones I was determined to remove forever. I had to fight power with power. The task at hand seemed clear. However, the dilemma of apparently breaking the systemic principles I value so highly plagued my thoughts (a point I will return to later).

What was needed involved a redesigning of the division to achieve Local Area Policing, which entailed an overhaul of procedures (some of which I had been able to implement on the way) that meant a huge cultural upheaval and consequently attracted strong political resistance.

The main task, using DEO terminology, was to move the management team from control to policy. In the eyes of the team this meant that they were being disempowered because they were no longer making day-to-day decisions. I established a five-weekly meeting where policy matters were dealt with. I also involved a wider spread of people including inspectors and Federation representatives (equivalent to a union). In addition to policy we discussed performance and action plans and have established procedures for review.

At first this new team went through a period of trauma. Before there were five of them including the commander. The four were used to being kicked around by the commander. If there was a split opinion on any matter, even if it meant that the commander was isolated, then he would override the other four. In my scheme, if I were in the minority I said, 'OK, if that is the majority view then that is what we will do.' So unused to this kind of response were they, that at first I was seen as a soft leader and this weakened my position. I was expected to come across as powerful and hard, not caring and conciliatory. It took some time for this to wear off and at times I felt at risk.

Over the last 12 months policy has evolved a service plan for the division. This plan sets out priorities, states standards of service we hope to achieve and establishes who is responsible in parts of the division to make sure the plan is met. The plan is a liberating document because it allows people to take the initiative and points out the kind of initiative that they could take whilst maintaining harmony with divisional activities.

The service plan set up a co-ordination group of three inspectors and two sergeants. Each is responsible for a key area of service. There are five key areas: response to calls, crime, public order, traffic and community policing. The co-ordination group manages competing demands for resources and any conflict that arises through this.

As far as intelligence is concerned, we see and promote the idea of everyone being a contributor. This is consistent with Local Area Policing. The information is distributed in a bulletin for routine matters, a package for specific operations, whilst trends are reported in special briefing reports.

The link to York Division's environment is being undertaken through activities already discussed, but is being made possible by Local Area Policing. Only through Local Area Policing can strong links be made with the community and social agencies. We are now advancing well with plans for implementation.

Even as I write, Professor Flood is facilitating some of the changes needed. Over the last few months he has been involved in internal marketing. He has been given the freedom to facilitate change with a working party dealing with Local Area Policing. The working party is a consultative body. They have come up with a plan for implementation which I had very little involvement in. But this kind of thing is possible as the new culture begins to mature and the political problems wane.

I understand that there have been many differences in opinion, but these have been debated and resolved using methods that encourage people to take into account the ideas of others. Recently I was passing an office from which I could hear much heated debate and guessed rightly that this was the working party thrashing out their differences with Professor Flood facilitating the use of Testing Polarised Viewpoints (TPV). Afterwards I was speaking to one of the inspectors on the working party whose minority view had been given a full airing through TPV. He said to me that the greatest value for him in the process was not so much that changes he felt strongly about were ultimately accepted into the plan, but that he was flattered his view was taken seriously.

The next big step is to implement the plan. This will involve each of the Local Area Teams going through idealised planning as part of Exploring and Choosing Designs (ECD). The team members will be designing their own mode of operation with only limited constraints set by the needs of everyday divisional co-ordination and control. In terms of the VSM, each team will be establishing their own operations to suit the local needs.

Finally, the aim is to have an effective organisational design and corporate culture that, even with still horrendous constraints, will provide communities as far as possible with the type of policing that they want, in an efficient manner, undertaken with knowledge about their concerns elicited by our closer contact with them.

REFLECTIONS

On reflection I find it interesting to discover that I never consciously decide to use TSI any more. Over years of use, TSI has become internalised. I have no choice about whether to use it or not because it is my management style. I just do TSI naturally. Thinking about this has made me wonder if now I am falling into a trap that TSI warns us about, that we can too easily internalise methods and not be reflective about their use and relevance. But the fact is, what I have internalised is an approach which is inherently self-reflective. TSI is self-reflective, and if it were not then I would not be worrying about such matters right now.

The main value of TSI for me is that it prevents managers from missing things. For example, in my situation it would have been very easy to have seen the management team as the problem when in fact TSI helped me to realise that the team was only a political expression of a wider problem. Also, TSI helps managers to use everything that is to their advantage and avoid everything that is to their disadvantage (which can only be true if the viewpoints of all stakeholders are fairly dealt with).

All this paints a picture of management without tears. Unfortunately it is never like that. Management is always demanding with or without TSI. For me, though, with TSI it is easier to be a more effective manager.

There are warnings that need to be flagged up, however. My red flag says be very careful if you are thinking about using TSI or any of its methods overtly in an environment where people are not familiar with them. Early on with TSI, I submitted a strategic document that put systems ideas in headlines. To put it bluntly, I was ridiculed because of all the obscure terms involved, such as autopoiesis and algedonic, expressions that Professor Flood has protected you from in this book. The problem was probably accentuated by the political nature of the organisation in which I work, that draws attention to Professor Flood's point in Chapter 7 that we must be sensitive to the issue of problem solving style. Anyway, it took me some time to recover from this experience. Is it perhaps the reason why in the early months as commander of York Division I chose not to be open about the methods I was using?

I can at this point almost hear readers saying, at the end of the day, 'Why bother?' 'Why make the effort?' My answer is a pragmatic one. I looked for help because the organisation in which I worked was hitting a crisis at the corporate level. I entertained only those ideas which I judged could help; others I ignored. So I bothered to learn about systems thinking and TSI for a very good reason – it is practically useful. At the end of the day this is the only thing that justifies the effort.

My advice to practitioners is, even if you are in large organisations, do it because ultimately you will be forced to. This is especially the case in the public services in the UK (which may differ from the home countries of some readers) because the bulldozers of change are on the way and will simply reduce to rubble those parts of the service that do not conform. Nothing can stand in the way of this wave of change in society today. But even if you are operating in a relatively stable environment with traditional management, then I can guarantee that the organisation will be underperforming, living in a comfort zone where people are achieving little.

I invite you to spend a little time thinking about the problems that you face now which are most threatening. Then think about TSI's ideas and work out what they can do for you. I am sure you will begin to see the advantages. Keep thinking about TSI in the real world. The amount of effort required to understand TSI as a problem solving system is a lot less than you might think. It is not too difficult. If you continue along this track then you will come into the sunshine of how TSI can help you.

And finally, I turn to the issue of my use of power to force change. I end with this one because it is the issue which I find difficult to resolve and continues to haunt me. As far as justification of using my power is concerned, there is no ultimate justification, but I did it with systemic principles in mind. I exerted my power with human freedom in mind. All interests were considered. In my judgement the situation was down to survival stakes and survival meant balancing individual needs with organisational needs taking into account the social environment. It was simply that TSI's ideal state of an organisation could not be achieved unless the constraints that prevented it were removed. I do not consider what I did as a licence for me or anyone else to exert power at will, only to recognise that sometimes it is proper for people in organisations to muster up sufficient power that will overthrow bureaucracy and autocratic management. That is what I believe I did. After all, at stake in North Yorkshire is the security and safety of three-quarters of a million citizens and the health and welfare of hundreds of police officers and support staff.

Case 10.5
Southern Life Association (South Africa)

WARREN TOPP, SENIOR PROJECT MANAGER

Focus: Critical evaluation within Business Process Reengineering (BPR).

Methods discussed: The 'For what reason?' Method, Critically Evaluating Designs and Decision (CEDD), Business Process Reengineering (BPR).

BACKGROUND TO THE WRITER AND ORGANISATION

Warren Topp has worked for Southern Life Association (SLA) for eight years. He began his career with SLA working for six years in information technology. During this time he moved through the ranks from programmer to senior project manager. Then he moved for one year to the service operations to gain wider experience. A year ago he joined the core reengineering team and is currently responsible for the mapping of current business processes and their redesign into image and workflow technology.

SLA is the fourth largest life assurer in South Africa. It has branches nationwide and currently has two head offices, one in

Cape Town and one in Johannesburg. The location of this project is the Cape Town head office.

SLA consists of four divisions or strategic business units. Life Division administers life policies, from new business capture to claims. It also contains the field staff who sell life assurance and investment products. The Employee Benefits Division sells and administers pension and group business. The Investments Division controls the investment of all policyholder and surplus funds. The Broker Division supports the broker community in marketing SLA's products.

The management structure within Life Division of SLA is classically hierarchical. However, there is mounting pressure on this through the introduction of learning organisation concepts and the idea of self-managing cross-functional teams who 'own' customer value streams. Since service is one of the few areas in which life assurers can differentiate themselves from their competitors, the quality of the information and human systems involved in processing customer service requests are critical to the company's long-term health.

A foreword is necessary for this case. Warren Topp was inspired as an individual by the principles of CEDD in his reengineering task and has interpreted them as he saw fit. It is interesting to see in this case how a manager's thinking can change. Warren explains how he was enriched by the process and in some respects that is the value of CEDD's use in this instance. The enrichment did not come easily, as you will read below, with Warren experiencing great personal turmoil. However, there still may be some contention about the use of CEDD in the private sector, so this case is best seen as contributing to a debate about possibilities for employing CEDD in the private sector. There may also be controversy concerning the wider social responsibility that companies have in the South African context in this period of social upheaval, being mainly white dominated and serving mainly white needs. At the end of the day it must be up to the reader to decide how far Warren has developed his thinking and how successful the application of CEDD has been in the context of SLA's needs as they compare with South Africa's wider social needs.

INTRODUCTION

The vision or purpose of SLA is stated as: *'To become first choice of customers, staff and shareholders in selected financial markets.'* This vision rests on three pillars as follows.

- The people of the organisation, who need to be competent and passionate.
- Our customers, who we need to gain and maintain.
- The profits we generate, which need to be long term and growing.

Another way of interpreting our purpose is to be first choice to all stakeholders. This could be problematical since the stakeholders involved (staff, shareholders, customers and others in the wider South African society) may have different interests. The Life Customer Services Divisional Steering Committee (DSC), which comprises the senior management responsible for the current functional areas, has determined a Life Customer Services vision within the context of the greater SLA vision. This was presented as a framework to all of Life Customer Services management at a recent working conference.

The Life Customer Services vision or purpose, within the context of SLA's overall purpose, is to 'Move from processing paper to delighting customers.' We hope to achieve this through *passionate people* using *quality systems* within a *flexible structure designed around customer needs*. Within Life Customer Services all interventions need to be tested to determine whether they are helping us move from processing paper to delighting customers (although we recognise that many South Africans economically are not able to consider being customers; a wider social debate that SLA wishes to be part of). During 1993 the DSC provided the following framework as a guide to how we might achieve our vision.

Our corporate culture. To achieve our corporate and divisional visions our corporate culture has to have the following attributes.

- People are connected to a larger purpose (including South Africa's wider social debate) and to each other.

- People are treated equally and can participate in the development of shared values.
- Our shared values and behaviour are incorporated in a monitorable creed of trust that can be evaluated by everyone.
- We are aware of the competitive environment in which we operate and support each other in achieving results – there is a minimal number of departmental or divisional jealousies and we try to transcend these in advance by making provision for different interests to be discussed.
- Information is valued as the life-blood of the organisation and is shared openly and rapidly both up and down.
- We value diversity and our culture reflects this.
- We are proactive in seeking to delight our customers with the quality of our service (not forgetting, as for all the points below, that there are economically disadvantaged people who cannot be our customers).
- We informally and formally survey our customers' needs on a regular basis.
- We welcome customer feedback and criticism as a rich source of learning.
- We constantly review our strategies in line with changing customer needs.
- We value and encourage flexibility in our thinking, in our structures and in our systems, in the knowledge that this gives us a unique competitive advantage.
- Learning orientation – people take responsibility for their own learning and development and staff are recruited more for their attitude and their ability to learn than for their current knowledge and skill levels.
- People are empowered and involved, being accountable decision makers.
- Commitments are seen as binding agreements, unless otherwise renegotiated, and people take personal responsibility for compliance through self-regulation.
- Employment/reward/job placement and development are competency-based.
- Our people are passionate about what they do; they see each day as bringing new challenges and they put maximum effort into their work.
- Rapid decision making.

- Managers act as role models and coaches.
- Results orientation.

Our structure. To achieve our corporate and divisional visions our structure has to have the following attributes.

- Flexibility of roles and structures to accommodate experimentation, growth and adaptation/change.
- Integrates the communal, individual and aspirational needs of people.
- Less formal.
- Devolved.
- Delayered with fewer job grades and very little hierarchy – wide spans of control.
- Multi-skilled, semi-autonomous teams with maximum accountability and authority.
- Multi-disciplined approach.
- Few status symbols.
- Little conformity and few rigid job descriptions.
- Project-based teams rather than functional organisation.
- Membership criteria are competency-based.
- Dual career pathing – technical vs co-ordinator.
- There are only three kinds of role – the doers, the co-ordinators and the strategic planners.

Our people. To achieve our corporate and divisional visions our people share and participate in discussion about the following attributes.

- Learning is self-motivated and experiential.
- Staff are recruited for their attitude and their ability to learn dialogical skills rather than their current knowledge and skills levels.
- Our people represent many cultures and both genders at every level in the organisation.
- People take ownership.
- Careful choosing with dialogical skills; and encouragement of this attitude.
- Management style.
  - Co-ordinators are coaches rather than managers.

- Co-ordinators are available to the people rather than the other way around (a lesson from the Viable System Model).
- Co-ordinators act as role models.
- A person's power base is gained through personal influence and openness rather than through position.
- Involve rather than exclude.
- Share rather than hold back.
- Information is shared openly and rapidly.

THE STUDY

Over the last two years SLA have employed a wide range of systems methods in efforts to achieve progressive organisational development. At the start we employed Exploring and Making Decisions (EMD) with our policy-making group to aid learning and understanding and to formulate a future vision of Life Customer Services. Diagnosis for Effective Organisation (DEO) was used to evaluate new team functions and structures that emerged from policy making. Exploring and Choosing Designs (ECD) was tried at the start of reengineering, but as things proceeded and reengineering itself took the stage, ECD faded and our pilot reengineering project took over with the explicit aim of building an example of how new teams would operate. Other forms of intervention came into play that are not covered in this book, including Building Shared Vision and Building Shared Values. This study focuses on the reengineering project.

The Life Division investigated the possibility of a reengineering project in July 1993. After some months of learning what reengineering was about, it was decided to begin with the Annuities Department as a first phase for the project. A pilot project is common with BPR. The main reason for the choice of the Annuities area was that its business processes largely reflected the rest of the division; it is considered a microcosm of Life Customer Services. It is expected that to reengineer the whole division will take about three years.

The purpose of the reengineering project is captured in essence in six project principles.

● To substantially improve quality and service to customers.

- To develop business processes that guarantee as far as possible sustained productivity improvement and thus customer delight.
- To reduce long- and short-term costs.
- To provide all involved people with a sense of ownership and accountability.
- To ensure that maximum benefit is derived from systems and technology.
- To increase the competence of our staff (i.e., knowledge, skills and appropriate behaviour) to ensure customer delight.

The following main deliverables of the reengineering project are planned.

- Efficient, effective processes.
- Co-ordinated technical effort.
- Competent people.
- Sustained sponsorship.
- Clear reasons for change.
- Competent enthusiastic change agents.
- Staff involvement and participation.
- Shared future structure.
- Delighted customers.

A small reengineering team was set up in October 1993. The team composition is given below.

- A general manager (GM), who has extensive human resource and project experience.
- An assistant general manager (AGM), who has risen through the ranks of the division and has extensive business experience.
- Myself, a senior project manager, who moved on from the Information Technology Division a couple of years ago in order to learn more about the business.

A steering committee was created which consisted of the above GM, AGM, as well as the executive head of Life Division, and the other GM in the division who is responsible for day-to-day operations. I am called to the committee on demand to clarify any technical and workflow design issues that are causing concern. There are given roles and responsibilities of team members as set out below.

Reengineering team.

- Meet project objectives.
- Develop communication strategy.
- Update key audiences (internal and external).
- Interface with all stakeholders.
- Manage integration of technical capability and business needs.
- Identify and agree on technology deliverables and timetables.
- 'Walk and talk' on the SLA and divisional vision.
- Monitor milestone achievements.

Steering committee.

- Main sponsors of the project.
- Ensure that ongoing project implementation is consistent with SLA's vision and business plan and principles established for the project.
- Provide support as requested by the reengineering team on key issues/activities.
- Monitor milestone achievements.
- Monitor financial requirements.
- Review outputs/quality requirements of the project as outlined in the project document.
- Act as change agents/role models in interactions with all staff within the division and company.

After the vision and values had been established the following broad process for reengineering was developed.

- Map the current business processes.
- Undertake walk-throughs and critical reflection on these and on deliverables too (asking 'Why?', 'Why?', 'Why?').
- Redesign the business processes in the light of new technology and the learning gained during the above two steps.
- Redesign teams and structure.
- Implement new technology and structures.

The first task that was tackled was a thorough analysis of the existing operation. There were two components of this task, mapping the existing business processes (method study) and statistical data gathering (work measurement). *This stage had as its premise the participation and learning of as many members of the Annuities team as possible.* It is our belief that nobody knows the current workflow better that those who perform it. Using a whiteboard, process flows (maps) were drawn employing facilitators. The facilitator's role was to describe the process using the participants' input. Facilitators initially were urged not to impose their own understanding of the business process, but rather to mediate a map of how the participants saw the process. As argued in Chapter 7, however, in some circumstances it is impossible for facilitators to play a neutral role.

Once the maps were documented on a computer drawing package, they were printed and checked for accuracy by participants. During these sessions everyone attempts to 'become ignorant' and ask as many questions of the current process as possible. Small, current, operation-based improvements (quick hits), based on the insights gained above, were instituted.

A large majority of insurance business is driven by paper. Service requests are usually triggered by a request letter or form (input to the process). The request is then serviced by inquiry into, or changes to, data on computer systems (the transformation process). Finally some sort of letter or schedule is produced and sent to the client (the output from the process).

Currently a paper file is kept for each and every policy. This not only contains the original application form and copies of schedules sent to the client, but is also filled with *ad hoc* notes and system prints reflecting the life history of any changes to the contract and related correspondence to the client. This file is therefore the main source of reference when attempting to service a client. The files are stored for safe keeping in a basement and are requested and shipped up to anyone who needs them. The advent of image technology presents powerful tools to help with the management and control of such paper-based operations. Image technology allows an image of a document (like a photocopy) to be stored electronically on a computer. The image is created by scanning the paper through a scanning device. Once an image is stored and indexed electronically, a number of things that are not possible with the paper document become possible.

- It can be viewed by more than one person at the same time.
- The image can be used to trigger work electronically.
- The distribution of work according to operator competency can occur.
- A person can work with a large computer screen without the need of paper.

Image technology is being used to automate and control paper-based workflows with the aid of computers in the Annuities area. An evaluation of several vendors was concluded and it was decided to purchase a package called Automatic Work Distribution (AWD). The new technology enables improvements in the business process. All business processes are therefore redesigned in terms of the new technology. This in turn enables the redesign of the structures that give rise to the processes.

The Life Division wants to move towards fast, flat teams that balance the needs of individuals and SLA and are customer responsive. Image technology and work distribution reduces the management requirements in service teams. Work is automatically distributed, selected for quality checking and measurement of all the stages of any business process occurs automatically. Historically within the Annuities area three functional teams existed. In the future model two cross-functional teams are planned. These teams will be supported by a paper-in team (which will scan and index all incoming service requests into the computer) and a paper-out team which will print and dispatch all outgoing letters. A new telephone team will be solely responsible for servicing telephone inquiries. The membership of the new teams was decided after consultation with the current Annuities staff, the main criteria being an even spread of business competencies between the teams and the existing relationships between people. The positions of co-ordinator for each of the new teams was advertised and open to anyone in the division. The respondents were shortlisted by the senior management of the division, the new cross-functional teams then interviewed them and selected the co-ordinator they preferred.

There were four main issue areas that we faced when implementing BPR. The first two issues, those of vision and values, are specific to SLA. The remaining two, the Problem of Reengineering and the Problem of Power in Reengineering, are not necessarily specific to SLA. It was this diversity of problems that raised in my thinking the need to chose methods appropriate to the task at hand. I employed TSI-based thinking to help us do this, as mentioned again later.

The reengineering within the Life Division is taking place against a company-wide process of value sharing. Every employee in the company has attended a two-day value-sharing workshop and whilst at the workshop, participants crafted the values they believe SLA should aspire to. Representatives from all areas of the company were then democratically elected to craft the final set of company values. The following represent values drawn up by the participants.

- *Customer focus (service excellence).* We attract and retain customers by identifying and satisfying their needs and exceeding their expectations through quality service, products and innovation.
- *Fairness and non-discrimination.* We value diversity by creating an environment of equal opportunity for all.
- *Flexibility.* We are open minded, flexible and welcome the opportunities that change provides.
- *Leadership.* We are all accountable to ourselves and each other and are effectively empowered to provide dynamic leadership that is value-driven, visible, transparent and focused.
- *Learning.* We have a learning environment for all individuals and teams to *acquire continuously skills and knowledge*, freely sharing it with others for the benefit of all stakeholders.
- *Mutual trust and respect.* We develop and earn mutual trust and respect through openness, honesty and a willingness to understand one another. We uphold human dignity and self-worth in all we do.
- *Open communication.* We have regular, open, honest, timely communication *leading to understanding and mutual appreciation*, and together we treat information responsibly.
- *Performance, recognition and rewards.* We recognise, communicate and reward *continuous improvements in productivity, quality*

and effectiveness, to enhance competitiveness in support of our vision.

- *Social responsibility*. We creatively apply resources for the enhancement of the environment and the community of South Africa.
- *Teamwork*. Through teamwork, interdependence and individual creativity we meet our outputs. We accept joint and individual accountability for our performance.
- *Wealth creation*. We create wealth and achieve long-term profitability through quality performance, products and investments to the benefit of all our stakeholders and ultimately to South African society.

There was some tension within the vision. The aim to become first choice to staff, customers and shareholders (whilst keeping the wider social issues in mind) is problematic, since these groups of stakeholders have very different interests and chances to express them. What makes a company first choice for staff may be very different from what makes it desirable to shareholders.

Then there was the reengineering problem. BPR has been defined by Hammer and Champy (see Further Reading) as rethinking and radical redesign of business processes to achieve dramatic improvements in critical contemporary measures of performance, such as cost, quality, service and speed. For Hammer and Champy 'fundamental rethinking' entails asking basic questions about our companies and how they work. We need to ask '*Why* ?' we do what we do (what is the purpose?) and '*Why?*' do we think the way we do? By doing this, it is believed that people will be forced to look at the tacit rules and assumptions that underlie the way they do business.

This sounds easier than it is in practice. In the age of learning organisations, where shared vision and values are the order of the day, how do planners involved in reengineering ensure that they are honest and working towards a transparent and legitimate purpose? How do we ensure that reengineering is not just a change of the management guard achieved through the restructuring and manipulation of staff? What is the real purpose of reengineering? Is this purpose a shared one? Is it to reduce costs, reduce staff, reduce middle management, change the culture, provide ownership to staff, empower employees, improve quality and contribute to societal development? Are individual interests driving the effort? Do the 'affected' in the form of those not involved in the redesign have a chance really to challenge the process and its designs? These are the types of questions that anyone involved in reengineering should ask themselves, if for no other reason than to achieve the systemic principle and therefore effective management, as Professor Flood mentions in Chapter 3.

When designers map any part of the real world (business process) they must make assumptions and judgements about what should be included in the analysis. For example, some designers involved in reengineering may implicitly consider people as part of the process or system being redesigned, whilst others may not. Existing computer systems may be viewed as part of the process to be redesigned. These assumptions may have far-reaching implications. They are boundary judgements that underlie and help form designer's maps of the real world.

There is an obvious need for an inquiry process that will reveal the boundary judgements that those involved in reengineering are inevitably making. Once the normative content (assumptions and boundary judgements) has been surfaced, it can be tested through critical reflection. This normative content can only be substantiated by the consent of those affected by the designs. It is the designers' *responsibility* to ensure the transparency of their assumptions and to discover their potential repercussions. The designer would have to enter into discussions with those affected by the designs in order to ensure the 'moral and democratic legitimacy' of maps and designs. Critically Evaluating Designs and Decisions (CEDD) is a conceptual framework that provides heuristic support in surfacing, testing and improving the normative content of maps and designs.

Ultimately one has to tackle the problem of power within BPR. Most reengineering efforts centralise large amounts of power in a small group of people. In order to understand this better, let us examine how Hammer and Champy answer the question 'Who will reengineer?' They recognise up-front that 'Companies don't reengineer processes; people do'. The following roles have emerged during Hammer and Champy's work with companies that are implementing reengineering. The leader role is filled by a senior executive who motivates and authorises the reengineering project. The process owner role is usually a manager who has responsibility for a team or process that is being reengineered. The reengineering team is dedicated to redesigning particular processes and the steering committee is a policy-making body. The people who fill these roles will only represent a small portion of the company, yet inherit power to influence radically the future structure and operations of the company.

It is inevitable that during large change projects, corporate politics and positioning for power in the 'new' redesigned structure will take place. It is possible that all the 'involved' roles named by Hammer and Champy may have a personal interest in the new structure. Mainly for these reasons CEDD has been chosen to evaluate problems of power in our reengineering task. It was used in Mode 1 as described in Chapter 9. It was vital that we made this choice of method. According to the philosophy of TSI, without such a choice the process would not be systemic and consequently reengineering would not be effective enough. I also share Professor Flood's view that it is morally desirable.

CEDD[1] poses 12 questions that must be addressed in the reengineering process. Let us examine the 12 questions relative to the reengineering effort that ultimately changes practically everything about the company. The critical intent of the questions is highlighted by asking them in both 'is' and 'ought' forms. The 'is' questions surface effective assumptions and implications concerning reengineering relative to the 'ought' answers, in other words, without the illusion of objectivity.

The first three questions largely address problems of motivation and power. Power is the ability of an individual or a group to impose its/their purpose on others. The concern in TSI is that this then alienates large numbers of people and therefore does not encourage them to work towards the purpose. The question of power in reengineering is thus an important one. This is especially relevant in organisations where the reengineering effort and its intended results are being marketed as

---

[1] I need to point out that the original source for CEDD given in Further Reading has been extremely influential on my work and the way it is reported.

progressive and empowering. The first three questions are explored below in the 'is' and 'ought' form.

- *Who is reengineering's actual client, i.e., who belongs to the group whose interests and values are served vs those who do not benefit and have to live the consequences?*
  - The steering committee provides direction, therefore their interests are being served to some extent.
  - The reengineering team benefits through experience, travel and learning.
  - New team members and co-ordinators created in the new structure will have to live the consequences.
- *Who ought to be the client (beneficiary) of reengineering?*
  - According to the company vision all stakeholders – staff, customers and shareholders.
  - According to the project principles; customers should benefit through improved quality and service. Shareholders and customers should benefit through cost reduction. Staff should benefit through increased knowledge and skills.

Comment. Ideally, all staff in Life Customer Services ought to be clients. There is a danger to be avoided, that the steering committee and reengineering team will serve their own interests. But neither the steering committee nor the reengineering team will have to live and work in the new structures (teams) and processes that are being built. This must be remembered.

- *What is the actual purpose of reengineering, measured not in terms of declared intentions of the involved, but in terms of the actual consequences (outcome)?*
  - The 'declared intentions' are contained in the project principles (essentially cost reduction, customer delight, more competent staff and contributing to the new South African society).
  - The actual outcomes produced so far are: the co-ordinators of new teams are selected by team members, the co-ordinators of the new teams do not have the privilege of offices and the new teams are very flat (two levels, team members and co-ordinators).
- *What ought to be the purpose of reengineering?*

- This depends on which stakeholder is answering the question.
- The purpose perhaps ought to be: to increase quality and flexibility and reduce cost and lead times, increase the levels of participation in decision making for all staff (empowerment), reduce the centralisation of power and provide an environment in which learning can flourish.

Comment. I have always found these questions about purpose to be very enlightening. There is not only a tension between the declared intentions and personal intentions normally found when comparing 'is' and 'ought' responses, but also possibly between declared intentions and actual outcomes. The only way I have found of dealing with this is to try and be as honest as possible and make transparent motivations for reengineering. The motivations are declared explicitly above. The values of the company are ideals that are created through the participation of all staff and as such they could represent an adequate purpose for reengineering. The purpose therefore could be stated as: Redesigning the division so that its operations reflect values of the organisation, which are (ongoingly) defined by all those involved.

- *What is judged by the design's consequences, the design's built-in measure of success?*
  - The reduction of operational service costs.
  - Improvement in service to customers through: the reduction of lead times on service requests, an increase in the quality and accuracy of service.
  - The ability of the new teams to improve constantly the above measures.
- *What ought to be the design's measure of success?*
  - In addition to the above, the following: the increase in participation and decision making for team members within the new structures and the development of all staff in basic skills and corporate thinking.

Comment. Organisations are groups of people, not just cost ratios, lead times, and quality statistics. We are more effective as designers involved in reengineering if reminded of this fact every once in a while. The result of this reminder in our effort was, as seen above, to re-emphasise participation and development of people, which had not been declared explicitly as measures of success.

The next three questions are essentially about sources of control. This set of questions is about decision makers within reengineering. The decision maker is the complex of persons who can produce and control changes in measures of improvement.

- *Who is actually the decision taker, i.e., who can actually change reengineering's measure of success?*
  - The steering committee could change reengineering's *required* measure of success, i.e., reduce the degree of cost reduction required.
  - The reengineering team members who help in redesigning the business processes take decisions that will affect the actual measure of success.
  - The new teams and their co-ordinators will make decisions that will affect the actual measure of success.
- *Who ought to be the decision taker, i.e., who has the power to change the measure of improvement?*
  - An implementation group consisting of representatives from the steering committee, the reengineering team and the area being reengineered.

Comment. This question can be interpreted in many ways. One can ask it referring to reengineering or referring to the new structures and processes that are created by reengineering. One of the assumptions related to reengineering is that we require 'outsiders' to be involved in the redesign. This is because they are less likely to be constrained by the current reality of the existing situation. My conclusion was that ultimately only a team that represented all viewpoints of involved and affected people, and which is sensitive to the South African situation, should be able to change the measure of success.

- *What components (resources and constraints) of successful reengineering are actually controlled by the decision taker?*
  - The Annuities Division reports to the AGM about the reengineering team.

- *What components (resources and constraints) of the area being reengineered ought to be controlled by the decision taker to ensure successful reengineering?*
  - All areas being reengineered should report to the GM or AGM for the duration of the phase. This will reduce the level of politics and increase the flow of information.
  - The information technology resources involved should be controlled by the reengineering team.

Comment. Some level of coercion will take place during the reengineering effort. Resistance to change and protection of interests and power is unavoidable. These issues need to be tackled with the values of the company, in which employees participated and societal issues were considered, foremost in our minds. The reporting system just mentioned goes some way towards this.

- *What conditions are not controlled by the decision taker, i.e., what represents environment to them?*
  - As technical designers responsible for workflows, we have taken the existing line of business information systems as given. The purpose is to avoid overdesigning the workflow system by integrating it with other information systems. The approach also bounds the scope of the first phase thereby improving the chances of timely implementation.
  - The Annuities Division is relatively self-contained with few of the business processes crossing into other business areas.
- *What resources and conditions ought to be part of the environment and not controlled by the decision maker?*
  - Ideally as little as possible. However, if certain things are not taken as given, one runs the risk of attempting to solve all problems within a business area. This in turn leads to a project that soon runs into diminishing returns. It also tends to make for large, long and costly reengineering projects.

Comment. In our project we have found it extremely useful to gain explicit agreement with involved and affected people, as far as that is possible, on what the scope is for the first phase on reengineering. This entails agreeing with those people what must be maintained and what can be changed.

The next three questions address sources of expertise. These questions are aimed at the sources of expertise required to map and improve business processes during reengineering. Expertise is a resource but it is not necessarily under the control of the decision makers.

- *Who is actually involved as planner?*
  - The GM concerned with special projects has been planning and co-ordinating the 'expert' resources on the project.
  - To a lesser extent the members of the steering committee, the reengineering team, and indeed other staff, are involved in recognising and enrolling further expertise into the project.
- *Who ought to be involved as planner?*
  - The actors mentioned above.
  - The existing leadership of the area being reengineered.
  - Everyone who will be affected by reengineering, since each one has an expertise in their own situation.

Comment. The 'planner' is a special case in that their crucial skill consists in bringing together all the people whose (ordinary) expertise is needed, rather than replacing any of them. This role has been adequately filled by the GM for special projects who has a strong network across the company and constantly brings together experts on the project. An illustration of this is that links have been established with a UK-based company that has just gone through reengineering using image and workflow technologies. This relationship has led to visits to that site by our experts and visits to our division by a senior project manager involved in their reengineering effort. The result of this bringing together of people has led to significant learning and mutual accountability on both sides.

- *Who is involved as 'expert', what is the nature of their expertise, what role do they actually play?*
  - The business expert: this role is filled by the AGM on the reengineering team with 20 years' hands-on experience.
  - The technical expert: the author fills this role. The source of my expertise is experience in large information technology projects.
  - The workflow expert: the above two actors plus a consult-

ant from the image and workflow software supplier and staff from Annuities, often called in to contribute their knowledge about specific business processes.

- *What kind of expertise ought to flow into the redesign of business processes, i.e., who ought to be considered an expert and what should be their role?*
  - The existing staff and leadership of the Annuities area and others affected.
  - All the actors under the 'is'; that those person(s) who has/have some relevant knowledge, experience or skill to contribute to the planning process, including those affected by the consequences.

Comment. This is problematic from a reengineering point of view, since although the people who work within the current business processes have experience to offer, one does not want to recreate the old business processes or structures. The 'affected' participated in SLA's initial mapping of the existing processes, the walk-throughs and questioning of those maps. Once processes have been redesigned onto the image workflow system, the staff of Annuities are once again walked through the flows and asked to challenge the new designs. This goes some way towards meeting the ideal answer of the 'ought' form of this question.

- *Where do the involved seek the guarantee that their design will work?*
  - *In the theoretical competence of experts?*
  - *In consensus among experts?*
  - *In the validity of empirical data?*
  - *In mathematical models/computer simulations?*
  - *In political support from interest groups?*
  - *In the experience/intuition of the involved?*
  Can these ensure the design's success?
  - Consensus among experts: the culture of the project is one in which it is considered acceptable to argue and discuss a point in design until a way forward is negotiated. For example, this frequently occurs both within the steering committee and the reengineering team.
  - General consensus: This is reflected in the following two

outputs (goals) of the reengineering projects: staff involvement and participation and shared future structure.

- *Who ought to be the guarantor of reengineering, i.e., where ought
  the designer seek the guarantee that his/her design will be
  implemented and will prove successful, judged by the client's measure of success?*
  - Ideally all members of the division should through their
    efforts guarantee success.

Comment. One major guarantor that needs to be clarified is the
type of consultation model used. The amount of participation
and consultation that takes place will reflect the relationship
between 'expertise' and 'practice'. As mentioned above in reference to the questions on experts, the relationship that is appropriate for reengineering is difficult to attain. On the one hand,
you seek fast, creative decisions during design and on the other,
your primary guarantee that designs will be successful lies in
widespread participation.

The last three questions are about sources of legitimation. The
questions so far have been aimed at the roles of those 'involved'
in reengineering and how those people are accountable. The
remaining three questions deal with those who will be 'affected'
by the reengineering effort. It is often more difficult for the
affected to contribute resources and expertise and for their purposes to influence the planning effort. These are the majority to
whom those involved in reengineering have a moral responsibility, a responsibility for all the practical consequences of their
designs. In reengineering this responsibility should go beyond
achieving any measures of success, it should extend to the costs
and consequences for those who are not in the client group.

- *Who among the involved witnesses represents the concerns of the
  affected? Who is affected without being involved?*
  - We do not have official 'witnesses' who represent the con-
    cerns of the affected.
  - The current management of Annuities have to some extent
    been involved and have on occasions represented the con-
    cerns of the rest of Annuities members.
  - We have an open door policy in the room where the re-
    engineering team is designing the new business processes.

- A group of five Annuities staff has been attending afternoon sessions where they are walked through the redesigned business processes and asked to comment critically on them.
- *Who ought to belong to the witnesses representing the concerns of the staff who will or might be affected by the changes reengineering brings. That is to say, who among the affected ought to get involved?*
  - We perhaps ought to have 'official' representation, or informal representation, or other channels through which opinions can be expressed, allowing expression of the concerns of people who may be affected by reengineering.
  - The affected who have relevant experience in the current business processes should be involved.

Comment. In my opinion this is an area in which we ought to improve. One improvement is that before the reengineering team begins work in an area, people from that area elect representatives who can perform the role of witnesses.

- *Are the affected given, or should they be given, the chance to emancipate themselves from the experts and take their fate into their own hands, or do the experts determine what is right for them? That is to say, are the affected treated merely as means for the purposes of others, or are they treated as 'ends in themselves'?*
  - The affected are given a chance to critically examine the new business processes.
  - The affected are not given the chance to emancipate themselves from the designs constructed by the reengineering team.
  - The affected were to some degree able to 'take their fate into their own hands' when they voted to elect their new co-ordinators.
- *To what degree and in what way ought the affected be given the chance of emancipation from the promises of the involved?*
  - The affected ought to be able to contribute on the issues that have a direct effect on, for example, their quality of work life. These include, for example: the physical layout of desks for teams, the constitution and leadership of teams and the issues surrounding possible changes in remuneration structures.

– The affected ought to be able to challenge any part of the reengineering process, therefore having a say in organisational values. The value of mutual trust and respect and open communication are two that are especially relevant to the affected.

Comment. Historically the culture of the organisation has not been one which openly challenges management or managers. These questions get to the heart of the problem of power in reengineering. How do we radically transform organisations in order to improve costs, quality, lead times and flexibility and yet also build organisations that are participative and have at their core negotiated shared values that are seen as relevant by all in the organisation?

● *What world view is actually underlying reengineering? Is it the world view of (some of) the involved or (some of) the affected?*
  – My own world view with regard to reengineering is that it should empower and develop the people who are affected by it. Empower them through participation in all decision making and an increasing ability to determine their own future.
  – Each person involved in reengineering will have their own world view. The responsibility of those involved is to make their world view explicit and open to challenge.
● *Upon what world views of either the involved or the affected ought reengineering to be based?*
  – The SLA's values represent to some extent negotiated organisational ideals. It is therefore appropriate to use them as the legitimate world view upon which reengineering should be based, as long as it is recognised that the values are always open to further debate.

Comment. These questions point to further problems which haunt reengineering. Is there a correct world view upon which reengineering should be based? What right does a designer have to impose his/her world view on others?

Perhaps this is an appropriate time to move on to reflections.

REFLECTIONS

Many of the case studies in Chapter 10 reflect upon the use of TSI in the process of management. I do not wish to repeat the points made elsewhere, although there are many which I firmly agree with. Instead, and since this case study is unique among the others in the way it attempts to use CEDD to address issues of power, I have decided to reflect upon the choice and use of CEDD to evaluate the reengineering process.

There has been considerable learning at SLA using CEDD in reengineering. The main points are recorded below.

- Questions asked about reengineering structures and business processes that it produces are never truly answered. As the context of a project changes over time the questions have been re-examined. Each time they have helped to see better how assumptions may affect designs and structures.
- In order to make transparent our own assumptions to others we have to surface them firstly for ourselves. CEDD provides a framework through which this can be done.
- The deep realisation that understanding of any business area or process will always be biased by our own assumptions has led me to state openly that the staff of the Annuities Division must not assume I am an expert, or that I fully understand the business they are in. I now make this declaration at the start of most walk-throughs of design sessions. This has had the following effects.
  - It has liberated me to act as ignorant about the processes at work, as I actually am. This has led to better listening and inquiry on my part (I can now ask uninformed questions without feeling embarrassed).
  - It has enabled the staff participating to take on the role of 'experts'. This gives them the confidence to contribute more than they might have if I were to assume an expert role.
- The use of the 12 questions has clarified for me my own biases and world view underlying reengineering. Now, the improvement of participation, and the development and empowerment of staff, drive most of my efforts. Yet the questions have led me to see that people's views, including my own, are incredibly limited and do not necessarily accommo-

date for the needs of other people. For example, it is all too easy in the private sector of South Africa to forget the wider societal needs and therefore play no relevant role in the social change underway.

Reengineering is taking place at a time when employees are becoming more aware of their ability to contribute towards decision making and the general purpose of teams and organisations. The fundamental rethinking and radical redesign of business process often requires new organisational structures that cross old boundaries. In today's competitive business environment, reengineering projects are given tight deadlines during which the redesign of structures and business processes must occur. If everyone affected by the changes had to participate in their creation, the projects would cost much more in time and money. An increasing moral burden is therefore placed on those who are involved in reengineering. They have to consider the consequences of their designs on those in the company who, because of time and cost constraints, are unable to participate fully. CEDD has helped those involved in reengineering to remain honest. Reengineering is as much about people as it is about the technical business process. The moral idea is a challenge to anyone involved in reengineering today.

Frankly, working with CEDD has been an intense and often lonely experience. The initial effect of immersing myself into the critical reflection that CEDD demands was to make me feel inadequate as a planner, designer and change agent. I became acutely aware of how dogmatic and arrogant I had become about some of my plans and designs. By following the questions I literally got to know myself as a change agent. I now try to be as explicit about my plans and the assumptions behind them as is possible. To help in this I have continually re-evaluated my actions through the principles of systems thinking as described by Professor Flood in Chapter 4 and according to the principles underlying CEDD given in the last chapter. Let me expand on the last point.

The principle of *purposefulness* has led me to examine in detail my own agenda as regards reengineering. It also led to a growing respect for the interests of others and the responsibility I have towards them.

The *systems idea* has helped me come to terms with the fact that any situation in which I work as designer or planner is much bigger and more complex than I can imagine. This has helped guard against falling into the trap of being too sure of my own knowledge, or believing that I really know what is going on.

The *moral idea* has forced me to consider all the people that may be affected by my actions within reengineering. In reengineering we need to design business processes that improve the human condition. One way of facilitating this is through the design of team processes that enhance participation, learning and the development of all. The striking fact that this idea highlights is that I will not have to work in such teams and therefore need to be vigilant about considering those who will.

The critical intent of the *guarantor idea* reminds me that the very things which I may feel guarantee a successful implementation may be misguided. This has led me to entertain many scenarios about how implementation will actually transpire and has convinced me that good implementation is best secured by focusing on the conditions that increase the likelihood of a wonderful accident happening. One such focus has been to increase steadily the level of participation by the new co-ordinators and team members and to introduce the idea of participation into their consciousness so that they operate this way. However, and this is a difficult one for me, I have for strategic reasons decided to use my influence on occasions to restrict participation. Although I make my reasons clear for this, and remain accountable for my actions, it is still difficult, and my only solace is in believing that the end product of reengineering will be better for it and for all.

In conclusion, using CEDD helped those involved in reengineering to get to grips with our inevitable limitations as designers and planners. It helped to improve reengineering itself, accommodating many more viewpoints, especially those normally neglected in such processes, and has therefore given rise to a more acceptable and sustainable design. It has guarded against the trap that designs or plans that we, as 'experts', construct are the best and only way of doing something. This is truly in the spirit of TSI.

Case 10.6
The Halesworth Partnership Pty Ltd (Australia)

TONY TREGURTHA AND ANNMAREE DESMOND, DIRECTORS

Focus: Consulting in the Australian financial sector.

Methods discussed: Metaphors, Quality Management (QM), Business Process Reengineering (BPR), Implementing Designs and Decisions (IDD).

BACKGROUND TO THE WRITERS AND ORGANISATION

Annmaree Desmond and Tony Tregurtha are joint founders and directors of The Halesworth Partnership Pty Ltd, a management services company providing consulting services and related products to the Australian financial sector. It has offices in Melbourne and Sydney in Australia. The company is unique in that its main goal is research and development into organisational problem solving and its tools and techniques, using commercial consultancy work as its means of generating funds to do this.

Prior to the establishment of The Halesworth Partnership (THP), Annmaree consulted in many Australian and New Zealand organisations across diverse industries including retail banking, life insurance, hospitality and manufacturing. She has also worked in executive positions within various service industries. The focus of Annmaree's consulting career, together with organisational improvement and redesign, has been the design and implementation of specialist management training and cultural programmes allied to the implementation of management information systems, including: client retention systems, work management systems, executive reporting systems, market feasibility systems, integrated forecasting packages and statistical quality sampling systems.

Prior to the establishment of THP, Tony worked within the management consulting sphere with a variety of Australian-based organisations. He consulted in many of Australia's leading companies in a range of industries including retail banking, life and general insurance, retail and manufacturing. The bulk of Tony's time was spent reengineering organisations and implementing management systems. With THP he has designed and implemented specialist management information systems, including proactive management and client retention systems, work management systems, executive reporting systems, market feasibility systems, integrated forecasting packages and statistical quality sampling systems. He also held management positions in the service industry.

INTRODUCTION

THP has a commitment to help organisations respond to the business context of the 1990s. Since the late 1980s organisations and their customers have become more sophisticated and innovative in their approach. The emphasis is on superior customer service at optimum resource efficiency with reduced costs. The process of management has moved away from dealing with technical aspects of organisations toward a human-oriented approach encouraging participation. This has involved much change. Changes include flattening of organisational structures and moving decision-making power to those closest to the customer, be they internal or external. Ultimately, this is all about adding value.

THP was founded on the premise that a consulting service

too must add value to the organisations that it serves. To do this consultants must systematically analyse the current and future needs and demands of a client's entire operation. Consultants should not leave reports for executive management to act on, they must take responsibility and assist the client to identify areas for improvement and make changes happen. Added value can be enhanced by developing the client's personnel and imparting to them expertise needed in today's highly challenging business environment.

THP therefore puts to work a philosophy about consulting practice that is directly relevant to the needs of organisations in the 1990s and beyond. There are four points relating to our commitment to leading-edge consultancy (a number of which come directly from TSI).

- Develop innovative proactive tools and proactive behaviour in the organisation through hands-on real time information – the technical dimension.
- Explicitly address cultural and political issues – the human dimension.
- View organisations holistically – be systemic.
- Stay in touch with new developments in problem solving – offer services at the forefront of consultancy.

There are four points relating to our commitment to the client.

- Promise and deliver only that which can be achieved.
- Work on the 'shop floor' with clients to develop solutions and make the solutions work.
- Impart knowledge about methods and tools for the client's future use.
- Link billing of the client to achievement of measurable deliverables.

To ensure that these commitments are fulfilled, THP undertook a critical review of current consulting practices. The main weaknesses in consulting practice that we uncovered and now address are discussed below. This makes an interesting addition to Professor Flood's discussion about consultants in Chapter 8.

- *There is a lack of knowledge about problem solving methods.* Com-

pany managers and consultants alike are often able to recognise symptoms of problems, backtrack to the causes, but then
are at a loss to know how to tackle the causes. This is mainly
due to a lack of awareness of the range of problem solving
methods that are available, or because there is no proper
understanding about which method or methods is/are most
appropriate to the problems faced. Problems are then either
'ignored' or are tackled with methods that are not capable of
getting to the root cause.

- *Difficulty in grasping the interacting nature of problems.* It is very
difficult for consultants to grasp and bring into focus the core
interacting problems in the limited time frames that they are
given. A tendency has therefore arisen to neglect differences
between organisations leading to one-fits-all approaches, for
instance we are aware of a large Australian consulting company that implements the same solution irrespective of the
industry, size of organisation, or the technical and human
problems, which all go to make organisations unique. This
has led to dramatic differences in the results achieved, with
some cases where clients have paid money to lose ground
both internally and in the market-place.

- *Political and cultural issues are ignored.* Consultants are often
employed to address a specific area or programme. Typically
these involve Quality Management (QM) or Business Process
Reengineering (BPR) looking only at things like workflow
analysis or design of reporting systems. As the focus is bound
by such programmes, cultural and political undercurrents
tend to be disregarded, which are usually key determinants
in success or failure. Possible forms of resistance are therefore
ignored, leading to failure. Sometimes solutions reflect only
the power structure of organisation which not only creates
resistance through alienation but fails to recognise and balance organisational and individual needs.

- *Difficulty in communicating core problems to the client.* Consultants are usually employed to assist the client in one of two circumstances.
  - When the client recognises a need for change but is not able
    to get to grips with what that change should be.
  - When a problem has been surfaced that requires the ser-
    vices of a specialist.

It is very difficult in either circumstance to ensure that a client fully understands the problems highlighted. This is often perpetuated by consultants holding back information for whatever reason or not communicating issues clearly. The results hinder both parties in the following ways.

- Confusing the client.
- Generating a misunderstanding of problems.
- Leading to the client and consultant working with a difference in understanding about the problems faced and the way to tackle them.
- Leading to the client hitting information overload.
- Leading to a loss of client support in the programme.

As a result of these findings THP chose to go through a phase of research and development. The following work was identified as vital.

- Research into the availability and utility of problem solving methods.
- Generation of tools for identification and measurement of cultural and political issues.
- Development of an approach to problem solving that treats organisation holistically.
- Development of an approach that recognises different types of organisation, hence different types of problem and the way they are interrelated.
- Development of a means of presentation of THP's approach that was easily understandable by both consultant and client, ensuring clear communication.

Our research into the availability of problem solving methods brought us into contact with TSI. We found TSI powerful in the way it addressed the remaining research and development tasks. It explicitly recognised cultural and political problems in a holistic way that separates out different types of problem to be dealt with. It also brings forward tools to make these things happen. It made sense to us to integrate our approach to consultancy with the TSI problem solving framework. We also saw TSI as an approach to problem solving that could easily be explained to consultants and clients. In fact, at the start of any consultancy we find it beneficial to explain to the client the approach that we are following and how this will help them, thus minimising chances for misunderstanding what we are doing. We do this by explaining the THP/TSI scheme up-front.

The THP/TSI approach to setting up a working relationship with organisations has five steps which have been the backbone of THP's approach to date. The five steps are given below.

- Initial meeting.
- Setting the approach.
- Analysis and project proposal.
- Implementation of project.
- Post-project support.

The five steps are now operated through TSI's three phases in the following way, making use of the recursive structure of TSI.

- *Creativity phase focusing on creative thinking*. To gain an overview of the core problems and how they interrelate. Continuation of the *creativity phase focusing on choice and implementation stages*. To examine the problems in more depth through a structured approach. This serves to gauge the severity, relative importance and complexity of the problems and to highlight other problems that may not have been apparent or seem relevant by the client. It leads to choice of problems to tackle.
- *Choice phase*. To document findings and problems surfaced and set out recommendations for implementation in an analysis report. To choose a project for implementation along with the methods appropriate to the programme.
- *Implementation phase*. To implement the chosen project.

The relationship between the THP approach and TSI is shown in Figure 10.6.1. The case study given below reports on a recent consultancy carried out using the THP/TSI approach.

THE STUDY

(A pseudonym is used for the organisation in this case study to maintain confidentiality as requested.) Delta is an Australian

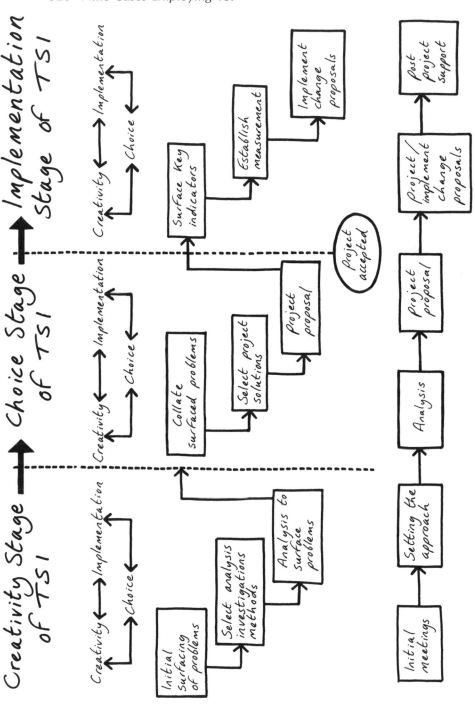

Figure 10.6.1   The relationship between the Halesworth Partnership's approach and TSI

insurance company. It is an extremely successful operation that has experienced excellent returns and substantial growth over the last ten years. It is a decentralised operation with branches throughout Australia. With a staff of 80, the Victoria branch is the largest of the organisation's operations.

THP was approached by the newly appointed Victoria branch manager who had heard of the THP's services through colleagues in the financial services industry. The branch manager was concerned that, although his personnel were committed to the company and the ethos in the branch was extremely conducive to getting the job done, those good efforts were being frustrated by a wide range of interrelated problems. His view was that the processes and culture had not developed in line with organisational growth that Delta had enjoyed over the last few years.

The three phases of the THP/TSI approach were brought into action. Throughout the three phases the client team were involved. The nature of the problems and all other matters were discussed with them. This ensured that there was awareness, understanding and commitment to the process. It also ensured a high level of commitment to solutions and their implementation. Moreover, it meant that consultancy played the dual role of problem solving whilst at the same time training Delta staff in problem solving – in the identification of problems and recommendations for solutions.

Creativity phase. THP employed several methods to highlight problems to be dealt with. This started with interviews. As part of the first two steps, 'Initial Meeting' and 'Setting the Approach', we held in-depth discussions with the branch and national managers. These meetings were structured with the purpose of identifying weaknesses in the branch and hence main areas in which they believed improvements could be made. The process began by explaining the THP/TSI approach to the senior management team. Discussion then moved on to questions about workflows, work management, organisation, work demands, management styles, the internal culture, interpersonal relationships, etc. The agenda of each manager was also investigated. From the discussions a number of problems were highlighted. Of a technical nature the problems were thought to be the following.

- Cumbersome and time-consuming workflows.
- No uniform reporting system.
- No routine planning.
- Poor internal communications.
- Unsatisfactory customer service.
- Poor team structuring.

Additional problems were raised of a human nature.

- The culture did not induce quality or customer service.
- High stress levels indicated by unusually high absenteeism and staff turnover.

The results of these meetings provided guidelines for THP to design a further set of structured interviews. These were held with the branch management team and a range of branch personnel. Again we started by explaining the THP/TSI approach. The discussions were then geared toward surfacing views about weaknesses of the branch and areas in which improvements were needed. Examples of these included customer service, productivity, efficiencies, error and rework, training, morale, absenteeism (four times the industry norm), etc. This process reinforced many of the senior manager's views, further clarified some of them and surfaced new problems that were not recognised by management such as management ineffectiveness and a lack of technical knowledge and training among staff. This exercise also helped THP to develop a working relationship with the client's personnel and further their training in problem identification and project-based solutions.

The next step of the investigation was a structured half-day working session with the branch management team. We went through a kind of brainstorming using the first stages of Implementing Designs and Decisions (IDD), undertaking obstruction analysis. Additional problems of obstruction were surfaced including career pathing. The session then continued with discussion being held about the managers' appreciation of the nature and extent of the problems surfaced. In the debate evidence mounted that the management team did not view Delta holistically.

There was no doubt, however, that the health and welfare of the staff had reached a critical state. Absenteeism was four times the industry norm and staff turnover was 45% per annum. There were serious health problems in the management team including: a heart attack, panic attacks and absenteeism. It was apparent to THP that stress levels were unusually high in the branch. Despite this evidence, some managers did not recognise stress as a valid concern, others pointed the finger to outside factors, but at the end of the day none of the team were able to bring forward a plausible explanation about why they were stressed – nor were they able to quantify the impact this had on branch performance.

We also used the five main metaphors/models introduced through Image Generation during the Creativity phase of TSI to tease out problems to be dealt with. (These metaphors are recorded in Chapter 9 but they are repeated below for convenience.) The five main metaphors that have been used as models in management and organisation theory are as follows.

- *Mechanistic* operations.
- Adapting, growing, evolving, etc.; the *organic* organisation.
- *Organic but intelligent*, conscious of and planning for the future.
- Behaving in the context of social rules and practices – *the corporate culture.*
- Events dominated by *a political dynamic.*

The detailed results of their use are recorded below; elaborated partly because they help to explain the choice of methods later, but also because some highlight common faults we encounter in the financial sector.

When looking at Delta in terms of mechanistic operations the following was noted.

- Customer service.
  - Little systematic control of customer service levels, i.e., follow-up procedures.
  - High telephone abandonment rate due to lack of appropriate procedures.

- Many inquiries avoidable through form and letter redesign.
- Good service to customers through standard correspondence is not happening.
- Management information systems.
  - No systematic procedure for monitoring or controlling work.
- Work process, flow and structure.
  - Poor structure definition resulting in unclear roles and responsibilities and considerable double handling of work.
  - No consistency between like processes being managed within the same area.
  - Workflows involve more people than is efficient or necessary.
  - Excessively long routing of work decreasing response times and increasing the likelihood of misplacing items or there being a build-up in backlog.
  - Bottlenecks in workflows that adversely affect output.
  - Methods of operation in some areas are not analysed for their possible adverse impact elsewhere (optimisation of parts rarely, if ever, leads to optimisation of the whole).
  - Many work procedures are cumbersome and ill-defined.
  - Not every job adds value to the process.
- Strategic planning and objectives.
  - No formal prediction of expected work demands on which to base plans.

When investigating Delta in terms of organic organisations the following was noted.

- Customer service.
  - High level of call backs due to poor management and overall levels of skill, slow turnaround times, customer retention, etc.
  - Lack of co-ordination and co-operation between areas within the branch and head office.
- Management information systems.
  - Management has very little control over the work.
  - The branch's productivity is determined by each individual processing work.

- Increasing backlogs determine resourcing rather than work volumes.
- Backlogs are not purely determined by work volumes, but are influenced by areas affecting work output, such as the amount of error, rework, etc.
- Rigid job designs create poor resource utilisation and uneven distribution of work.
- Little or no understanding about productivity level.
- No systematic or standard method for reporting and therefore no common means of comparing one area's performance to another.
- Lack of information about cultural aspects of the organisation, e.g., stress levels.
- Little front-line management of work.
- No clear objectives for management accountability.
- Individuals are not accountable.
- Design of jobs and workflows has created a lack of ownership of work and its results, adversely affecting morale and motivation.
- No systematic method of continually analysing and improving workflows.
- Little co-ordination or co-operation between areas.
• Strategic planning and objectives.
- No mechanisms are in place to set objectives and plans.
- Management roles and responsibilities are not designed.

When looking at Delta in terms of organic but intelligent organisations the following was noted.

• Customer service.
- High abandonment rate due to a lack of knowledge and training.
- Poor definition of roles.
- Lack of technical knowledge.
- Lack of identification and understanding of internal and external customers.
- Lack of people development in customer service.
- Mismatch between resources and skills, and needs of the customer.
• Management information systems.

- No management information regarding error, quality, hours of work in and out, productivity, service levels, etc.
- No planning tools for management to utilise within any area or the branch as a whole.
- Lack of uniform reporting from branch to head office.
- Unstructured and infrequent communication between teams.
- Strategic planning and objectives.
  - There is no strategic planning.
  - There are no branch objectives.

When looking at Delta in terms of corporate culture the following was noted.

- Customer service.
  - The current culture does not induce a quality service.
  - Currently there is a poor image of the customer held in the branch.
  - Very poor teamwork prevents delivery of a joint customer service approach.
- Management information systems.
  - Staff feel that they have too much work to do, demonstrating inadequate resourcing measures.
- Work process, flow and structure.
  - Little or no teamwork or communication between areas or parallel levels of management.
  - Working environment does not allow for accomplishment of the job.
- Strategic planning and objectives.
  - The culture does not induce strategic planning due to its micro-level focus and fire-fighting approach.
  - Crisis management has increased branch stress levels.
- Other issues.
  - Conflicting demands on time at work.
  - A job well done is never commented on.
  - People are unhappy in their jobs.
  - High levels of error.
  - Lack of feedback and support.
  - Unclear how to divide time.

When looking at Delta in terms of political dynamics the following was noted.

● Customer service.
  – Disagreement in the management team about the importance of customer service as an issue in Delta.
  – Other factors that did not surface?

Recorded above, then, is information about Delta's problems that surfaced during the Creativity phase of THP/TSI. We found problems in all of TSI's four key dimensions of organisation. The judgement made at this stage by ourselves in discussion with the Management team placed greater importance on problems of 'process' and 'culture'.

At this point we collated and grouped in an easily understandable format the information about problems faced. Methods of measurement were also assigned to each of the problems. We identified how the problems were linked and impacted on each other. This was our form of preparation for an in-depth study of the problems in advance of choosing appropriate tools. It prepared the way for discussion about choice of method and how successful implementation using each method under consideration would be. There was, however, one further preparatory task.

As mentioned earlier, one area that is often overlooked in organisational problem solving is the socio-cultural dimension. Even when corporate culture is recognised as important, as it was in our case with Delta, little advice is given about how to get to grips with it. THP has been researching this part of problem solving and has come up with a structured way of understanding important aspects of organisational culture. It is in effect a tool for measuring and subsequently monitoring and managing key elements of corporate culture. To be consistent with TSI's recognition of organisational individuality it is necessary to develop one of these for each consultancy, but a basic proforma underlies each one. This approach was used in the Delta intervention. The actual survey form used is shown in Figure 10.6.2 and as you can see it is certainly context specific, e.g., with questions relating to stress. We administered and ana-

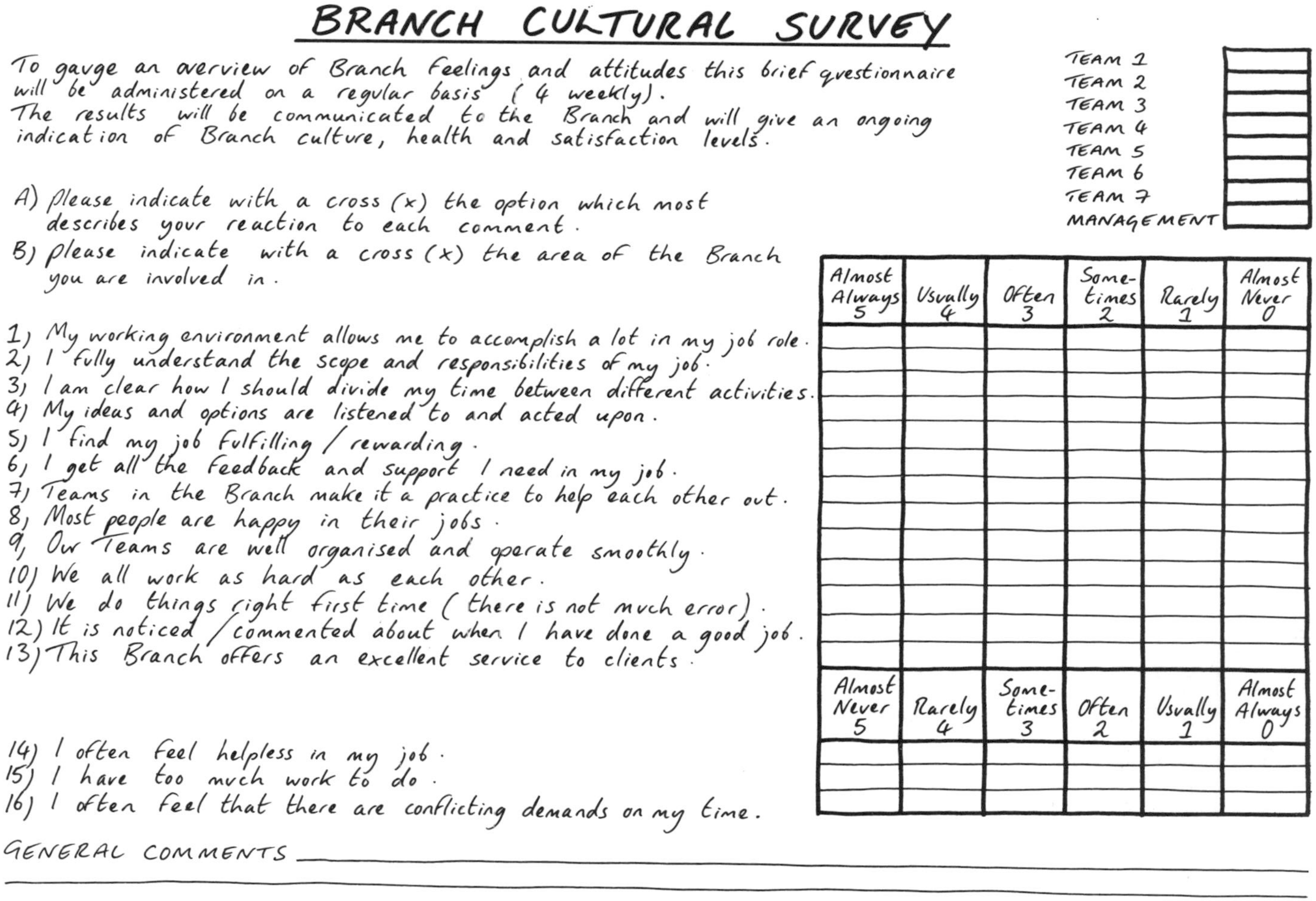

BRANCH CULTURAL SURVEY

To gauge an overview of Branch feelings and attitudes this brief questionnaire will be administered on a regular basis (4 weekly).
The results will be communicated to the Branch and will give an ongoing indication of Branch culture, health and satisfaction levels.

TEAM 1	
TEAM 2	
TEAM 3	
TEAM 4	
TEAM 5	
TEAM 6	
TEAM 7	
MANAGEMENT	

A) Please indicate with a cross (x) the option which most describes your reaction to each comment.
B) Please indicate with a cross (x) the area of the Branch you are involved in.

	Almost Always 5	Usually 4	Often 3	Some-times 2	Rarely 1	Almost Never 0
1) My working environment allows me to accomplish a lot in my job role.						
2) I fully understand the scope and responsibilities of my job.						
3) I am clear how I should divide my time between different activities.						
4) My ideas and options are listened to and acted upon.						
5) I find my job fulfilling / rewarding.						
6) I get all the feedback and support I need in my job.						
7) Teams in the Branch make it a practice to help each other out.						
8) Most people are happy in their jobs.						
9) Our Teams are well organised and operate smoothly.						
10) We all work as hard as each other.						
11) We do things right first time (there is not much error).						
12) It is noticed / commented about when I have done a good job.						
13) This Branch offers an excellent service to clients.						

	Almost Never 5	Rarely 4	Some-times 3	Often 2	Usually 1	Almost Always 0
14) I often feel helpless in my job.						
15) I have too much work to do.						
16) I often feel that there are conflicting demands on my time.						

GENERAL COMMENTS ______

Figure 10.6.2 *Survey form for getting to grips with organisational culture used by the Halesworth Partnership*

lysed it monthly and from this assessed how changes were proceeding.

Choice phase. Preparation for discussion about choice of method was carried out in the following fashion. We linked problems to the four key dimensions of organisation. We then identified relevant methods for each dimension (see Tables 10.6.1 and 10.6.2). In conjunction with the management team we debated the way each method would cut across the interacting problems, how the results could be measured and the costs and benefits that would result from their use. Problems were prioritised. Recommendations outlining methods and solutions and means of implementation were made. They were grouped under generic headings as follows.

- Review and streamline workflows, structures and procedures.
- Define responsibilities and accountabilities.
- Identify work and service standards.
- Identify internal and external customer requirements.
- Design and install an integrated operating system.
- Develop a training programme to promote learning and understanding and to encourage people to have a common understanding and sense of belonging in the organisation.

Each one of these is expanded upon below. As can be seen, some problems prevail in more than one generic area revealing the extent of the difficulties they present to Delta.

Review and streamline workflows, structures and procedures.

- Main weaknesses relating to processes.
  - Rigid job designs creating uneven distribution of work.
  - Job designs minimising ownership and morale and motivation.
  - Cumbersome workflows.
  - Ill-defined workflows.
  - Bottlenecks in workflows.
  - Lack of consistency between like processes.
- Main weaknesses relating to people.
  - Little control over or understanding of work demands.
  - Little communication of information to teams.

Table 10.6.1 *The Halesworth Partnership and TSI analysis; problems and measures*

Technical problems		Human problems	
Process	Organisation	Culture	Politics
Cumbersome and time-consuming workflows	Poor team structure	Poor attitude towards the customer	(None recorded)
Bottlenecks in work	No routine information or system	Reactive rather than proactive management	
Like tasks being performed in different areas	No recursive planning/reporting systems	No focus on continuous improvement	
No method to identify skills required	Poor communication between teams	High stress levels	
Poor/unclear letter and form design	No targets or goal setting		
Outdated work procedures	Many integrated systems		
Poor layout	Management not managing		
No time standards for work completion			
No error, quality, turnaround standards			
No routine planning			

Measurement indicators

	Measurement indicators
Productivity, efficiency, backlog, turnaround times	Error and quality indicators
Error rates, variances, performance to budget	Job performance indicators
Profit/staff cost ratios, income/staff cost ratio	Training assessment
Abandonment rates, utilisation, best practice	Skills assessment survey
	Staff turnover, staff absenteeism/sickness
	Performance and quality review
	Customer survey
	Cultural survey, error and quality indicator

Table 10.6.2 *The Halesworth Partnership and TSI analysis; tools*

	Technical problems	Human problems	
Process	Organisation	Culture	Politics
Operational Research • workflow analysis • layout analysis • diagnostic interviews and questionnaires • predetermined time standards study • work study job role analysis • error and quality analysis • work measurement review Systems Analysis • information system diagnostics • computer system analysis • systems engineering • systems dynamics	Diagnosis for Effective Organisation • organisational structure review • flow process analysis	Testing Polarised Viewpoints • diagnostic interviews and questionnaires • diagnostic management workshops Exploring and Choosing Designs • diagnostic interviews and questionnaires • diagnostic management workshop Exploring and Making Decisions • diagnostic interviews and questionnaires • brainstorming sessions • cultural surveys • performance and quality reviews	Critically Evaluating Decisions and Designs • diagnostic interviews and questionnaires • diagnostic management workshops

- Management are not trained to identify anomalies in work-flows.
- There was little front-line management time spent on work management.
- Tools lacking.
  - A systematic method for continuous assessment of work-flows.
  - A means of identifying when work adds value.
- Recommendations.
  - Clearly define procedures and processes for call-backs, follow-ups, customer retention, complaints handling, etc.
  - Analyse content of workloads identifying non-value adding functions.
  - Identify and structure communication channels.
  - Review and streamline workflows, removing double handling, rework and bottlenecks.
  - Identify clear one-stop responsibility for processes within an area.
  - Analyse and streamline team structures.
  - Analyse and flatten management structure.
  - Redefine individual input, i.e., less structured 'job by title' descriptions.
  - Establish standard review procedures.

Define responsibilities and accountabilities.

- Main weaknesses relating to processes.
  - No clear objectives for management accountability.
  - Little systematic control of customer service, e.g., follow-up and call-back procedures.
  - Lack of co-ordination and co-operation between areas and between the branch and head office.
- Main weaknesses relating to people.
  - Little front-line management spent on work management.
  - Little co-operation between areas and levels of management.
  - Unclear definition of roles and responsibilities.
  - Little control over or understanding of work demands.
  - Management roles and responsibilities not designed using planning criteria.

- Tools lacking.
  - No system or tools to support objectives or plans.
- Recommendations.
  - Clearly define roles and responsibilities for individuals and areas.
  - Identify key business indicators.
  - Identify global reporting requirements.
  - Identify clear roles and responsibilities for the management team.
  - Identify clear roles and responsibilities for planning and goal setting.
  - Analyse and identify key business indicators for strategic planning, e.g., budget control, costs, resource requirements, scheme costing, etc.

Identify work and service standards.

- Main weaknesses relating to processes.
  Job designs are rigid leading to decreased customer satisfaction due to poor cross-utilisation of staff.
- Main weaknesses relating to people.
  - A very poor image of the customer.
  - Lack of technical and customer training and knowledge.
- Tools lacking.
  - Little or no information to drive customer service standards.
- Recommendations.
  - Set clear customer requirements to compare results against.
  - Identify and set work standards.
  - Identify key business indicators.
  - Identify global reporting requirements.
  - Set criteria for ongoing measurement and review of key business indicators.
  - Analyse and identify key business indicators for strategic planning, e.g., budget control, costs, resource requirements, scheme costing, etc.

Design and installation of an integrated management-operating system.

- Main weaknesses relating to processes.

- Little systematic control of customer service, e.g., follow-up and call-back procedures.
- Lack of co-ordination and co-operation between areas and between the branch and head office.
● Main weaknesses relating to people.
    - Little co-operation between areas and levels of management.
    - Lack of technical and customer service training and knowledge.
    - Culture does not induce strategic planning.
● Tools lacking.
    - Little or no information to drive customer service standards.
    - Little or no information to identify skills and resources.
    - There are no systems to monitor and control work.
    - No tools for determining resource requirements.
    - No planning tools exist.
    - No method for reporting.
    - No means to identify what work adds value.
    - No systematic method for continuous analysis and improvement of workflows.
    - No system or tools to support objectives or plans.
    - No formal prediction of expected work demands for planning.
● Recommendations.
    - Continuous improvement to address problems of documentation, correspondence, lost time, procedural deficiencies, etc.
    - Error and quality systems to understand and assess whether customer requirements are being met.
    - Design of an integrated operating system that enforces set planning and reporting standards.
    - Design of an information system that provides knowledge on work volumes, scheme fluctuations, etc.
    - Identify key business indicators.
    - Identify global reporting requirements.
    - Design an effective method of reporting.
    - Design a method for measuring resource requirements.
    - Design an effective operating system focusing on work control, planning and training.

- Identify and structure communication channels.
- Design an operating system that continuously identifies and removes inefficiencies within workflows.
- Identify clear and structured communication channels within and between areas.
- Set criteria for ongoing measurement and review of key business indicators.
- Design a systematic operating system that requires strategic planning and goal setting.
- Analyse and identify key business indicators for strategic planning, e.g., budget control, costs, resource requirements, scheme costing, etc.

Identify internal and external customer requirements.

- Main weaknesses relating to processes.
  - Job designs are rigid leading to decreased customer satisfaction due to poor cross-utilisation of staff.
- Main weaknesses relating to people.
  - No understanding of internal or external customer requirements.
- Tools lacking.
  - Little or no information to drive customer service standards.
  - Little or no information to identify skills and resources.
- Recommendations.
  - Set clear customer requirements to compare results against.

Develop a training system.

- Main weaknesses relating to processes.
  - None identified.
- Main weaknesses relating to people.
  - A very poor image of the customer.
  - Lack of technical and customer training and knowledge.
  - Little front-line management spent on work management.
- Tools lacking.
  - Little or no information to identify skills and resources.
  - Little or no training occurring.
- Recommendations.

– Set clear customer requirements to compare results against.

Provide a management training programme.

- Main weaknesses relating to processes.
  - Everything noted above under process.
- Main weaknesses relating to people.
  - Management levels are not trained to identify anomalies in workflows.
  - Very poor image of the customer.
  - Little control and understanding of work demands.
- Tools lacking.
  - Everything noted above under tools lacking.
- Recommendations.
  - Design an education programme that focuses the operation on the customer.
  - Design a training programme that supports a quality service and professional image.
  - Design an education programme to focus on work control, resource planning, variance management, planning, proactive management, etc.
  - Establish leadership through management training.
  - Design a training programme on workflow management and continuous improvement.
  - Design an education programme that supports a culture of planning, goal setting and achievement of objectives.

Through this process THP produced an analysis report for Delta that clearly identified the core problems that had to be dealt with if improvement within the branch was to be achieved. The core interrelated problems referred mainly to process and culture. Recommendations of methods were also given to address those problems. Some of those methods were actually developed during the analysis stage, making them highly relevant to these unique problems faced by Delta and adding continuity between the analysis (Creativity and Choice) and implementation.

THP, through the employment of the THP/TSI process, productively and systematically utilised the limited time available for the analysis. A thorough analysis led all involved to believe that the core problems had been surfaced and the way they interrelate established, providing a full picture of current organisational difficulties. This put THP and Delta in a strong position from which to move on to the Implementation phase.

Implementation phase. A genuine benefit of the THP/TSI approach was the ease with which we were able to highlight problems within Delta and summarise those in a format that was readily understood by the client and lead straight into a logical format for the analysis report. The analysis report listed findings under specific groupings as indicated above. We then mapped recommendations for change against each of the problems, or opportunities for improvement as we prefer to see it. As the extent and scope of each problem had been identified and tools aligned to them, it was possible to work out a realistic time frame for implementing each of the solutions or groups of solutions. This provided an excellent base from which we quoted deliverables and costs. This reinforced THP's philosophy, to propose only that which can be delivered and to tie deliverables to the costs of the programme.

The branch and national managers reviewed the analysis report, commenting that they found a significant amount of relevant detail, some of which was news to them, in an easily digestible format. THP was retained to implement the recommended solutions. It is our view that TSI had assisted in streamlining the process, assisting the client to grasp the problems and their impact and to appreciate the need for the steps toward solutions.

The programme schedule was set at 23 weeks. Achieving this clear time frame was possible because problems, tools to be used and solutions to be worked on had been established. Nevertheless, changes had to be managed well to ensure success in such a short time frame, especially as the programme meant the organisation refocusing on proactive management and continuous improvement. The global programme flow, the detailed programme schedule and specific deliverables are shown in Figures 10.6.3 and 10.6.4.

The programme is still running. There have been several challenges that have meant further involvement on our part, such as changes in the management team and a legislative change.

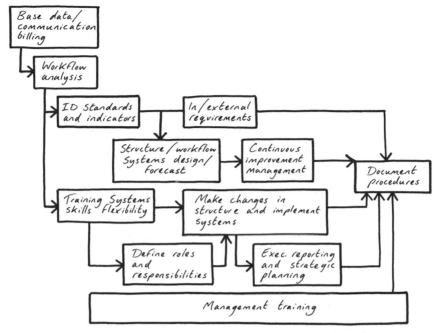

Figure 10.6.3   *Programme flow for the Halesworth Partnership's intervention in Delta*

The flexible nature of the THP/TSI approach allowed us to deal with these hiccups whilst still keeping on track. A key factor in this success was that the client fully understood what to expect, what was expected of them, the problems faced, solutions recommended as well as the stages of the programme.

The cultural survey played an important role. It allowed THP and the client to maintain a measure of the branch from a cultural point of view. With the managers trained in analysis of the survey and action planning, the onus was on the organisation to manage the change rather than relying on consultants. This had a twofold impact. Firstly, the client learnt tools to develop new skills and was creating its own results. Secondly, THP spent more quality time on positive improvements rather than dealing with negative attitudes.

Results achieved to date are extremely encouraging. They have been achieved in under four months, with the client now in possession of tools to identify its own problems and manage them in an ongoing basis. Projected improvements in the first

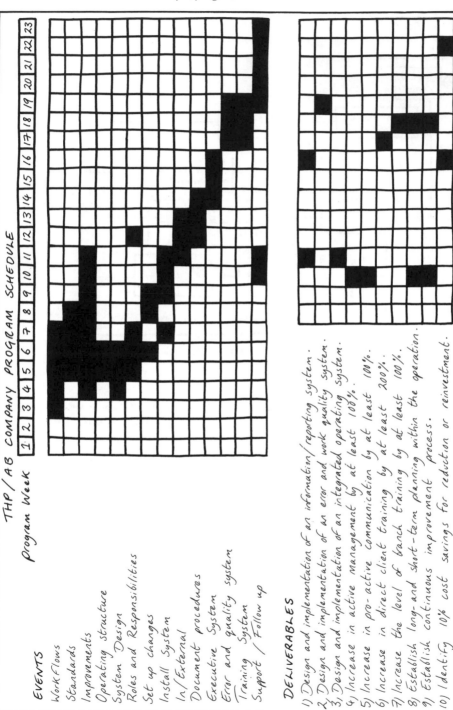

THP / AB COMPANY PROGRAM SCHEDULE

| Program Week | 1 | 2 | 3 | 4 | 5 | 6 | 7 | 8 | 9 | 10 | 11 | 12 | 13 | 14 | 15 | 16 | 17 | 18 | 19 | 20 | 21 | 22 | 23 |

EVENTS

Work Flows
Standards
Improvements
Operating structure
System Design
Roles and Responsibilities
Set up changes
Install System
In/External
Document procedures
Executive System
Error and quality system
Training System
Support / Follow up

DELIVERABLES

1) Design and implementation of an information/reporting system.
2) Design and implementation of an error and work quality system.
3) Design and implementation of an integrated operating system.
4) Increase in active management by at least 100%.
5) Increase in pro-active communication by at least 100%.
6) Increase in direct client training by at least 200%.
7) Increase the level of branch training by at least 100%.
8) Establish long- and short-term planning within the operation.
9) Establish continuous improvement process.
10) Identify 10% cost savings for reduction or reinvestment.

Figure 10.6.4   Programme schedule for the Halesworth Partnership's intervention in Delta

year will be well in excess of those promised. The main results of the programme are summarised below.

- Costs reduced by 15%.
- Backlogs reduced by 61%.
- Abandonment rate down by 52%.
- Overtime hours down by 64%.
- Efficiency up by 48%.
- Productivity up by 41%.
- Increase in customer contact up by 900%.
- Increase in proactive management activities up by 336%.
- Improvement in the cultural survey indicator up by 10%.

In our and our client's view, and according to all the measurable deliverables, the THP/TSI intervention has been a tremendous success.

REFLECTIONS

There are obvious benefits that TSI has given THP, such as taking a holistic approach, achieving relevant and co-ordinated intervention, and so on. Below are a few unique aspects that we have selected to offer as points of reflection.

- TSI and its format enables limited time frames to be utilised most effectively, ensuring all angles are considered.
- TSI enables, or even ensures that, the correct tools in the circumstances are chosen and applied.
- The client found the format easy to grasp, making the task of explaining tools, their purposes, the programme of intervention, etc., to it so much easier.
- TSI helped us to structure our own consultancy tools and methods in a coherent way.
- TSI ensures that cultural and political dimensions of organisation are not neglected.

For these reasons it is our considered opinion and experience that any group practising consultancy will benefit by reviewing their practices through TSI. The review process must focus on the nature and scope of the methods under use. Using the Critical Review Mode of TSI operationalised in Chapter 9 is an excellent way of starting this process. Additional methods almost certainly will have to be introduced to tackle dimensions of organisation not currently catered for. This is a challenge worth accepting because TSI is highly relevant to today's organisational problems.

Case 10.7
ABC and Co. (Hong Kong and Taiwan)

PETER C.Y. WONG, MANAGING DIRECTOR

Focus: Implementing Quality Management (QM) principles in an ageing family-owned company.

Methods discussed: Quality Management (QM), Exploring and Choosing Designs (ECD), Diagnosis for Effective Organisation (DEO), Implementing Designs and Decisions (IDD).

BACKGROUND TO THE WRITER AND ORGANISATION

Peter Wong is Managing Director of the Hip Wah Gingell Holdings Ltd, engaging principally in toy manufacturing and marketing, property development and investment and electrochemical trading business in Hong Kong and China. In the past 22 years Peter has worked in various disciplines in different industries. Organisations he has worked for include Hang Seng Bank, Fair Wind Secretarial Services, Hysan Development and Kader Holdings. Peter serves on the Hong Kong Institute of Company Secretaries. He is an external examiner of a postgraduate course in business administration at the City Polytechnic of Hong Kong and also works in an advisory capacity at Hong Kong Polytechnic and City Polytechnic of Hong Kong.

(A pseudonym is used for the company in this case study to maintain confidentiality as requested.) ABC and Co., a company to which Peter gave advice and which is the focus of this case, was a well-established Taiwanese manufacturer of consumer products. It was founded as a family firm in the 1950s. In the mid-1980s it was taken over by the next generation of the family. Since then it has been under the control of Ms Li, the eldest daughter of the founder, and Mr Li, her younger brother.

The company had a substantial office in Taipei with about 200 staff responsible for sales and marketing, purchasing, material control, product design, accounting and finance and administration. It had two plants in different industrial parks with a total workforce of about 4,000. The company was fully vertically integrated making all moulds, plastic, metal and electronic parts itself.

INTRODUCTION

With the development of the Taiwanese industrial and export sector in the 1980s, ABC and Co. expanded rapidly. Its annual turnover, at one time, reached a peak of US$1 billion with a profit of US$100 million. In recent years competition in the market for consumer products has become extremely keen making it difficult to maintain market share. The company also suffered from increasing problems with quality in many parts of its activities, partly due to the ageing process. Combined, these factors led to a substantial 60% drop in turnover. The company had to downsize from 10,000 to 4,000 employees to stay in business. Profits stabilised at about break-even.

THE STUDY

The whole process of intervention discussed below was guided by the principles of TSI. All methods used are reported in this book, except those used for financial analysis. I began my job as adviser to ABC and Co. by making exploratory investigations to come up with as much basic information as possible. To do this I interviewed people and went to secondary sources rather than use any of the creativity-enhancing techniques (at least not at this stage). Interviews were held with Ms Li and Mr Li, various departmental heads and some workers when conducting office and factory visits. The initial profile that emerged is summarised below.

- The company was operated under the joint leadership of Mr Li and Ms Li. Mr Li was the managing director. Ms Li was the purchasing manager, but, being the elder sister, was respected by Mr Li and other colleagues. Her informal authority often got its way over the formal authority of Mr Li.
- Mr Li was thought of as a nice gentleman by the staff of ABC and Co., although he was not decisive enough. He adopted his father's (and indeed a typically Chinese) top-down authoritarian management style. He worked very hard but spent too much time helping his sister sort out daily problems. He was too involved in daily operations, in particular in engineering and production.
- Ms Li, a single woman, was devoted to her work. She had a very strong will, being clear in her mind about what was right and wrong. She was very clever, observant and keen on detail. She continually came across problems in operations and lodged complaints about this with Mr Li expecting action to be taken. Ms Li did not trust the majority of old employees doing things in the old ways. She was certain that only her department performed well and that her staff saved substantial moneys on behalf of the company. Each year she took her staff for a short trip as encouragement, a privilege not enjoyed elsewhere in the company.
- Both Ms and Mr Li believed that, despite the obvious operational difficulties, the company's major problem was the Sales Department.
- Mr Tang was the deputy managing director who tried tirelessly to balance the situation and eliminate the effect of serious internal departmental conflicts.
- Turnover rate of remaining employees was high.
- The organisational structure was not balanced; it was clearly purchasing oriented emphasising low-cost operations.
- Quality of products was deteriorating. Deliveries were often late. Customer dissatisfaction led to rising complaints.

- The company's working system operated through word-of-mouth. There was no documentation, little co-ordination and excessive communication problems.
- The late Mr Li built a corporate culture based on team work within a fully integrated internal environment, which made the company one of the most successful manufacturers in its field. The culture was breaking up.
- The company stayed afloat only through sound financial management.

In summary, ABC and Co. appeared to suffer from an ageing problem. The company had a static structure, a fading corporate culture, a loosely controlled operational system, an unbalanced organisational structure and many self-imposed constraints, leading to poor quality, late delivery, high costs and a slow response to the rapidly changing business context.

I agreed with the Lis that there was a sales problem; however, it could not and should not be solved in isolation. For example, customer dissatisfaction also reflected poor quality products and late shipment. Going back to fundamentals, the competitiveness of a manufacturer is constructed on good quality products. Ultimately, only reliable products attract and keep customers. In order to build sales back up, widen profit margins and secure some guarantee of survival, improvement in quality was needed. In fact this had to be regarded as the first priority. In TSI terms, the organisational processes were failing and had to undergo redesign. A TQM strategy would mean a reallocation of resources alongside organisational redesign. The complete redesign could best be done I judged through a Quality Management (QM) programme aided by Diagnosis for Effective Organisation (DEO).

To introduce QM using DEO meant a whole new strategy for ABC and Co. A TQM strategy was needed. A change of the scale required to save ABC and Co. through TQM would require a drastically altered management and leadership style as well as people's working attitudes. In particular, the Lis needed to understand that their style of tight control was partly responsible for the lack of flexibility in the company and unless they relinquished some of their overbearing power the company would surely self-destruct.

It was recommended that process redesign would be built up from the bottom by employees through project teams. This meant culture change inside a very large organisation that could only be achieved through learning and understanding, requiring debate. This led me to think of the two methods Exploring and Making Decisions (EMD) and Exploring and Choosing Designs (ECD), both good at stimulating debate. Furthermore, there was a need for solid management support to changes, a management reshuffle, an empowering organisational redesign and all the political problems that these entail.

The task at hand was clearly far from simple. All in all, the changes being considered involved significant changes to the four key dimensions of organisation as TSI sees it: process design, organisational design, organisational culture and organisational politics. This amounted to a company reform. To reflect upon this reform Critically Evaluating Designs and Decisions (CEDD) was therefore very appropriate, although did not happen for reasons given later.

Much work was undertaken using ECD. The redesign into a QM organisation was shaped using DEO. Several of the case studies in this chapter concentrate on these methods, so I shall make my contribution by focusing on Implementing Designs and Decisions (IDD). This was the crux point for the intervention as we shall see.

The method in a nutshell is: undertake a systems analysis to work out how the system operates, look for obstructions to change, then make a reference projection assuming that things do not change, make a reference projection on the basis of the chosen design or decision, compare the two and identify the gap, work out how to close the gap, determine the resources needed to do this, design the implementation process and then implement. Let us see how IDD went in ABC and Co.

A detailed systems analysis was undertaken to ascertain exactly how the organisation currently operated, who and what were affected and how. The analysis covered the following organisational matters.

- Business processes.
- Work processes.
- Policies, strategies and tactics.

- Management style.
- Past and present performance.
- Relationships between employees, shareholders, suppliers, customers and the general public and their views on the company, etc.
- Task environment.

Obstructions to development were identified as twofold. For growth, the constraints were primarily found in the company's environment. For development, constraints were largely self-imposed, often unconsciously, and were of two types.

- Discrepancies in what the main players believed about Utopia and further discrepancies between these viewpoints and what was actually the case; involving organisational ends (where the ends were vague anyway), means employed to reach those ends, resources available for such pursuits, the organisation and carrying out of the pursuits, external stakeholders, etc.
- Conflicts of different types; including conflict between people, people and the company, within units, between units, units at different levels, within the company as a whole, between the company and external groups such as suppliers and clients.

There was such a mess that identifying discrepancies became a full-time job. The company was riddled with conflict and as suggested had no mission, no goals and no objectives. It was directionless.

A reference projection was made assuming that nothing was done and that the environment would remain relatively static. The projection was clear enough. Goods and services could not be delivered to meet customer's requirements. The sales would continue to fall, slowly at first. The company would remain borderline for a while and then begin to slide out of the market. Profit could not be protected from inflationary pressures such as salary rises and increasing cost of supplies. The financial position would weaken. Morale would drop. The internal problems would amplify leading to worse quality in goods and services. There would be multiplier effects so that the slow decline would accelerate and, after a couple of years, ABC and Co. would be driven out of the market. Quantifying in terms of time frame proved difficult, but it was reasonably clear that changes had to begin more or less immediately.

The causes of the reference projection were reasoned to be the following.

- Family-type business.
- Authoritarian style of management.
- High centralisation of power and responsibility.
- Non-participative tradition.
- Purchasing-oriented bias.

With the results of this as projected above.

The key features of the idealised design were as follows (an output from ECD).

- Open-minded management.
- Decentralised and balanced power and responsibility.
- Participation.
- Team spirit.
- Customer orientation.

With projected results of better quality goods and services, increasing sales, enlarged market share and higher profit.

Gap analysis was frightening. The gap between the causes of the reference projection and the idealised design was tremendous. So, how could the gap be closed? In order to achieve strategic, structural and cultural changes, the attitude of the Lis had to change first. Much discussion was held with them and they did agree to the implementation of a Quality Improvement Action Plan (QIAP) to close the gap.

My task was to prepare the QIAP for the company to bring about a total company reform. The purpose of the plan was to achieve quality improvement in the goods and services provided by the company to the total satisfaction of all customers. The action plan was a master plan to guide and facilitate all participants to make their own individual plans which would permeate throughout the company. It would provide a ground for participative planning.

The mission was to achieve total customer satisfaction. This was unattainable in the short run, but it did provide a direction for the whole company to work towards. A main objective was to establish a viable company structure, management system and a corporate culture that would ensure customer satisfaction. The goal was to implement ISO 9000 with TQM principles so as to achieve continuous quality improvement. This would reduce costs, increase sales, enlarge market shares, enhance profits, promote morale and generate better returns to both shareholders and employees. Though it was branded under the heading of quality improvements, the plan was for company-wide reform of ABC and Co.

There were eight actions to be taken.

- *Managerial change.* The company had to proceed with managerial change (as regards the Lis). If so, questions on how it would change and affect the quality improvement process should be considered. If not, then the question of how the quality improvement process could be strengthened so as to balance out the existing political and power problems should be reviewed.
- *Strategic changes.* ABC and Co. should change its purchasing-oriented approach to a customer-oriented approach. Total customer satisfaction would be the ultimate target. Top management should make clear their quality commitment and policy providing a direction for all employees to follow.
- *Structural changes.* The existing organisational structure did not cater for quality improvement. It could not cope with rapid internal and external changes. Thus a new structure based on the Viable System Model (VSM) was recommended. This could come in the form of a shadow organisational structure. A steering group was recommended. Members would be drawn from executive directors and managers. There would be three layers of project teams.
  - Departmental working groups.
  - Section working groups.
  - Unit working groups.

The steering committee and the project teams would be organised in the form of a circular organisation with some modification (see Russell Ackoff's work under Further Reading). It was designed for participative planning. The steering committee would be the promoter and final decision maker of the quality improvements. It would be responsible for overseeing a cultural change within the company in collaboration with the Human Resources Department. The Steering Committee and project teams would create a structured environment for the following.

- Improving the quality of goods and services.
- Developing employees' skills.
- Establishing communications and team work.
- Enhancing the quality of working life.

- *Reallocation of resources.* Reallocation of resources was almost a must. A detailed plan could only be made by the steering committee after the submission of the first plan made by individual working teams.

- *Cultural changes.* Understanding and adoption of ISO 9000 and TQM principles was vital. The seed of quality had to be planted in everybody's mind. Continuous training and education was therefore paramount. A unique corporate culture in quality and team spirit had to be established. A proper programme was badly needed.

- *Establishment of a quality system.* The new quality system would be established through individual working groups under the guidance of the steering committee and advice from consultants based on IS0 9000 using TQM principles. Though ISO 9000 did not cover financial and administrative aspects, the company was going to set up a total operational system for total quality improvement. Establishment of a quality system called for participation. Team work was important. Initial projects should not be too remote. The success of short-term projects would help to encourage people to participate. Employees should be educated that they were the best designers for their own future. Any system, procedure, practice and method established would be operated by themselves. So it was better for them to plan than be planned for.

- *Implementation.* Although the programme was scheduled to be company-wide, early stages of implementation of systems, procedures, practices and methods were planned on a pilot basis. If proven to be successful, full implementation subsequently would be carried out. Otherwise necessary corrective actions would be taken before further implementation proceeded.

- *Evaluation of performance.* Both the performance of these systems and the people needed to be evaluated. Appraisal, reward and control systems were designed. The results of the evaluation would be fed to management for review. The quality improvement cycle would start again.

After serious discussion Ms and Mr Li decided to adopt the QIAP without managerial change. This was considered to be a big mistake but not so surprising. Even worse, the Lis stopped the process half way through after one year. And the end result? The accelerated effect of the reference projection happened.

REFLECTIONS

The QIAP made was the final product of the whole TSI and ECD processes: it was practical. The QIAP aimed at providing guidance to the company for quality improvement. It covered all areas of the company from strategy, structure, resources allocation, culture, systems and feedback. It was considered to be systemic in nature. The QIAP emphasised communication, control and participation. But continuity was the spirit of QIAP and the break in implementation destroyed the process.

QIAP was the first step towards quality improvement for the company. A great deal of effort was required to make it happen. However, the top management of ABC and Co. wanted a quick fix and did not appreciate the whole plan. So the first step, managerial change, did not happen. Managerial power also prevented use of CEDD. That meant fundamental changes in management style would not happen and the company reform was doomed to fail. It is not uncommon for senior executives or managers to look for a quick fix to cure company problems. Quick fixes seldom go back to fundamentals. In that case they will fail. If nothing else, this study should act as a warning against narrow-minded management action and encourage you to follow a systemic approach.

On reflection I am convinced that TSI was eminently suitable for the problems ABC and Co. faced. The selection of ECD as the dominant method for problem solving was also appropriate. ECD was complemented by other supporting methods that dealt with problems as they arose. Ultimately, no method can force the powerful to give up their power, although we can try and reason with them. Reasoning in this case failed, despite the immanent collapse of the company as correctly predicted by the reference projection.

Case 10.8
Utopia-Aire Pty Ltd (Singapore)

JEREMY CHIA, MANAGING DIRECTOR
(Singapore Entrepreneur of the Year, 1993)

Focus: Entrepreneurship, creativity and change – building innovativeness into organisational processes.

Methods discussed: Brainstorming, Metaphor, Design for Effective Organisation (DEO), Exploring and Making Decisions (EMD).

BACKGROUND TO THE WRITER AND THE ORGANISATION

Utopia-Aire Pty Ltd was founded in 1980 by Jeremy Chia. Its success is marked by Jeremy being named Singapore's Entrepreneur of the Year for 1993. Since 1990 Jeremy has been implementing TSI in Utopia-Aire to help to reassess organisational processes and design. Apart from the obvious aim to achieve efficiency and effectiveness, it has been Jeremy's mission to weave into the organisation an entrepreneurial spirit, to get innovativeness into the fabric of organisation so that progressive change is maintained.

Utopia-Aire's business is computer room site preparation, design and construction of clean rooms. The company prepares everything in the environment where computers operate. They design and construct the whole environment – doors, walls, floors, precision air-conditioning, control over temperature and humidity and dust, uninterruptible power supply, fire protection, security, signal cabling, etc. The company has three subsidiaries. Today, Utopia-Aire employs 110 people and enjoys sales of Sing$20 million, up from Sing$0.5 million in 1980.

In the study below the main stages in the TSI problem solving process are recounted, avoiding detail for reasons of confidentiality.

INTRODUCTION

I first came across systems ideas in 1990 in a seminar given by Professor Flood in Singapore. By 1991 I had developed enough confidence to start trying out some methods in my own work environment. I did not feel a master of these tools and the staff of Utopia-Aire knew nothing of them. Now, in the fourth year of practising systems ideas through TSI, I feel very confident. In 1992 I began the process of educating my managers with the same tools, such as introducing the fundamental principles of the Viable System Model (VSM) and aspects of Exploring and Making Decisions (EMD). It was exciting to see how the managers responded to these new tools, using them to solve problems and to appreciate the complexity of them. TSI is being subtly introduced into the thinking process. It has become part of the management process.

THE STUDY

To kick off we tried some fairly crude creative analysis using a standard brainstorming technique and what I call reverse thinking. Reverse thinking is a simple technique that asks people to look at situations from other people's perspectives. Impartially, I introduced different viewpoints, seeking to appreciate the perspectives of other involved people. It is rather like aspects of the Creativity phase explained in Chapter 5 where other people's viewpoints are explored. It asks us to sit in another person's chair, to see through their glasses, to define their interests and motives, etc. Even better, when it is possible, I meet up with those people, for example by mingling at work, and encourage discussion among interested parties.

It is important in a TSI context not to dominate the process when holding the position of president or senior manager. These roles are better understood as coach of a team. This is especially important during interviewing sessions where questions are raised, not only to seek objective information or data but also to form an inner process of communication. This enhances both individual and team learning.

I have also benefited by drawing upon metaphorical analysis. Recently, when in Shanghai, China, a metaphor for understanding organisations emerged out of the cultural context. I observed the Chinese 'cult, community and religion'. I have explicitly used these ideas as metaphors for understanding organisational behaviour but unfortunately have no room to expand in this case study.

This is exciting new stuff, but I had better take you back to those earlier, much cruder uses of creative thinking. Idea generation through brainstorming surfaced the following issues to be dealt with.

- Structure is of great importance. Unfortunately communications and reporting lead to confusion.
- There is no way to synthesise departments. Each department is partially isolated.
- The MD's span of control is too wide with a ratio of 7:1. Handling seven senior managers is too time consuming for the MD.
- There are no common goals or objectives.
- There is poor utilisation of and excessive fighting over scarce resources.
- There is a lack of organisation-oriented values and beliefs.

Analysing these issues and assessing their interactive nature led us to appreciate that the main issues were technical in substance. How could we possibly be entrepreneurial with poor communication and isolated departments, weak goals and objectives, ineffective use of resources, etc.? What was needed was a technical approach that improved the design and processes so that the entrepreneurial process could flow again. The VSM was chosen to guide the redesign process. Also, the VSM prom-ised to implant intelligence throughout the organisation sup-porting the idea of enabling people to become innovators. Thinking forward to the Implementation phase, we could see that once organisational design was in place it would then be a matter of defining people's tasks and duties. This could be done using job descriptions to form efficient organisational pro-cesses within the new organisational design.

Before intervention using the VSM, extensive discussion was held with key managers and staff. We used forms of brain-storming to generate ideas about the problems of organisational design. This led to increased commitment to ideas generated and began the drive toward growing involvement and auto-nomy in the decision-making process.

The most noteworthy change was breaking away from operating according to a traditional hierarchical tree (see Figure 10.8.1) to thinking about our operations in terms of effective organisation. The process began with a review of the basic oper-ations. We consolidated HV Air Quality, Clean Air and Indoor Air Quality into two departments, being HV Air Quality Equip-ment Parts and Supplies and Project Management Consultancy. After-Sales Service Department became Customer Services Department. These three departments were grouped under one division called Engineering. A second division was Industrial Supplies.

This consolidation helped in the following ways.

- Activities became more focused.
- Activities were more logically ordered and therefore better understood.

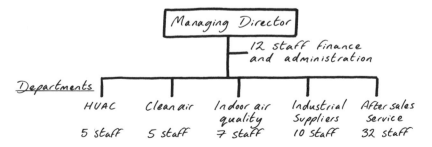

Figure 10.8.1 *Organisational chart of Utopia-Aire in 1990*

- Activities were managed by those who were responsible for them leading to improved decision making.
- Human resource capability was increased.
- Policy making was in a better position to support the organisation as a whole, which enhanced the company's strategic position and enabled it proactively to modiflex internally and with the environment.

There were some difficulties encountered using the VSM.

- Our existing systems such as management information systems did not suit the redesign so we had to reengineer computer software to match VSM requirements.
- The physical stock in the warehouse was not reidentified in line with the new system, causing a lot of stock variance, unaccounted stock, overstocking and obsolete stock.
- Staff found it difficult initially to take on responsibility for autonomous units. Guidance, policy and procedures had to be clearly defined to start with. Also, staff feared taking on jobs where they were fully accountable and at times resented being audited feeling that they were not trusted.
- Growth meant that we had to introduce a well-organised operation, but the traditional friendly and close means of operation appeared to some staff to undergo a sudden uncomfortable change to professionalism and apparently 'sitting across a table'.
- Use of the VSM did not help change organisational culture. Values and beliefs were hard to change, such as the internal economies where staff did not believe that they would be rewarded after redesign in either monetary terms or quality of working life. This point is taken up below.

Despite some teething problems, the VSM helped Utopia-Aire to achieve effective design and led us to clarify organisational processes. In this process of change we hit cultural problems with some staff in the form of beliefs, fears and distrust. I even had one of my managers resign. This was despite significant involvement of the staff in the redesign process, especially with their own job descriptions. The culture had changed but not everyone had come along with it. It was time to refocus on the cultural issues within Utopia – to emphasise debate, learning and understanding.

Various viewpoints about the problem of culture change were encouraged through informal meetings with staff, walking about and chatting and listening to what was going on. In effect I was a facilitator and the meeting was 'ongoing'. I used CATWOE analysis from EMD to identify the players and then asked them for their advice and opinions. This helped to redefine the players and to introduce many viewpoints. In this way change proposals were generated and were tested with many different players. The outcome of the debate was recognition of the need for more structural change. Not surprisingly this affected the processes and so we had to return to redesign. This included a new incentive and staff reward system encouraging innovation in line with well-defined job accountability.

REFLECTIONS

I have shared with you a few of my experiences in using systems methods and how I used TSI to guide the organisational processes of Utopia-Aire, in particular as they relate to the entrepreneurial processes. You may be interested to hear how it has been for me, especially since not everything after TSI was hunky-dory. Well, there have been benefits, real benefits, that you should seriously take note of.

● I am more confident in facing up to problems in crisis times. I know that there are ways to work out well-informed understanding of problems faced. I do not have to bring in consultants at all (even notwithstanding the guidance given in Chapter 8). Consultants are frustrating because they do not understand the value of your words. They do not read your lips. They do not and cannot have the same deep understanding of the organisation as those who work in it. My advice is to tackle issues internally with a system like TSI, making everybody a problem solver. Make everyone an innovator and intrapreneur. Encourage everyone to be an innovator and you will get progressive change everywhere. Any expert consultant's written opinion looks thin against this.

- The staff became more skilled, being taught a number of simple problem solving techniques.
- Managers became more skilled and familiar with systems problem solving so that continuous improvement was enhanced.
- Utopia-Aire is now more organic, less mechanistic, and is better able therefore to grow. The staff too share in the organic understanding.
- The whole management process has been tremendously creative. Many more choices for the future were explored and methods to help in the process were identified. This opened new avenues and built innovators into the organisation.
- TSI is relevant to today's complex world.
- TSI purifies thinking – it helps to explain things more clearly.
- In many ways systems practice has become a daily prayer.
- TSI gives freedom. It releases time by reducing inefficiency and ineffectiveness. There is no need for fire-fighting.
- TSI kills complexity. Complexity kills freedom.

Case 10.9
Trent Health Authority (United Kingdom)

WENDY GREGORY, NORMA ROMM AND MICHAEL WALSH, RESEARCH CONSULTANTS

Focus: User participation in defining quality standards within the National Health Service.

Methods discussed: Quality Management (QM), Critically Evaluating Designs and Decisions (CEDD).

BACKGROUND TO THE WRITERS AND ORGANISATION

This case reports on the Trent Quality Initiative in the National Health Service (NHS) of the United Kingdom. Three members of Hull University's Centre for Systems Studies were employed on the initiative as research consultants: Wendy Gregory, Norma Romm and Mike Walsh. The project was instigated as a response to the perceived need for greater user participation in defining quality standards within the NHS. The practical phase commenced in September 1993 and finished in July 1994. Prior to this there was a preliminary investigation. The investigation discovered that the majority of quality initiatives in the NHS rely on standard setting and audits, using formulae, and on outcome measures – none of which in themselves necessitate direct user involvement. Where user involvement was detailed in NHS quality standard setting, the capacity of users to participate on an equal footing with NHS professionals was taken for granted. Such approaches do not acknowledge the degree to which users may be intimidated or diverted from stressing their concerns.

The research was based in Sheffield, cutting across traditionally recognised organisational boundaries of the NHS, by involving purchasers, providers and users. It was originally hoped to engage in the region of 50 individuals directly in the research, but this proved to be impossible for a variety of reasons. For example, clinicians (especially doctors) could not get time off from their duties, despite their willingness to participate – in spite of six months' negotiation with senior staff within the Trusts and the health authority. Two doctors were eventually recruited and participated in most workshops.

Participants in the intervention were as follows.

- *Users.* The user group including members of the Royal Sheffield Institute for Blind people (RSIB) and the (Visually Impaired Persons (VIPs). It therefore comprised people with impaired eyesight, ranging in age from about 30 years to over 85 years.
- *Providers.* The Central Sheffield University Hospitals Trust and the Northern General Hospital Trust. Trusts were represented by individuals drawn from several domains within the provider organisations (e.g., nursing staff, medical professionals, quality assurance personnel, managers, etc.).
- *Purchasers.* Sheffield Family Health Services Authority, Sheffield Health Authority, Family and Community Services and Trent Regional Health Authority.
- *Other interest groups.* The Community Health Council (CHC) was represented by six members.

INTRODUCTION

The main objective of the research was to establish a forum for dialogue between stakeholders, including purchasers, providers and users of NHS services. Such a forum had to be developed and facilitated since it had not evolved on its own. We proposed that a formal method be developed within an NHS setting to reflect contemporary views of quality, i.e., 'to satisfy agreed customers' requirements'. It was anticipated that the process would enable gaps to be identified between NHS service specifications and standards, users' requirements of services and new ways forward considered, by pitting viewpoints against one another in mutual confrontation.

THE STUDY

The research employed TSI. We chose TSI because it is a participatory approach and provides a means for improving communications where perceptions of a problem differ. Furthermore, no expertise in terms of knowledge of the context of application is specifically required for the effective use of TSI.

A number of preparatory activities were undertaken before the project officially commenced. In TSI terms, these activities represented work in the Creativity phase of the Problem Solving Mode. The analysis undertaken is outlined below in order that choice of method and its implementation can be situated in the broader context in which intervention took place.

Two main lines of inquiry were conducted prior to the project, both (in different ways) seeking to establish the views of providers and users about the quality of NHS services. The first of these was a postal survey of clinical, managerial and other NHS staff, conducted during early 1992. The second involved extensive unstructured interviews of members of the RSIB and the VIPs, the user groups who we selected to exemplify instances of user views in our subsequent workshops. Through the postal survey we hoped to establish what quality initiatives members of staff were aware of and the degree of success (or failure) that these had had (in the views of the respondents). The main findings are summarised below.

Many responses indicated 'imprisonment' in patients' perceptions of the health service. For example, professional staff limit choices only to those regarded clinically as safe. Ultimately, choice of this sort represents professional power over patient autonomy. One of the main characteristics of professionals is that they tend to monopolise expertise, leaving the lay-person little option but to trust them in difficult matters of choice.

Patients are not the only people to be 'imprisoned' by the NHS system. Staff may also be imprisoned. There is a boundary defining safe allowable choices over which he or she will not or cannot step. When a clinician has no option but to (perhaps unwillingly) enforce the restriction of choice, jailing the patient, the clinician too is imprisoned. This constraint on the clinician can arise from legal, professional, organisational or normative regulation.

Furthermore, NHS staff encounter problems when grappling with demands for increased accountability together with improvements in efficiency and effectiveness in service provision. The extent to which a quality-oriented customer culture is creeping into the provision of services is uncertain, but comments taken from the survey responses suggest that the change is, at least, occurring in some domains. Should such an orientation provide for greater patient autonomy and choice, together with the empowerment of staff, then it might be deemed a success.

In the second piece of preparatory work we elicited stories from visually impaired people about the quality of NHS services *as they perceived it*. Approximately 100 people were approached within the RSIB, of whom 80 agreed to participate in further small group meetings. Two similar meetings were undertaken with members of the VIPs. All of these meetings used storytelling to elicit issues of concern about NHS services. Although individuals were not prompted to provide negative stories, the predominant accounts were of a negative nature. Issues raised concerned the future existence of the NHS, the support and security of 'treatment when needed' currently provided by the NHS, the attitudes and manners of (some) NHS staff and the quality of information available to NHS service users. Again, perceptions of the NHS suggested it acts to imprison people.

Data collected through the postal survey and the unstructured interviews highlighted differences in perceptions in relation to possibilities for addressing issues. Furthermore, the interview data revealed that problems experienced by people with visual impairments closely resembled concerns of the general public, whereas problems are normally starkly enhanced by difficulties associated with their disabilities.

As a result of the postal survey and the interviews, we were able to identify a number of objectives for the Trent Quality Initiative.

- Ascertain what quality initiatives are being implemented in the NHS and determine how they affect a group of NHS users (and potential users).
- Reveal differences in perspectives on quality between stakeholders in the NHS setting and from this define and investigate problems in healthcare provision.
- Develop a formal method, in the light of the above, that will involve stakeholders (especially patient users) in dialogue. The method must encourage facilitation of critical discussion between purchasers, providers, users and people with other related concerns, on the nature and means of service delivery.

The last objective coupled up with our decision on choice of method. We chose CEDD to guide the process of intervention. CEDD is particularly useful in situations like the Trent Quality Initiative, where there is conflict characterised by groups pursuing their own interests at the possible expense of others (in our case, probably because of the following reason). Many respondents painted a picture of the NHS as a prison, where their concerns are not accounted for.

A process was identified through which CEDD would be employed. This amounted to six meetings/workshops. The meetings/workshops were planned for peer groups and multi-agency groups. The meetings/workshops were organised so that preceding meetings/workshops fed the next ones. They were organised in three cycles, with peer group meetings preceding multi-agency meetings in each cycle. The peer groups were the following: manager-providers, nurses, CHC members, RSIB and VIPs members, mixed professionals and purchasers. The multi-agency groups comprised volunteer representatives from the peer groups.

The first cycle started by exploring views on the current functioning of NHS systems as experienced by people in different peer groups. Four questions were addressed, questions that have a bearing on concerns. In fact, these may be regarded as the core questions in CEDD. Ideas generated using the core questions were then summarised at the start of the first multi-agency meeting/workshop. The multi-agency meeting/ workshop then set about differences in opinion, attempting to establish how these could be dealt with. In terms of CEDD this meant starting to look for what 'ought' to be done.

The four questions posed initially to the peer groups are listed below.

- Who is the beneficiary of the system's design?
- Who decides on measures of success?
- Who is involved in planning the system?
- Who represents those affected by the system's design? Who is affected by the system?

Three facilitators were used. The approach to facilitation adhered to the guidelines on facilitation presented in Chapter 7 of this book. Some details of the output of the first cycle are presented below.

Who is the Beneficiary of the System's Design?

- *Manager-providers.* The discussion began with an indication that the staff of the Trusts, including the managers, can be seen to benefit in various ways. The staff may benefit in that quality systems offer a form of feedback mechanism on performance. Staff can use the systems to ascertain whether they have achieved some standard. They also may benefit by becoming part of the standard setting team, in which they can contribute to the setting of feasible standards of performance. It was suggested that managers benefit because quality systems provide guidelines for reviewing cost effectiveness. Some persons in the group were in disagreement about the possible contradictions between management benefits as opposed to patient benefits. It was felt by some that the degree to which patients benefit was yet to be seen – that so far there was no definite indication that patients were benefiting substantially from the currently functioning quality systems. Although there were means for inviting patients' views in the form of surveys, complaints, etc., there were difficulties with these procedures. For instance, patients may withhold from complaining because of fear of prejudice (victimisation) against (further) care. This is related to the lack of confidentiality or lack of anonymity of their complaints.

As regards the surveys which are undertaken, the questions seem to be largely those that the staff find relevant – rather than being patient-initiated questions. Furthermore, there do not seem to be forums in place for ongoing feedback between staff interpretations of (and action upon) the surveys and patient conceptions of options. Some participants in the group felt that this was a matter of time and that at least quality systems had been introduced allowing some patient involvement. Others felt that we must be careful not to assume that we were necessarily going in the right direction and that benefits would necessarily follow in the best way possible. Whether patients are seen as beneficiaries therefore depends on the viewpoint being adopted.

- *Nurses*. There was some disagreement over whether patients indeed could be said to benefit from current designs. Some felt that although patients *should* benefit, the mechanisms for achieving this were still not sufficiently in place. There was also some doubt expressed about relevance of statistics and whether other measures (and ways of evaluating the measures) could be designed. Nurses pointed out that ward staff (and delivery staff) benefit from the designs because they have a clearer idea about the kinds of goals that they are working towards and they get feedback regarding their achievement. It was felt that the government does benefit – because it has statistics at its disposal to prove how it is faring. The government can use (or manipulate?) statistics to point to its successes. GP fundholders, it was felt, also benefit from the system; as does the district health authority.
- *CHC*. Consensus was rapidly achieved, agreeing that some patients benefit some of the time, but that there is a dilemma – namely, 'to help the one' to their maximum benefit, or 'to help the many' to their much less minimal benefit? It was suggested that the dilemma was affected by limits of time (on

the part of NHS staff), which was seen as a resource issue, and by the attitudes of both patients and professionals. When prompted to say who (really) is benefiting, the group had several suggestions at individual and group levels.

- Managers who are achieving high salaries, getting promotion, enhancing their job satisfaction, increasing their power, or who have 'delusions of grandeur'. Managers as a group are necessary, but they are often employed at the expense of clinical staff.
- Other staff (including non-clinicians) under certain circumstances.
- Patients and employees – in particular some patients benefit from new technology that the system makes available.
- (With some disagreement) contractors (who are involved in building or refurbishing staff offices).

It was argued that if someone gives good service and receives recognition then many people will benefit – doctors, their support staff and patients will all share in the benefits. In other words, there is a ripple effect when people give credit where it is due. This suggests that patients should give recognition to their doctors.

A more cynical participant suggested that managers can build up their own numbers (at the expense of clinical staff) through the development of quality posts and may thus benefit. It was suggested (more charitably) that patients benefit through the introduction of new technology which may occur as a result of quality schemes. Budget prioritising implies managers benefit from NHS quality systems because they help to cut costs and identify inefficiencies. The only people who seem not to benefit are the consultants.

- *RSIB and VIPs.* Generally, the system is for someone else's benefit and management. The NHS quality system serves those who cut costs.
- *Professionals.* Wards, departments and nurses benefit. It was argued that patients are not the direct beneficiary – because of fire-fighting. That leaves no time for direct and useful liaison. On some occasions, pharmacy does benefit – 'when we tell them what's what'. The experience in physiotherapy con-

trasted. The direct beneficiary is the patient but the service is inadequate. When it is adequate the patients notice. Only finance managers and lazy patients can be benefiting from the current inadequate service.

- *Purchasers.*
  - Patients (should be, in theory).
  - Planners and managers from the providers and purchasers.
  - Different levels will benefit from the quality systems, e.g., the organisation itself, the professions employed within the organisations and the patients.

Doubt was expressed about information systems and their usefulness in guiding users to what they want or need to know. For people with visual impairment (or hearing difficulties, or other disabilities, or from ethnic minorities), the information is often not presented in a format that is readily accessible. For example, a person with hearing difficulties is told to phone the hospital to rearrange an appointment, or a person with visual impairment is sent a lengthy letter in normal print with a (scrawled) date and time for their appointment. By not providing adequate information systems, the ability of a person to access services, and thus benefit from them, is seriously hindered.

Who Decides on Measures of Success?

- *Manager-providers.* Government can be said to provide a measure of success by defining, for instance, standards within a patient charter that quality systems have to take into account. Purchasers are another group that may decide on quality specifications; they set objectives defining what they expect a service to provide. These objectives become their measure of quality success. The provider staff too are involved in deciding aspects of quality in that they play a part in defining a feasible service contract. And lastly, it was indicated that patients too may be involved in defining measures of success in that they have an input at the level of 'voting with their feet'. Some discussion ensued on the degree to which patients may, and do, 'use their feet' to express their concern with quality. Although there are hospitals from which they can choose among consultants within hospitals, it may be difficult in practice to exercise these choices. The degree of difficulty for different types of service may be different.

- *Nurses.* It was suggested that the government 'sets the standards' and that this is the primary influence on the planning process. The ward staff – within certain parameters – also may contribute to setting ward standards. They can help define what is achievable. Purchasers (again in terms of government-set standards) define how to draw up contracts with quality requirements and evaluate achievements in terms of these requirements. The clinical management teams in the Trusts have their evaluation terms. GP fundholders also define quality (through the power that they exercise). Patients have some say – through complaints, comments (satisfaction surveys) and focus-group input. And quality co-ordinators are also involved in evaluation.

- *CHC.*
  - Provider Trusts. There was what some might regard as a cynical view expressed that measures of success are determined in Trusts by the chairman and members of their boards, perhaps exclusively, often through hidden decision making in advance meetings.
  - Purchasers, including fundholding GPs.
  - To a lesser extent it was argued that non-fundholding GPs and the patient were also able to determine measures of success.

- *RSIB and VIPs.* There was a great deal of ambivalence in the discussion prompted by this question, with participants saying that they really didn't know who was setting the standards. Everyone present was in agreement that they did not know how success (or failure) is measured. It was suggested that perhaps those in higher places were responsible for deciding, for example, how many patients are allowed on a ward, or how many operations have to be done in a year, etc. Managers are earning thousands with the creation of the Trusts. We used to know how measures were set (in the old NHS) and who made the decisions, but we don't now. Clear lines of management have disappeared. Some people have a lot of power, whilst patients have less autonomy.

- *Professionals.*
  - Physiotherapy. Patients can measure the success of a treatment through instant feedback. Doctors express their satisfaction or dissatisfaction.
  - Pharmacy. The pharmaceutical society and other external bodies measure the success of drugs and pharmaceutical aids. Various audits, including the recent Kings Fund audit, measure success.

    It remained unclear whether measuring success was the same as deciding on measures of success. Standards in the one area were seen as coming from the patients' and doctors' expectations, whilst in the other they were seen as originating from professional bodies.
- *Purchasers.* It was strongly argued that the main force behind decisions about measures of success is the government – via legislation/directives. In second place come the managers who have some scope for choice. Thirdly, professional bodies can influence standards, although it was felt that this is usually a negative influence. Mention was made of the Strategic Planning and Purchasing Group (SPPG). This is a unit made up of various personnel drawn from different functions within the purchasers and providers who are tasked with setting standards within the health service. Finally, it was argued that the Health Authority Executive is a powerful player in establishing measures used by providers.

    The main problem to be dealt with in deciding on measures of success is that people's expectations vary; since patients cannot vote with their feet the question remains, 'How do managers decide?'

Who is Involved in Planning the System?

- *Manager-providers.* Planning could be ascribed to various sources: to external agencies, sometimes to those selected by the provider, sometimes to the providers themselves and sometimes to focus-groups of users. It was suggested that the users had a small input. There was contention over the amount of input on the part of users. It was suggested that their involvement consisted of telling providers that it was necessary to change a system. The way in which the collation of information and planning of changes to the system took place was seen as a response partially to patients' complaints, but largely to control of the clinical management team. The role of the patient's advocate in helping to set up focus-groups, and the way in which patient involvement on various scores was invited as part of the planning process, became a central topic in this meeting.

- *Nurses.* Nurses, managers, the Trust board, pressure groups and the Family Health Services Association saw nurses as involved. The discussion focused on the possible input of nurses. It was argued that they may act as spokespersons on behalf of patients; but if their input was to be treated seriously, this depended on there being a receptive manager. Often nurses' input would be judged in terms of resource implications. This raised the issue of how nurses are involved in budgetary issues or decisions. It was pointed out that thus far their involvement was minimal when it came to contributing ideas on the way hospital (or even ward) budgets could be utilised.

- *CHC.* The following people or institutions are presented in order of the amount of impact they can have on the planning of the system.
  - V. Bottomley (Health Minister) and K. Clarke (Chancellor of the Exchequer), in their respective roles, and the Department of Health and the Treasury.
  - The purchaser (i.e., Trent Regional Health Authority).
  - CHC can influence but not take decisions. The CHC can now only give advice and feel frustrated when it is not acted upon. At this point, a discussion opened up about the extent to which the CHC can give advice to NHS personnel. The advent of the Trusts' status has meant that the CHC has not always been allocated a role or a seat on the decision-making boards and as a result there are few opportunities to influence decisions. The CHC can influence by offering advice, criticism and by lobbying.
  - Professional bodies have independent control of their own members and plan for their members, although this is usually with their members' support.

- *RSIB and VIPs.* Again, NHS users expressed their disenfranchisement – the person who plans the system is the one who controls the budget.

- *Professionals.* Mainly senior physiotherapy and a physiotherapist in audit. Similarly in pharmacy.
- *Purchasers.* SPPG, providers, GPs, finance, planning, information, medical, nursing, health promotion, quality directorate and patients (through initiatives such as focus-groups and special projects).

Who Represents Those Affected by the System's Design? Who is Affected by the System?

- *Manager-providers.* It was suggested that those affected could be represented by: the staff (in particular the named nurse), the CHC, patient's representative/advocate, managers who represent staff and social services. Those not represented were identified as: lower grades, social services and GPs.
- *Nurses.* Patients, relatives and staff are affected by the system. Some nurses wondered about their degree of representation, others suggested that they could be seen as being represented in some form. The patients and relatives are represented by: the CHC, the patient's representative, nurses, relatives and MPs. The staff are represented by: themselves, unions and managers.
- *CHC.* Members of the CHC were keen to demonstrate that those affected by an NHS service provision system could have recourse in the event of problems occurring. This led to a lengthy debate about the many individuals and agencies who exist to support and represent those in need of representation. There was an unresolved disagreement about the extent to which health authorities could be advocates for patients' interests and not have a conflict of interest (i.e., their own!).

  Employees of the NHS, in turn, could be represented by their trade unions, or in the law courts if a matter warranted legal action. Carers can call upon the CHC and other voluntary bodies to represent their needs. Any voluntary bodies can represent themselves, or turn to the Council for Voluntary Services, the Community Health Council or other reference groups for representation.

  There was some discussion about the extent to which the media may be affected by NHS reforms which include the introduction of quality systems. Most of this focused on whether the media had benefited from the purchaser–provider split. The opinions expressed here included the view that the media had been able to sell papers by producing stories about (for example) the (horrific) waste of money in some areas and the (scandalous) inadequacies of the NHS in others. Most participants felt that the media were capable of representing themselves whenever an issue arises, but there was continued disagreement about whether or not they should be included as a group which is affected by the system.

- *RSIB and VIPs*. There are several ways of being affected – as a patient, as a worker and as a manager. The role of the CHC as a representative of patients was virtually unknown. What CHC goals and objectives are and what they do were largely unknown. What is the role of the CHC?

  Patients can represent themselves, but they have a limited involvement in planning. Whilst it was agreed that NHS workers are affected (as potential patients), the influence of workers (or their trade unions) would be small because of their concerns over jobs – people are afraid of losing their jobs. The ethics seem to be, do not rock the boat. Workers could represent their own views, although it should be remembered that they may be affected by doing so. It cannot be right to be silenced, but workers have to follow the person with the purse strings. Workers cannot change the system.

- *Professionals*. This last question was unanswered, mainly because the group was late starting as the expectation had been that others would be arriving to join the group and so the commencement of discussions was delayed. Also, the debate of other issues had been extensive.

- *Purchasers*. The question of representation was seen as a complex issue that needed much discussion. It was felt that representation is inadequate at present. However, it was agreed that purchasers may act as advocates. It was stressed that there are no representatives for those affected at present, but special projects exist. It was felt that these projects did not go far enough. Most representation at present tends to be through the random selection of patients and this can often miss the cases where things have gone wrong. Random selection is not adequate on its own.

It was generally felt that representation is poor, with outpatients being particularly bad, but it was stressed that information systems are improving. Problems include reducing resources, i.e., there is less money coming into the purchasers with more demands being raised for expenditure.

Subsequent discussion in the multi-agency groups helped to lend clarity where differences existed in perceptions of who benefits from current designs, who defines quality, mechanisms for involvement in planning and of representation of the affected. Participants, though not all agreeing to the same degree, were willing to see that certain difficulties in the current system (as far as the four questions were concerned) needed to be, and indeed could be, addressed. This is not to say that they all would see the problems in exactly the same way. But at least the problem areas were now becoming symbols for further communication indicating how difficulties may be approached. This created the climate for a discussion in the next set of peer group meetings about what participants felt 'ought to be'.

Subsequent to the multi-agency meetings, a letter was sent out reminding participants when the next peer group meeting was. Included with the letter was our summary of the multi-agency discussions, indicating that at the next meeting we would consider suggestions on how quality systems may be designed. To this end, we asked participants to think about and bear in mind 12 questions adapted from CEDD.

• Who should benefit from the system's design?
• What should the purpose of an NHS quality system be?
• What should the measure(s) of success be?
• Who should decide on changes to the measure(s) of success?
• What resources should they control?
• What resources should they not control?
• Who should be involved as designers of the system?
• What expertise should be used in the design process?
• Who should be able/expected to guarantee the design?
• Who (from those affected) should be involved?
• How should they be involved?
• Which point of view should determine the design?

The second cycle began with the peer groups reviewing a summary of findings from the first cycle. Peer groups then explored 'ought to be' questions, indicating what the system ought to be like. Participants were shown how four 'ought' questions corresponded with 'is' forms that were part of the output of the first cycle. The second multi-agency meeting/workshop reviewed the output of the last peer group meeting/workshop and considered what could be done. Six issues were highlighted and passed on to the third and last cycle. Some of the output of the second cycle is summarised below, starting with a consolidation of 'ought to be' opinions for each of the adapted 12 questions.

- **Who should benefit from the system's design?**

Patients and staff. The organisation should benefit.

- **What should the purpose of an NHS quality system be?**

To satisfy the patients and everyone. You cannot cure everything, you cannot alleviate all pain. To give an A1 (good) service. To provide maximum service in health preservation at reasonable cost (money is not the only thing).

- **What should the measure(s) of success be?**

The satisfaction of all involved parties. Satisfaction may be a poor measure of quality, for example counselling services are widely offered in medical centres and are very popular but counsellors are often untrained and services differ widely. Another measure is improvement in health (morbidity and inspection rates).

- **Who should decide on changes to the measure(s) of success?**

Management, staff and patients. Everyone involved including monitors. There should be consumer involvement/contribution to quality assessment tools. Baseline outcome measures should be consumer led. There should be schemes like the purchasing and commissioning framework which considers both the involvement of various participants and the measures of success to be employed.

- **What resources should they control?**

Discussion should occur between experts, e.g., statisticians and patients. This question triggered a number of other questions in the minds of those present. For example, some wished to know how purchasers decide where to spend research money. What is research money spent on? Who should be the policy-making authorities? They should be democratically elected bodies. This may occur through a general vote or some electoral mechanism (indirect electing of appointments).

- **What resources should they not control?**

People should only control budgets where they can demonstrate experience and willingness: but experience is something that can be invited in a way that encourages input and perhaps increased participation over time.

- **Who should be involved as designers of the system?**

Everyone should be represented, including patients, monitoring agents, staff, users and clients. Elected or nominated representatives? Representation that overcomes disability – you are the person who best understands your needs – you cannot really speak for someone else.

- **What expertise should be used in the design process?**

All the professions – multi-disciplinary teams at ward level. Not just written qualifications but also grassroots experience including patient/user experience. Some medical, some lay. Those who have responsibility/expertise in an area (need to be within restrictions/limitations). Patient involvement.

- **Who should be able/expected to guarantee the design?**

Needs to be monitored but not always by the people who are delivering the care. Need to develop a quality culture. Audit results should be available to all, e.g., CHC and purchasers. Monitors and those appointing the monitors.

- **Who (from those affected) should be involved?**

Everyone, but especially people who can speak to everyone involved and pick out salient points. Also consultants, as chosen and agreed upon by patients. Medical and lay persons must be involved. Pressure groups and those who can influence change.

● **How should they be involved?**

Through complaints being heard, perhaps along the following lines.

- Effective monitoring bodies.
- Becoming involved in the construction of questionnaires.
- Patient councils.
- Open hospital surgeries.
- Attendance by patient representatives (as long as they have credibility), patients and patient councils at bigwig meetings.
- Staff should not be asked to provide repeatedly information that will not be used (i.e., to management). They should be involved in deciding how to use information they provide.
- By collecting information, co-ordinating meetings and going to the House of Commons to lobby. The problem is that people are evasive and information may be deliberately distorted or withheld. It is impossible to get promises in writing.

● **Which point of view should determine the design?**

People committed to the delivery of a high standard of appropriate quality service with equal access to all (for all users and equal ability to voice opinions and be involved in discussions for all staff/providers). Perhaps finance, perhaps management. Patients' views must be considered. But patients are transient – how do we get them together? GPs' views too must be considered.

From this great diversity of results surfacing out of 'ought to be' thinking, six main issues were identified for translation into action steps. Examples of issues put forward are given below, including peer group names that were suggestions from the multi-agency groups about who should debate the issue in workshops to follow.

Issue 1 (to be discussed by managers-providers). Administration services need improving, e.g., medical reports. Co-ordination between services (departments) is poor, e.g., reports to consultants or GPs take ages or are never received. There is clerical inefficiency too. Mistakes occur in dates or times of clinics, lost papers, etc. Clerical staff are part of the quality chain.

Issue 2 (to be discussed by purchasers). Patient involvement:

who are they?, what do they want? Steps need to be taken to improve patient representation, for example each person could be provided with a quality card on entering hospital and should state on it their expectations/needs. On leaving, each could complete an evaluation form. There must continue to be an external body for patient complaints/representation.

Issue 3 (to be considered by mixed professionals). Informed decision making of patients – requires improvement. Patients decide on services with little or no information to guide them. Informed decision making is rarely possible and needs to be improved upon.

Issue 4 (to be considered by nurses). Flexibility such as budgets and suggestions. It was felt that there is little flexibility in how budgets are spent and that this could be due to the history of the NHS, but it needs to be improved. Directorates get budgets and there is a perception that it has to be spent as predetermined. There needs to be some built-in spare budget to respond to new ideas, suggestions, and so on. For example, a float for interpreters and signers not held by directorates.

Issue 5 (to be considered by the CHC). How are authorities selected? To whom do they account? Who decides who is on the board of a Trust or of a purchasing authority? Boards seem to be held in secret. It should be possible to move to a council-type format (i.e., elected members and listeners/the public) to enable better accountability.

Issue 6 (to be considered by RSIB/VIPs). The role or profile of the CHC. The CHC provides a significant view on what quality is or should be. However, the role of the CHC is not clear to many members of the community. Its profile needs to be raised.

The third cycle concentrated on carving out and concretising action steps. The peer groups began this cycle, the output of their efforts was sent on to participants of the multi-agency group. A summary of some action steps is given below (in the report itself there are detailed suggestions about how these action steps can be realised).

- More effective use of resources.
- Improve administration.
- Develop an integrated quality system.
- Formalise a new way of setting budgets.
- Greater patient involvement.
- Patients to be informed about decision making.
- Provide information about services.
- Set up an operation that makes contact with patients and the public in person, by letter and/or by phone.
- Introduce a complaints and suggestion-handling system.
- Formalise a new way of selecting authorities.
- Publicise CHC to gain interest of local people in representing their community.
- Find a representative from local people to sit on the CHC and to lead a local informal committee.
- Introduce a worker volunteer recruitment activity.

Above is an account of the process followed and outcomes realised. We now want to outline some of the main lessons that we learnt as research consultants in the Trent Quality Initiative.

REFLECTIONS

In the Trent Quality Initiative we elicited, challenged, explored and developed ideas as options to address quality issues in the Health Service. Facilitators played the part of temporary participants in group meetings, aiding and contributing to the dialogical process. Facilitators did not attempt to stay outside the process but took part in a way that allowed participants to reconsider their original viewpoints. To a large extent this amounted to a trust-building process. We encouraged negotiation with and between purchasers, providers and users. The discussions led to fruitful insights and recommendations and has shown that people can shift perspectives. A number of tangible results have already arisen from the project, e.g., adjustments to service contracts, easier ways for users to offer suggestions on services and provisions made for three-pronged discussion between patients/providers/purchasers.

The process that we developed allowed for the creation of

insights through the process of eliciting, challenging, exploring and extending stakeholders' views. This did not preclude stakeholders from referring to quantitative data. We stressed, however, that the relevance of data and its interpretation also had to be negotiated. This involved questioning what possible use can be made of the data and how it may help to extend conceptions of options. The relevance of statistically prepared data for health authorities also could become negotiated through *in situ* communication. However, any focus on collecting data must be weighed against the problem of its becoming a substitute for communication. Also, data may serve to entrench feelings of lack of control of those offering it, especially if they receive no prior or subsequent feedback and have no prior or subsequent opportunity to interpret or discuss its relevance.

Involving people in defining relevance of data may well save time of creators, collators and fillers-in of information. Initially it will take time to build up a climate where people can become involved by expressing and challenging viewpoints and offering ideas on what is acceptable. In our case we believe the time we spent on this can be justified. Our discussion networks, based on a model of the dialogical process, prevented time and energy being wasted on the creation of data holding little value, even to the audiences to which it was addressed.

There were, however, a number of significant difficulties that we encountered. The main one was the threatening nature of the dialogical forum experienced by some participants. The professionals in particular felt that the forum simply created a further avenue for complaint and criticism of their efforts. For our part, it was very difficult to keep on top of group dynamics arising from such circumstances. For example, it appeared that discussion had enabled users to understand the kinds of pressure that professionals are under, with users' antagonism being redirected to government. Not all professionals perceived progress of this sort, as made abundantly clear to us at the end of the initiative by a doctor who felt that the increased knowledge about her work simply provided further ammunition to shoot at doctors.

Another problem we had to tackle was attrition on the groups that we set up. Dealing with large numbers of people over an extended period of time inevitably leads to drop outs. For example, one volunteer for the multi-agency forum, unemployed at the time he put his name forward, found employment after several meetings and had to withdraw. The effects of attrition clearly impact on the process, with particular viewpoints being under-represented. Adding more people half way through would not necessarily solve the problem since they would come at things cold, without the benefits of learning and understanding already enjoyed by existing participants.

Turning to the process itself, we have the following observations to make. The process, built on the principle of participation, an integral part of TSI, evolved as learning and understanding was generated. This possibility is mentioned and encouraged in Chapter 9 where choice of method is discussed. In our view, it would not have been productive to prearrange methodological intervention in a situation as diverse and complex as the Trent initiative. Our advice is: be clear of your principles prior to intervention, be creative with methods employed through these principles during intervention.

The guidelines that we followed in terms of setting up and facilitating the cycle of peer and multi-agency meetings/ workshops are not, of course, set in concrete. In this setting, with the complexity of involving varied participants in (confrontative) dialogue, it can be argued that the cycles were an appropriate way of proceeding. However, it is also possible that had we decided to devote more time to outlining in detail to participants what we intended to achieve in our project, it might have been possible, in the course of the project, to alter the structure of the cycles of discourse, taking account of varied views of participants about the structure itself. It is also possible that more time devoted to outlining and discussing with participants our facilitation style, and its purpose, would have helped them to be more attuned and indeed resilient to being confronted by challenging views as levelled by others (including the facilitators!). This is a reflection *post facto* of something that we, and perhaps others, may want to do, depending on the context of their research engagements. Not all the facilitators involved in this project agree on what the complexity of this structure suggested in terms of possibilities for renegotiation of the very structure of peer/multi-agency/peer/(and so on) meetings, or indeed about the amount of time (to be) spent on discussing facilitation purpose and style. In keeping with the critical spirit of our thinking it is also important to note that we do not all equally endorse or give the same meaning to all of the statements in this study.

Finally, as regards the actual report proposed for our sponsor and sent to all participants, we do not wish our discussion of relevance of ideas to be seen as fixing them and making them non-negotiable. What is important is that people reading our report feel that they gain some insight from the interpretations included and that they are able to defend their own insights by considering and taking into account how others would respond. In this sense, we hope that our work demonstrates the importance of increased sensitivity on the part of participants in problem solving, towards learning and experiencing a process of encountering competing arguments, in a dialogical fashion, and using this as a basis for considering ways forward.

Overview

In this overview of the case studies just presented I intend to point things out which transcend the cases and consequently are not highlighted in any one of them. This will help to round off the lessons learnt from TSI in action, complementing the reflections given by the authors of the case studies. I will start with a rather obvious point before digging out less evident ones.

- An international perspective on TSI has been achieved with cases in this chapter (and Chapter 9) from Australia, Hong Kong, Japan, Singapore, South Africa, Taiwan, the United Kingdom, the United States of America and a country in the Middle East.
- TSI is shown to be effective across many management processes. The cases span a range of management processes including strategic management, quality management, innovation and change, planning, organisational development, joint venturing and, of course, consultancy.
- A point that struck me about the cases is the much wider use of Exploring and Choosing Designs (ECD) over Exploring and Making Decisions (EMD) as methods for debate. This may reflect the sources drawn upon by the authors to get guidance about how to use the methods and the terminology used in those sources. It is fair to say that the original sources for EMD are far more academic than those for ECD and hence far less accessible to managers. Terms and concepts found in the original sources for EMD are certainly more obscure when it comes to a lay person. On the other hand, what we have

found in *Solving Problem Solving* may simply accord with Russell Ackoff's opinion, the originator of idealised planning and procedures behind ECD, that what is mainly wrong in management today is poor planning.

- One of the first things to be noticed by those working hard to introduce methods in problem solving that question why something should be done and whose interests will be served, or in coercive contexts, is the moderate amount of use of Critically Evaluating Designs and Decisions (CEDD) in the cases. This issue comes to the fore when thinking about the prevalence of politics in organisational dynamics, highlighting in my view a genuine difficulty that will always cause tension for TSI managers and problem solvers. The tension is that, just at the time CEDD is most needed, the political dynamics are going to make the possibility of its use very unlikely. This is a dilemma that Norma Romm and I discussed at length in a paper detailed under Further Reading. The essence of the argument is that we must find a way to use methods that tackle political dynamics when political dynamics prevail. Our recommendation, which is used in *Solving Problem Solving* in Chapters 5 and 9, is to learn how to use methods for design and debate in an oblique way that adheres to the principles of CEDD. In my view, there is herein a classic illustration of this kind of approach. Jason Magidson's use of ECD, reported in Chapter 9, is clearly carried out with principles of human freedom at the fore right throughout the process.

- Several cases refer to the scale of TSI and the time needed to employ it properly. In each case, however, it was ultimately accepted that the enhanced results justified the time and effort. Authors stated that participants were convinced in the end. This possibly reinforces the point that problem solving now using TSI prevents large amounts of time wastage that inevitably arises during crisis management later on. Nevertheless, when using TSI this concern has to be managed and dealt with. That is why I attach importance to an idea put forward earlier in the book, and actually put in my mind by Peter Checkland who is the originator of the original version of EMD, that we need to have versions of our problem solving methods that can be used in different time frames. There needs to be the five-minute TSI, the one-hour TSI, the one-day TSI, the one-week TSI, the one-month TSI, the three-month TSI, the six-month TSI, the one-year TSI, and many more. It can be done. For example, I quite often use TSI to run through problems in my mind over short periods of time. Of course, this is a compromise, but then we live in a world of compromise. I feel justified in doing this as long as I do not violate TSI's principles and I am moving things some way toward the ideal state of organisation that TSI proposes. Something is better than nothing.

- Two cases in particular stress the importance of the problem context in determining the permitted degree of openness about the methods used with those involved and affected by the process they entail. Annmaree Desmond and Tony Tregurtha of The Halesworth Partnership make it policy to explain to their clients what methods they are using and why. TSI is explained up-front. The benefit is that the transfer of knowledge about problem solving is made more complete. Steve Green of North Yorkshire Police operates in a totally different organisational context. The corporate culture reflects a long and traditional history. It is a culture that can be harsh on people who do not conform. One way of not conforming is introducing new management methods. It is easy to get a reputation as a 'loony' by breaking with tradition. The social pressures were so strong on Steve that it was out of the question that he would be open about the methods chosen to guide his management style. Ultimately these observations reinforce TSI's argument that everything we do in problem solving must be treated and respected as context dependent.
- And in the same vein as the last point, many of the cases made reference to the importance of respecting the individuality of every organisational context and the uniqueness of each problem solving situation.

The case studies in this chapter and the discussion that they have generated are a fitting place to end the presentation of the problem solving system TSI. All that remains in this book is Chapter 11, that provides essential concluding comments.

11
Concluding Comments

The problem solving system TSI has been developed to provide managers with a practical and useful systems-based approach to problem solving. It offers procedures to integrate all methods for problem solving in a process which ensures that they are employed to tackle only the issues they are best suited to. TSI achieves this through three modes of its use: Critical Review Mode, Problem Solving Mode and Critical Reflection Mode. Ultimately this builds up a system of methods for creative thinking, choice of method for implementation, and methods for implementation within a reflective process that has three main phases. The phases are Creativity, Choice and Implementation. Each of the three phases has three subphases, creativity, choice and implementation, which follow in a recursive structure.

The process of TSI remains true to four principles. These principles are, being systemic, achieving meaningful participation, being reflective and achieving human freedom. The principles support each other. A valid use of TSI would be able to demonstrate to those involved and affected that each of these principles has been met as far as is reasonably possible in practice.

The process of TSI has matured over about eight years of practice and reflection upon this and its original theoretical foundations. TSI has been used by many consultants and managers in many countries. Its use has occurred in two ways: in consultancy and in the process of management. The process of

TSI arguably operates well in practice as seen in the case studies, although there is always scope for further evaluation such as checking across the board whether all organisational members agree about TSI's relevance. Research into this is currently in progress in the Centre for Systems Studies at Hull University. I can see no reason at this time to want to change the process as it is expressed by its three phases (although further reflection on TSI may change this?). The task of each activity and the expected outcome have become well established through application. There are a number of points that I wish to make, however, about the tools of each activity of TSI in the Problem Solving Mode.

There is enormous opportunity to develop further the tools of the Creativity phase of TSI. Additions and/or replacements for Idea and Image Generation and Evaluation need to be explored. It would be wise to continue to apply the fundamental idea of creative thinking to the Creativity phase itself.

The Choice phase has presented the most exacting challenge of the three phases. The idea, and principles, of choice of method are clear enough. Difficulties have arisen when translating these into an agreeable procedure. The latest development used in this book is to organise methods into groups. The groups are categories that comply with TSI's four key dimensions of organisation. These categories are further characterised by the type of question that they raise for managers and consultants. These are reproduced below.

- 'How can we design the most efficient organisational processes and arrange their implementation?'
- 'How can we achieve effective organisation?'
- 'What options should we decide upon that debate technical and human issues which arise in organisations and lead to decisions on what to do about them?'
- 'Why should a design or a decision be adopted that merely serves the interests of dominant groups, rather than balancing the needs of individuals and the organisation, taking into account the physical, biological and social environments?'

Core problems reflect one or more of those questions. Every type of problem has a set of relevant methods that can be chosen, where relevance is determined by those involved and affected by the problem. Therefore a basis exists for aligning methods to problems. This categorisation and the procedures used to operationalise it might be improved following further investigation.

The Implementation phase has involved the most extensive work to be done. A number of extant problem solving methods have been translated into lines of questioning and embedded in the process of TSI in a system of methods. This provides a satisfactory way of including them in TSI's process. It overcomes difficulties that otherwise occur because the original versions of the methods were designed outside of the philosophy, principles and process of TSI. Further translation work is likely to be beneficial. For example, you probably use methods not discussed in this book and can incorporate them in your own system of methods using the Critical Review Mode of TSI.

I believe that much has been achieved using TSI in practice. Much more can be achieved if adequate efforts are invested in further work. I hope that I, and the rest of the team at the Centre for Systems Studies at the University of Hull, succeed in persuading many more people to contribute to the exciting programme of further research that we are engaged in.

At the outset of *Solving Problem Solving* I raised the concern that it is in the interests of managers to improve their problem solving skills. I stated that improving problem solving skills will help managers to cope even more effectively with organisational problems that they face and will broaden their perspective on how to face them. The worry I had, you may remember, concerned the obstacles that get in the way of managers who want to improve their problem solving skills. I named three main obstacles, repeated below, and asked what could be done about them.

- Time available for managers to make improvements is limited.
- Help given to managers seeking to make improvements is not good enough.
- Making improvements means change that may seem threatening to managers and not in their interests.

The conclusion that I deduced spotlighted the primary concern as a need to improve substantially help given to managers. In fact, that happened to be the main motivation that led me to write this book. To this end I came up with nine Critical Success Factors (CSFs) that will improve help given to managers if they are achieved. It seems appropriate in the conclusion to this book to reflect on these CSFs, to highlight where in the text the CSFs are dealt with and achieved. That task is carried out below.

CSF1   *A problem solving system is needed that guides managers through the process of choosing methods relevant to the main problems that they face.* Chapter 5 explains a process for choice of methods, Chapter 9 operationalises this, and the case studies in Chapter 10 show in varying degrees of detail how choice works in practice.

CSF2   *A problem solving system is needed that cuts back on the number of concepts used to explain methods, and translates those that are kept into everyday language and then integrates them into one coherent whole system.* Chapter 9 describes a coherent system of methods in everyday language.

CSF3   *A problem solving system is needed that incorporates powerful tools to stimulate and provoke creative and perceptive thought about organisational problems.* The Creativity phase reported in Chapter 9 incorporates creativity-enhancing tools into the system of methods in the Problem Solving Mode.

CSF4   *A problem solving system must be supported by an explanation of what is happening when people use the system properly, according to the principles of the system.* Chapter 6 explains what is happening when you problem solve with TSI.

CSF5   *A problem solving system must be used in the light of knowledge about potential pitfalls to avoid.* Chapters 7 and 8 categorise and discuss potential pitfalls in problem solving with TSI.

CSF6   *A problem solving system must not be shallow or gimmicky.* TSI's problem solving system is carefully thought out. It is based on a deep theory that can be followed up from Further

Reading. A form of that theory applicable to this book is explained herein, with Chapter 3 providing the philosophy and Chapter 4 the principles.

CSF7 *A problem solving system has added value if it is demonstrated to be applicable at an international level.* There are many case studies provided in Chapters 9 and 10 that report on the use of TSI and problem solving methods in the following countries: Australia, Hong Kong, Japan, Singapore, South Africa, Taiwan, the United Kingdom, the United States of America and a country in the Middle East.

CSF8 *Problem solving should be fun.* This book cannot force you to have fun when problem solving, but it suggests you ought to if at all possible. The creativity element is an obvious place where chances exist for fun. Creativity is spread across the three modes of TSI: the Critical Review Mode, the Problem Solving Mode and the Critical Reflection Mode. Because of the recursive nature of the Problem Solving Mode, creativity is found in the three phases: Creativity, Choice and Implementation. Of course, I recognise that problem solving is sometimes undertaken in conditions where fun is not the order of the day and this has to be respected, as Johan Strumpfer did in his search and recovery task discussed in Chapter 10.

CSF9 *A problem solving system must include procedures that are critical of the outcomes it generates and must include procedures which ensure that the system remains critical of itself.* TSI is built on a deep theory called Critical Systems Thinking. By its very nature, then, TSI is critical. Procedures which, if followed, will ensure that managers remain critical, in a positive sense, are found in the Critical Review Mode and Critical Reflection Mode of TSI reported in Chapter 9.

And finally, as already stated, there is much more work yet to be done to develop our knowledge about intervention. Whatever developments occur with TSI, however, I believe that there will be one common thread. The common thread is that problem solving will be based on lines of questioning like the version of TSI set out in this book. In this way it will remain critical.

It must be just so. But this kind of notion is not new. As far back as 1902, Rudyard Kipling established the importance of questioning, questioning and questioning again to promote everyday thinking (although perhaps not expressed in politically correct or fair terms, hence my bracketed addition in italics).

> I keep six honest serving men *[sic]*
> (They taught me all I knew);
> Their names are What and Why and When
> And How and Where and Who.'

Rudyard Kipling, 1902
Just So Stories
Macmillan, London

Further Reading

The first official account of TSI was published in 1991.

- Flood, R.L. and Jackson, M.C. (1991) *Creative Problem Solving: Total Systems Intervention*, Wiley, Chichester.

It contains an extremely detailed analysis of six methods that are mentioned in this book. The first thoughts on the Creativity phase are given, as are the origins of the Choice phase. A completely different set of case studies illustrates the 1991 text. Further research on TSI has subsequently been published as follows.

- Flood, R.L., Jackson, M.C. and Schecter, D. (1992) 'Total Systems Intervention: A research programme', *Systems Practice*, **5**, pp. 79–84.
- Flood, R.L. (1993) 'Practising Freedom: Designing, Debating and Disimprisoning', *OMEGA*, **21**, pp. 7–16.
- Flood, R.L. (1993) *Beyond TQM*, Wiley, Chichester.
- Flood, R.L. (1994) 'Total Systems Intervention: A reconstitution', *Journal of the Operational Research Society*, **45**, pp. 174–191.
- Flood, R.L. (1994) 'What is happening when you problem solve?: A critical systems perspective', *Systems Practice*, **8**, pp. 215–222.
- Flood, R.L. (1995) 'An improved version of the process of Total Systems Intervention', *Systems Practice*, **8**, (in press).

TSI is theoretically founded on an approach to the management sciences called Critical Systems Thinking (CST).

- Flood, R.L. (1990) *Liberating Systems Theory*, Plenum, New York.
- Flood, R.L. and Jackson, M.C. (eds) (1991) *Critical Systems Thinking: Directed Readings*, Wiley, Chichester.

● Jackson, M.C. (1991) *Methodology for the Management Sciences*, Plenum, New York.

TSI and CST apply systems thinking to problem solving. An introduction to systems thinking in problem solving and many other disciplinary areas can be found in the following book.

● Flood, R.L. and Carson, E.R. (1988) *Dealing With Complexity: An Introduction to the Theory and Application of Systems Science*, Plenum, New York (2nd edn in 1993).

Articles on TSI, CST and systems thinking and its application can be found in the learned journal *Systems Practice*.

The following classic texts on systems thinking are highly recommended reading.

● Ackoff, R.L. (1974) *Redesigning the Future*, Wiley, New York.
● Ackoff, R.L. (1978) *The Art of Problem Solving*, Wiley, New York.
● Ackoff, R.L. (1981) *Creating the Corporate Future*, Wiley, New York.
● Beer, S. (1973) *Designing Freedom*, Canadian Broadcasting Company, Toronto.
● Churchman, C. West (1968) *Challenge to Reason*, McGraw-Hill, New York.
● Churchman, C. West (1968) *The Systems Approach*, Delacorte Press, New York.
● Churchman, C. West (1971) *The Design of Inquiring Systems, Basic Concepts of Systems and Organisation*, Basic Books, New York.
● Churchman, C. West (1979) *The Systems Approach and its Enemies*, Basic Books, New York.

The discussion on facilitation in Chapter 7 drew upon on the following paper.

● Gregory, W. and Romm, N. (1994) 'Developing multi-agency dialogue: The role(s) of facilitation', *Working Paper No. 6*, Centre for Systems Studies, University of Hull.

The following text provides an insightful account of developments in organisational analysis mentioned in Chapter 7.

● Reed, M. and Hughes, M. (eds) (1992) *Rethinking Organisation: New Directions in Organisation Theory and Analysis*, Sage, London.

The discussion on measurement in Chapter 8 can be pursued through the following source.

- Flood, R.L. and Carson, E.R. (1988) *Dealing With Complexity: An Introduction to the Theory and Application of Systems Science*, Plenum, New York (2nd edn in 1993).

Further details on the methods presented in Chapter 9 can be found in the following texts, many of which provide full accounts of the original methods from which the system of methods in this book has been derived. The enhanced process of Choice is discussed at length in the following journal article.

- Flood, R.L. and Romm, N.R.A. (1995) 'Enhancing the process of choice in TSI and improving the chances of tackling coercion', *Systems Practice*, **8**, (in press).

The example used to illustrate an oblique use of methods is detailed in the following article.

- Magidson, J. (1992) 'Systems practice in several communities in Philadelphia', *Systems Practice*, **5**, pp. 493–508.

Sources on creative thinking found particularly useful and recommended for further reading are listed below starting with two general texts.

- Ackoff, R.L. and Vergara, E. (1981) 'Creativity in problem solving and planning: A review', *European Journal of Operational Research*, **7**, pp. 1–13.
- De Bono, E. (1990) *Lateral Thinking*, Penguin, London.

The following book gives a useful account of Brainstorming and Nominal Group Technique (NGT).

- Shuster, H.D. (1990) *Teaming for Quality Improvement: A Process for Innovation and Consensus*, Prentice-Hall, New Jersey.

Metaphors are explained in two key texts.

- Morgan, G. (1986) *Images of Organisation*, Sage, London.
- Lakoff, G. and Johnson, M. (1980) *Metaphors We Live By*, University of Chicago Press, Chicago.

Further details on Quality Management (QM) as reported in this book, alongside illustrative case studies backed up with a comprehensive set of references to the main QM gurus, are given in the following book.

- Flood, R.L. (1993) *Beyond TQM*, Wiley, Chichester.

Business Process Reengineering (BPR) can be followed up using two reference texts to start with.

- Johansson, H.J., McHugh, P., Pendlebury, A.J. and Wheeler, W.A. (III) (1993) *Business Process Reengineering: BreakPoint Strategies for Market Dominance*, Wiley, Chichester.
- Hammer, M. and Champy, J. (1993) *Reengineering the Corporation: A Manifesto for Business Revolution*, Nicholas Brealey, London.

The method for Implementing Designs and Decisions (IDD) has the following original sources.

- Ackoff, R.L. (1974) *Redesigning the Future*, Wiley, New York.
- Ackoff, R.L., Vergara, E. and Gharajedaghi, J. (1984) *A Guide to Controlling Your Corporation's Future*, Wiley, New York.

The method for Designing Effective Organisation (DEO) was derived from the following trilogy.

- Beer, S. (1979) *The Heart of the Enterprise*, Wiley, Chichester.
- Beer, S. (1981) *Brain of the Firm*, 2nd ed., Wiley, Chichester.
- Beer, S. (1985) *Diagnosing the System for Organisation*, Wiley, Chichester.

The description of the method for Designing Effective Organisation (DEO) made some use of the XY case study published in the following book.

- Flood, R.L. and Jackson, M.C. (1991) *Creative Problem Solving: Total Systems Intervention*, Wiley, Chichester.

The case study for Designing Effective Organisation (DEO) was taken from the following thesis.

- Beckford, J.B. (1994) *The Viable System Model: A More Adequate Tool for Practising Management?*, University of Hull, PhD thesis.

The method for Exploring and Choosing Designs (ECD) has the following original sources.

- Ackoff, R.L. (1974) *Redesigning the Future*, Wiley, New York.
- Ackoff, R.L., Vergara, E. and Gharajedaghi, J. (1984) *A Guide to Controlling Your Corporation's Future*, Wiley, New York.

The case study for Exploring and Choosing Designs (ECD) was taken from the following report.

- Rovin, S., *et al.* (1994) *An Idealised Design of the U.S. Healthcare System*, INTERACT, Bala Cynwyd.

The method for Exploring and Making Decisions (EMD) has the following original sources.

- Checkland, P.B. (1981) *Systems Thinking, Systems Practice*, Wiley, Chichester.
- Checkland, P.B. and Scholes, S. (1990) *Soft Systems Methodology in Action*, Wiley, Chichester.

The method for Testing Polarised Viewpoints (TPV) has the following original source.

- Mason, R.O. and Mitroff, I.I. (1981) *Challenging Strategic Planning Assumptions*, Wiley, New York.

The method for Critically Evaluating Designs and Decisions (CEDD) has the following original source.

- Ulrich, W. (1983) *Critical Heuristics of Social Planning*, Haupt, Berne.

The case study for Critically Evaluating Designs and Decisions (CEDD) was taken from the following research report.

- Cohen, C. and Midgley, G. (1994) *The North Humberside Diversion from Custody Project for Mentally Disordered Offenders*, Centre for Systems Studies Press, University of Hull.

At the end of Chapter 9 a number of methods, not included as part of the system of methods in this book, were recommended for further consideration. One main source is given below respectively for Operational Research, the 'seven tools' of Quality Management (QM), Just In Time, Supplier Development

Strategies, ISO 9000, System Dynamics, Cognitive Mapping, and Project Planning.

- Daellenbach, H.G., George, J.A. and McNickle, D.C. (1983) *Introduction to Operations Research Techniques*, Allyn and Bacon, Boston.
- Karatsu, H. and Ikeda, T. (1987) *Mastering the Tools of QC: Learning Through Diagrams and Illustrations*, PHP, Singapore.
- Hay, E.J. (1988) *The Just-In-Time Breakthrough – Implementing the New Manufacturing Basics*, Wiley, New York.
- Isaac, M. (1994) *The Theory and Practice of Supplier Development Strategies for Small and Medium Sized Enterprises*, University of Hull, PhD thesis.
- Flood, R.L. (1993) *Beyond TQM*, Wiley, Chichester.
- Wolstenholme, E.F. (1990) *System Enquiry: A System Dynamics Approach*, Wiley, Chichester.
- Eden, C., Jones, S. and Sims, D. (1983) *Messing About in Problems*, Pergamon, Oxford.
- Burke, R. (1992) *Project Management, Planning and Control*, Wiley, Chichester.

The following book was referred to in Chapter 10.

- Porter, M.E. (1985) *Competitive Advantage*, Free Press, New York.

The Trent Quality Initiative, a case given in Chapter 10, can be found in full in the following report.

- Gregory, W., Romm, N. and Walsh, M. (1994) *The Trent Quality Initiative: A Multi-agency Evaluation of Quality Standards in the National Health Service*, Centre for Systems Studies Press, University of Hull.

Index

ABC and Co (Hong Kong and Taiwan) 349
Ackoff, Russell 92, 356, 391
Acropol Johnson Controls (Singapore) 249
Advance Bank (Australia) 136, 139
Aesthetics 66–67
Allied Health Company (Gulf region) 203
Annuities Division, SLA (South Africa) 299, 310–311, 317
Asian Development Bank 251
Audit Commission 281
Automatic Work Distribution (AWD) 303

Bohr, Niels 101
Bono, Edward De 93
Bottomley, V (Health Minister, UK) 378
Brainstorming, Idea generation and evaluation 94–97, 125, 128, 173
British Army of the Rhine 279
Broker Division, SLA 295
Business Process Reengineering (BPR) 109–110, 131–136, 143, 299, 304–306, 323

CARCO (UK) 161–171
CATWOE 188–189, 196, 365
Central Sheffield University Hospitals Trust (UK) 368
Centre for Advanced Construction Studies, Nanyang

TechnologicalUniversity (Singapore) 250
Centre for Systems Studies, University of Hull (UK) 217, 227, 268, 282, 367, 394–395
Chartered Institute of Arbitrators (Singapore) 250
Checkland, Peter 391
Check Lists 129
Cheng, Richard 250
Chia, Jeremy 360
Choice 107–114
Chuen, Loo Wing 188
Citizens Charter (UK) 282
City Council, York (UK) 287
City Developments Ltd (Singapore) 249
City Polytechnic of Hong Kong 349
Clarke, K (Chancellor of the Exchequer, UK) 378
Cognitive Mapping 231
Cohen, Claire 217
Community Healthcare Board (USA) 183–184
Community Health Council (CHC) 368, 371, 373, 376, 378–380, 385–386
Competance, Training and 68
Construction Industry Development Board (CIDB, Singapore) 104–107, 249
Consultants, Choosing and Using 75
Council for Voluntary Services (UK) 379
Creativity 88–107

Creativity, Choice and
    Implementation 9–15, 29, 32–41,
    86, 393, 397
Critical Reflection Mode 29–30, 41–
    43, 227–229, 393, 397
Critical Review Mode 29–32, 84–86,
    229, 348, 393, 395, 397
Critical Success Factors 3–8, 396–
    397
Critical Systems Thinking 70, 397
Critically Evaluating Designs and
    Decisions (CEDD) 109–110,
    122, 136, 161, 175–176, 181, 192,
    203, 211, 213, 217–218, 295, 306–
    307, 317–319, 353, 358, 371–372,
    381, 391
Crosby, Philip 78
Cross, Robert 203

Debate – 'What?' 50–52
Deming, W. Edwards 78
Department of Environment (UK)
    288
Department of Health (UK) 378
Design – 'How?' 48–50
Desmond, Annmaree 320
Diagnosis for Effective Organisation
    (DEO) 109–110, 118, 139,
    146,181, 189–192, 203, 241, 243–
    244, 246–247, 258, 261, 267, 282,
    288–289, 299, 352–353
Disimprison – 'Why and for
    whom?' 52–56
Divisional Command, North
    Yorkshire Police (UK) 285

Employee Benefits Division, SLA
    (South Africa) 295
Exploring and Choosing Designs
    (ECD) 110–114, 160, 177, 190,
    203, 218, 227, 241, 243, 245–247,
    257–258, 267, 273–274, 291, 299,
    353, 355, 358, 361, 390–391
Exploring and Making Decisions
    (EMD) 109–110, 172, 185–186,
    192, 194, 196, 257, 353, 365, 390–
    391

Facilitation style 61–64
Fair Wind Secretarial Services
    (Hong Kong) 349

Family Health Services Association
    (UK) 378
Fayol, Henry 69
Federal Government (USA) 184
Feigenbaum, Armand V. 78
Fishbone diagram 125–126
Fong, Chow Kok 104–107, 249
Fudosan, Kurosawa 251

Green, Steve 279
Gregory, Wendy 367
Gremlin story 72–73
Gross Domestic Product 281
Gumi, Kurosawa 251

Halesworth Partnership Pty Ltd
    (Australia), The 320
Hammer and Champy 305–307
Hang Seng Bank (Hong Kong) 349
HARDCO (UK) 192, 194, 196
Hasewaga, Fumio 252
Hearse, Phil 235
Health Authority Executive (UK)
    377
Helderberg Boeing 747 Disaster
    268–293
Hierarchical levels
    the system 26
    the subsystem 26
    the suprasystem 27
Hip Wah Gingell Holdings Ltd
    (Hong Kong) 349
Home Office and Department of
    Health (UK) 221–222, 224–225
Hong Kong Institute of Company
    Secretaries 349
Hong Kong Polytechnic 349
Housing Development Board (HDB,
    Singapore) 250
Hysan Development and Kader
    Holdings (Hong Kong) 349

Idea and Image Generation and
    Evaluation 394
Image LAN (Local Area Network)
    138
Implementation 114–227
Implementing Designs and
    Decisions (IDD) 110, 112, 121–

122, 135–136, 161, 171, 176–177, 181, 192, 203, 241, 245–246, 328, 353
Information Technology Division, SLA (South Africa) 300
Inland Revenue Service (IRS, USA) 183
Institute for Futures Research (South Africa) 268
Institute for Maritime Technology (South Africa) 268
INTERACT, Healthcare Consortium (USA) 112, 181
Interacting issues 23 (footnote)
Investments Division, SLA (South Africa) 295
Ishikawa, Kaoru 68, 78, 125, 229
ISO 9000 93–94, 231, 356–357

Japanese Credit Bank 252
Juran, Joseph M. 78
Just In Time (JIT) 230

Kaizen 94
Kipling, Rudyard 398

Leadership style 59–61
Li, Ms and Mr 350
Life Division, SLA (South Africa) 295, 300, 303–304
Life Customer Services Divisional Steering Committee, SLA (SouthAfrica) 296, 308
Local Area Policing (UK) 289–290

Magidson, Jason 111
Measurement 67
Metaphors, Image generation and evaluation 100, 103
'Methods', How to problem solve 83–232
Midgley, Gerald 217
Miller, Mark 248
Monte Carlo simulation 272–273
Motivation style 58–59

NACRO (UK) 221
Nakamaya Corporation (Japan) 249–267

National Health Service (NHS, UK) 367–389
Nominal Group Technique (NGT) 97–100, 173
Normet Pty (Australia and Asia) 235–248
North Humberside Diversion From Custody Project (UK) 217
North Humberside MIND (UK) 218
North Yorkshire Police (UK) 279–293
Northern General Hospital Trust (UK) 368
Northern Territory Department of Mines and Energy (Australia) 235

Obstruction Analysis 173
Operational Policing Review (UK) 282
Operational Research (OR) 229, 267, 269, 272–273, 276
'Organisation', what is meant by 69
Organisational
   activities 22
   culture 21, 26, 36, 109
   design 21, 26, 36, 109
   events 22
   forms 22
   management style 23
   politics 21, 26, 36, 109
   processes 21, 26, 36
Osler, Karin 278
Other Problem Solving Methods 122, 229–232

Pareto
   Analysis 138
   Charts 129
Participation, meaningful 27
Personal style 64
Police and Magistrates' Court Act (UK) 282
Police Staff College, Bramshill (UK) 279
Political dynamics 20
Pride Coupon Programme (USA) 113
'Problem', what is meant by 71–74
Problem solvers 23

Problem solving
  style 64–65
  system,
  new 3
  overview 9
Problem Solving Mode 29–30, 32–41, 86–229, 369, 393, 397
Process Control Charts 230
Programme for Systems Management, University of Cape Town 268
Project Planning 232

Quality Improvement Action Plan (QIAP) 355, 358
Quality Management (QM) 68, 110, 115–118, 120, 122, 125, 131–133, 136, 172, 182, 231, 238, 240, 245–246, 282–283, 323, 352–353
Quickmap 135

Reductionism 58
Reflection 27
Reichman Hotel (Singapore) 251
Rich picture 186–188, 194–195
Romm, Norma 367, 391
Rowan, Mark 136
Royal Corps of Signals (UK) 279
Royal Military Academy, Sandhurst (UK) 279
Royal Sheffield Institute for the Blind (RSIB, UK) 368, 371, 374, 376, 378, 380, 385

'Safer Cities' (USA) 288
Sasaki, Akiro 252
Seven tools of QM 125
Sheffield Family Health Services Authority (UK) 368
Sheffield Health Authority, Family and Community Services (UK) 368
Shingo, Sheigo 78
Sintech Construction Pty Ltd (Singapore) 249–267
South African Airways 268
Southern Life Association (South Africa) 294–319

Strategic Planning and Purchasing Group (SPPG, UK) 377, 379
Strategy, Supplier Development 68
Strümpfer, Johan 268, 397
Style
  motivation 58–59
  leadership 59–61
  facilitation 61–64
  personal 64
  problem solving 64–65
Supplier Development Strategies 231
Suzuki, Toshiyo 252
SWOT function 154
System Dynamics 231
Systemic Principle 47–48

Tang, Mr 351
Taylor, Frederick 69
Telebanking Centre (Australia) 138
Territorial Policing Unit, York HQ (UK) 280
Testing Polarised Viewpoints (TPV) 97, 109–110, 122, 136, 161, 176, 181, 197–198, 203–204, 273–274, 276, 291, 357
Time constraints 66
Topp, Warren 294
Total Quality Management (TQM) 116, 352, 356
Total Systems Intervention (TSI)
  philosophy of 19–25, 47
  principles of 26–28, 47
  process of 47
Toyota (Japan) 230
TQM, Beyond 71
Training and competence 68–69
Treasury (UK) 378
Tregurtha, Tony 320
Trent Health Authority (UK) 367–389
Trent Quality Initiative, NHS (UK) 367, 371, 386
Trent Regional Health Authority (UK) 368, 378

University of Cape Town 268
University of Hull (UK) 268, 282

Utopia-Aire Pte Ltd (Singapore)
   360–366

Viable System Mode (VSM) 118,
   140, 146, 157, 161–162, 191, 258,
   261, 263–264, 267, 282–283, 288,
   291, 356, 361–364
Visually Impaired Persons (VIPs)
   368, 371, 374, 376, 378, 380, 385

Wah, Lew Yue 122
Walsh, Michael 367
Weber, Max 69
Wong, Peter CY 349
Wong, Sharon 104–107
World Bank 250–251

York Division, North Yorkshire
   Police (UK) 285, 292

Further Reading From Robert Flood....

Critical Systems Thinking
Directed Readings
Edited by **ROBERT L FLOOD** and **MICHAEL C JACKSON**
Critical Systems Thinking brings together a unique collection of classical and new papers that have influenced the development of systems ideas in recent years.
0471 93098 9   October 1991 364pp   £55.00   hbk

Creative Problem Solving
Total Systems Intervention
ROBERT L FLOOD and **MICHAEL C JACKSON**
Creative Problem Solving is designed to help managers and decision maker choose and use the most appropriate problem solving approaches available for managing the complexity and diversity of the difficulties that they face. By describing and analysing a range of different approaches, this book investigates the strengths and weaknesses of each and provides its own approach for the complementary and integrated use of different system methodologies.
0471 93052 0   July 1991   268pp £19.95   pbk

Beyond TQM
ROBERT L. FLOOD
Many organisations have experienced unexpected difficulties when implementing TQM. The difficulties arise from basic, yet widely held, misconceptions about quality, management and organisations. Understanding and implementing TQM therefore presents a challenge - this book explains how to meet this challenge.
"Provides some fresh air in an intellectual space that has been enclosed and stagnant for sometime. The book deserves a 'hurrah'!". - Professor Russell Ackoff, Institute of Interactive Management
0471 93967 6   May 1993   328pp £19.95   hbk

Available from your local Bookshops or Direct from the Publisher

All prices correct at time of going to press

WILEY